ALBERT REYNOLDS

RISKTAKER FOR PEACE

Conor Lenihan

MERRION
PRESS

First published in 2021 by
Merrion Press
10 George's Street
Newbridge
Co. Kildare
Ireland
www.merrionpress.ie

All quotes from *Albert Reynolds: My Autobiography* by Albert Reynolds
published by Transworld Ireland. Copyright © Albert Reynolds 2009.
Reprinted by permission of The Random House Group Limited.

978 1 78537 405 0 (Paper)
978 1 78537 407 4 (Ebook)

A CIP catalogue record for this book is
available from the British Library.

Typeset in Minion Pro 11/15.5 pt

Front cover: Albert Reynolds at the Fianna Fáil Ard Fheis,
7 March 1992. (© Independent News and Media/Getty Images).
Back cover: Gerry Adams, Reynolds and John Hume shake
hands outside Government Buildings, 6 September 1994.
(© PA Images/Alamy Stock Photo)
Cover design by riverdesignbooks.com

Merrion Press is a member of Publishing Ireland.

Table of Contents

Preface

During my time working as a political journalist and later as a minister in the Dáil, Albert Reynolds was a friend to me. He was a man who courted controversy in a number of ways in his time in politics and, as such, I agonised over writing this book for several years. I felt conflicted between the duties of a friend and the need to give him the recognition that is his due for his role in the process of creating peace on the island of Ireland, even if that meant exploring some difficult periods of his life. This book is the first full-length biography of his life and career and will, I hope, complement Tim Ryan's assessment of a remarkable man as told in *Albert Reynolds: The Longford Leader* – an incomplete biography, having been published in 1994 when Reynolds stepped down as Taoiseach.[1] Reynolds' period as Taoiseach was so short and intense that many of his immense achievements are, in detail at least, forgotten. The hope is that this book will prompt future scholars and writers to take a closer look at his not insignificant contribution to Ireland in the late twentieth century. Consequently, the focus of this book is on Reynolds' public life.

Whilst I knew members of Reynolds' family over many years and marvelled at the close family ties that bound them together, despite their father's prominence in public life, I have not quoted them to any great extent in the book. Much of what they have to say is recorded elsewhere, particularly in Reynolds' autobiography, *Albert Reynolds: My Autobiography*.[2] Throughout this book, I have quoted extensively from it, but, beyond this initial reference, I will not give more specific or repeat details for these quotations. Instead, they will be indicated by a comment in the text, such as 'in his own words' or 'according to Reynolds'.

The autobiography, Tim Ryan's book, *One Spin on the Merry-go-round* by Seán Duignan, and numerous assorted articles have been invaluable in helping me write this biography.[3] I would also like to thank all the people who agreed to be interviewed for the book and, just as importantly, those who gave me advice but, for one reason or another, felt they did not want to be quoted in the text.

On a personal level, I would like to thank the publishers and my cousin Pádraig Lenihan, a professional historian, who made suggestions as I wrote. My wife, Nikita, has put up with a lot while I wrote this during the prolonged Covid-19 lockdown and I thank her greatly. My five children, Brian, Jack, Alexandra, Aoife and Patrick, need no thanks – they are my pride and joy.

CHAPTER ONE

Early Years

Rooskey, County Roscommon, is a tiny place sitting beside Ireland's largest river, the Shannon. The village is part of Roscommon but is at the conjunction of Counties Roscommon, Longford and Leitrim. These Shannon counties have, historically, been amongst the poorest counties in Ireland. In a Central Statistics Office survey of Irish counties in 2018, Roscommon emerged as the second poorest after Donegal. It was into this county that Albert Reynolds was born on 3 November 1932. His mother, Catherine Dillon, was from the nearby county of Leitrim, the county of origin of the Reynolds clan. As a young woman, she had emigrated to the United States in search of work, like so many others from the impoverished west of Ireland counties. On a return visit to Ireland to see her sister, then living in Rooskey, she met John P. Reynolds, also a resident of the village. They married and settled down.

Albert Reynolds is by far the most famous person to have been resident in the village. The only other person of great note was a Michael Whelahan, who, in 1878, became both captain and co-founder, with a Fr Hannan, of the Scottish soccer club Hibernians. The club's founders recognised a need among the poor Irish populations living in Edinburgh and so the club was born. The website of the Hibernian Historical Trust gives some background on living in Roscommon at around the time Albert Reynolds' father, John, would have been growing up: 'The Whelahan family was typical among those living in the Western province of Connaught at that time – they scratched a meagre existence from the soil. The great famine had traumatic effects on peasant families like the Whelahans, as their communities were decimated and their folk customs, pastimes and Gaelic language lapsed with the increased need to speak English.'[1]

The literature about Ireland in the 1940s and 1950s, when Albert was growing up, suggests a rather joyless existence in terms of popular entertainment. High emigration and a low-growth economy seemed to have made Ireland a place that young people wanted to leave. Reynolds himself elegantly described the world and the village of Rooskey in which he grew up following his birth on 3 November 1932:

> The main street, although surfaced, was more like a dirt track, ploughed up by the hooves of the herds that passed through on their way to market. Cars were a rarity: there were carts and the odd truck, and the rare bus but mostly you either walked or travelled by bike. A picture of quaint rustic simplicity appears in the mind's eye, but it was also a time of great hardship and deprivation. Money and jobs were scarce, houses stood empty and cottages crumbled: sure signs of abandonment where people had been forced to move away, usually to emigrate, in their desperate search for employment.

Albert's father, John, was a hard worker, starting out as a coachbuilder until the arrival of the motor car in the 1950s sounded the death knell for that business. He went on to maintain his family on the strength of a number of businesses. His son, Albert, referred to him as a carpenter, undertaker and auctioneer, and he also owned a small parcel of land, which he farmed. Additionally, he provided a local coach and horse carriage link between the village and Longford town for many years. Whilst this assortment of local businesses kept the family afloat, money was always tight as John and Catherine's children – Joe, Jim, Teresa and Albert – were growing up.

In spite of this, the family offered a wealth of support to the young Albert and his parents remained a powerful example to him throughout his life:

> My family have always been the centre of my life, my support and cornerstone. My profound belief in strong family values definitely comes from my mother. She was a purposeful, deeply religious woman, who believed in the value of prayer and a hard work ethic to get you through life, as did my father. They both had enormous energy, a trait I inherited.

Apart from the dedication to hard work conferred on him by his family, Albert's autobiography also gives a strong sense of a childhood enjoyed, as his father switched from building horse-drawn coaches to converting a shed into a basic dancehall where locals from thirty miles around would come to dance. This was Reynolds' first taste of a business that would propel him to prominence as the 1950s gave way to the 1960s:

> I have distinct memories of these times because as youngsters we were always called upon to sweep and polish the floor so that couples could glide across it more easily. We used buckets of a mixture based on paraffin; I can smell it still, it stayed on your hands for days and was powerful stuff. We were also expected to help out on the farm but I avoided that as much as possible; farming was not for me and I'd sneak off while no one was looking.

The fact that Albert was the youngest of the four children probably meant that he had a much easier time than the rest. While he had to muck in like the others, he was, in all likelihood, not expected to pull his weight to the same extent as the others born earlier and in less forgiving times; a world before the arrival of the motor car.

With the other siblings well on their way to being reared when he was still young, his mother formed the view that Albert had academic ability and decided to transfer him from the local school to one three to four miles away from the village. She had heard good things about the schoolteacher there, Elizabeth McLaughlin, and while Albert's siblings had attended the local national school for the whole of their primary education, they had not gone on to secondary education, which was not free but fee-based at the time. Albert's mother was intent on Albert getting a competitive education which would allow him to win a scholarship to go on to secondary school. Without this, the family would find a secondary education for him hard to afford. McLaughlin's Carrigeen National School had a good record in terms of winning County Council scholarships for her pupils.

Albert arrived in Carrigeen National School with just two years left at primary school; this was too late for him to achieve a full scholarship but time enough to attempt to win a bursary to Summerhill College in Sligo. Apparently, he had a talent for Latin and Greek. Such was McLaughlin's impact on Reynolds that his youthful ambition was to become a teacher. As was typical of the national schoolteachers of the time, McLaughlin often gave her time for extra tuition outside school hours, and she did so for young Reynolds to help him secure the bursary.

Most of the people who left Summerhill College were destined for jobs as teachers, or as priests in the country's many seminaries. Reynolds recalled of his time in Summerhill:

> Going to boarding school was a momentous change in my life. It was September 1946 and I was approaching my fourteenth birthday; I had never been away from home before, so leaving my family and Roosky was not easy, and it was with a great deal of trepidation that I said goodbye to my siblings.[2] We were all very close and I watched as the little figures of my sister and two brothers disappeared into the distance, still waving, as the bus took me away to what felt like the ends of the earth.

As the youngest, and probably most mothered of the Reynolds children, Albert found the first year of boarding in Summerhill College particularly tough. The Second World War was still casting its shadow over Irish society and unemployment and emigration were still high a year after the conflict had finished. Ireland's isolation from the rest of the world meant that food was still in short supply, with wartime rationing continuing despite the ending of the conflict. Boarders at Summerhill depended on the day students for extra food as well as the parcels sent by post from home. Potatoes, according to Albert, were the only basic foodstuff they had to eat. Despite this, he had happy memories of the place, but he also recalled many beatings for 'various misdemeanours'. Though soccer (the 'English game') was forbidden in the school, he and a few others would play in a field far from the prying eyes of staff and priests. Summerhill, like many other schools in the country at the time, was a strictly GAA-playing school, though pupils were given a taste of a lot of other sports, too, including rugby. Reynolds, in opting to play soccer, was stepping away from the consensus of the time and showing he had a mind of his own, as well as a determination to observe his own preferences.

The school, despite its hardships, was about to become a kind of platform for his entrepreneurial skills. Reynolds had a sweet tooth and he began to buy extra supplies of sweets and confectionary, when he had any extra money on hand, to sell to the other boarders. Somehow the school authorities learned of his little enterprise and decided to make the most of his skills, putting him in charge of the school tuck shop which had poor sales:

> I set myself the task of reorganizing the shop, threw out all the old stuff and opened up once or twice a week. With a subsidy given to me by the school, I'd go off to the local wholesaler, look for whatever bargains were offered, carefully select only what I knew I could sell, and return with my bags of goodies which were eagerly awaited by the other boys.

Reynolds confesses it was his 'first taste of making money and I liked it, and what was more, I was good at it.' This entrepreneurial instinct clearly had its origins in his family background, given his father's ability to turn his hand to all kinds of different activities.

In the village of Rooskey, there was a meat factory owned by the Hanley family and Reynolds' association with the Hanleys also seems to have contributed to his early insight into the world of wealth and business success – as well as his developing interest in politics. He acknowledges fulsomely the influence the Hanley family had on his life decisions and, most importantly, the two significant careers he went on to build in business and in politics:

> The Hanley family was the most successful in the village in those days. They gave me my first taste of association with wealth and business success, and I was very impressed. The father owned the meat factory in Roosky and employed most of the locals. They were also a big political family, well connected with the leaders of Fianna Fáil and very active supporters at election time. Through my friendship with the boys I was a regular visitor to the house, and so it was natural that

I was frequently asked to help out with the political work too, and it was through them that I really began to understand the more recent history of Ireland.

Some of the Hanley family were also hugely keen card players, with regular games hosted in the house. Reynolds' early and enduring interest in card gambling was another thing that started in the Hanley home.

At school, the annual notes that he is as an enthusiastic participant in several pursuits, including billiards, snooker and table tennis, where he was viewed as one of the best players amongst his peers. In academic terms he was viewed as excellent in the classics and his ambition to become a teacher, first expressed at national school, endured through secondary, according to the Summerhill College Annual. He seems to have been an all-rounder and popular with his classmates. 'He was a great guy who had his wits about him. If he got bread from home, he'd know where to get butter,' according to Joe Jennings, a classmate.[3]

When home from school at holiday time, the young Reynolds showed little or no interest in work, least of all, it seems, work on the farm, which clearly was drudgery for him. There are many references to his liking for the sunshine and the River Shannon. In his autobiography he tells us, 'For me the call of the river and being with my friends was irresistible. I can still feel the sun on my back on those endless summer days, lazing and swimming and playing down by the Shannon and hiding whenever one of my elder brothers came looking for me.' And in Tim Ryan's biography, his brother Joe is quoted as saying:

He would even dodge the haymaking when we'd be piling the ricks. You would always find Albert at the bottom of our field where the Shannon flowed, swimming in a place we called 'The Canal'. Joe Egan, the Caslins and the Hanleys would be racing across the river with him. It was a safe place and he was a very good swimmer.[4]

The young Albert held high ambitions to realise his mother Catherine's faith in his potential in academic terms. In spite of the promise he had shown in winning his bursary to Summerhill College, however, when his Leaving Certificate year arrived in 1952, he was struck by bad luck which affected his results. He broke his leg after falling awkwardly during a clumsy football tackle and when surgery for the football injury did not work, he was forced to sit the exams in excruciating pain. He didn't manage to complete all of them. While he still managed to attain honours in Irish, English, Greek and Latin, it was not enough to go on and study teaching as he had hoped. He could have stayed back a year and re-sat the exams, but he was anxious to move on into the wider world of work. By his own admission, 'money was in short supply at home' and he clearly didn't want to become an additional strain on the family.

It seems that the basic elements of Albert Reynolds' character were already fleshed out even before he left school. He was a popular student and participated widely in school life. He had a flair and a liking for making money; throughout his life, this became not just a necessity to survive but a passion that he enjoyed. His liking for gambling and politics were encouraged by his neighbours and the boys he was friends with in the Hanley household, and it seems that the Hanleys' home gave him an ambition to do better for himself. His own family was a strong anchor in his life, and the religious values and attachment to family which he carried with him through life can all be attributed to his mother, who appears to have had a huge influence on him. It was she who pushed him to do better by travelling the extra miles beyond the village to attend Elizabeth McLaughlin's school. It was she who sent food parcels to Summerhill at a time of great food shortages. Catherine Reynolds was a driving force in her son's life through the determination so amply exemplified by her emigration to the United States as a young woman. And it was thanks to his father's decision to turn a shed into a dancehall that Albert developed his lifelong love of music and dancing.

CHAPTER TWO

Risktaker

If things were tight for the Reynolds family in Rooskey, it was the same for most people who lived in the Ireland of 1952. The 1950s are known as a 'lost decade' in Irish economic life. The decade was frequently described as one of 'doom and gloom'. As if to demonstrate this, unemployment and outward-bound emigration continued at a high rate, with 500,000 people leaving the country in the 1950s. In the years 1949–56, the European economy grew by 40 per cent, whereas, in Ireland, the increase was a mere 8 per cent. Ireland was not able to take advantage of the Marshall Plan, the massive American aid plan, to the same extent as countries which had been actively involved in the Second World War, because of the country's wartime neutrality. Albert Reynolds makes the reality of life plain in his autobiography:

> It was a very difficult time in Ireland. The economy was in a dreadful state, there was very little employment and the majority of young people – people of all ages in fact – were still being forced to emigrate to countries across the world: Britain, America, Australia, Canada. My brother Jim was one of them. Joe was running the family farm and business, which provided work for only one person and his family, so Jim left to start a new life first in Canada, then in Australia. But I had no desire to leave Ireland – quite the opposite: I was determined that I would not be forced to leave and that, come what may, I would make my future in my own country.

It would have taken a particularly tough mindset to believe that one could stay in Ireland in the 1950s and make a living. Right up to the early 1970s, remittances (money sent from abroad) remained a feature of the Irish national accounts, as hard-working emigrants sent home income they had earned abroad to help their families. There was a pervasive fatalism to the 1950s and, in this period, a number of articles and books appeared which seemed to suggest that the Irish race might actually disappear.

Albert Reynolds' mother, Catherine, was as determined as ever to get the best for her son. She was on good terms with a local bank manager and asked if he would recommend Albert to sit the banking exams. She succeeded in persuading him, which was no mean achievement on her part. Local bank managers were often sparing with their recommendations and inclined to confer such favours on relatives rather than strangers. As late as the 1970s, I remember my mother discussing, with a friend, efforts to get a similar recommendation for her nephew. In the 1950s, jobs in the bank were like gold dust. Ireland's middle class was a tightly knit group and frequently only mixed with their social equals in local golf clubs and the like. The position of bank manager was one of great influence and often a manager actually lived above the bank branch in the fine, stone-cut buildings that stood out on the main street of many country towns.

In any event, having secured a recommendation, Reynolds dutifully made his way to Dublin to do the interview and sit the exams that might see him become an employee of the bank, in accordance with his mother's wishes. He took the interview and sat down to do the competitive exam the following day. After the exam, the candidates broke for lunch. While they were hanging around, before sitting down for the second exam paper in the afternoon, Reynolds took in the scene:

> I saw some of my fellow applicants walking around, chatting and joking with the interviewers and exam supervisors, and came to the conclusion that I was wasting my time. This was not for me. There's a saying, 'It's not what you know, it's who you know.' I didn't know any of them, so I left. To my mind the man who merits the job should get the job, what I was witnessing – or concluded I was witnessing – was a 'jobs for the boys' situation. Rightly or wrongly, I thought the decisions had already been made, and that I, as the boy up from the country, the

outsider, didn't stand a fair chance. There and then I decided I'd make my mark elsewhere. So I did not go back for the second half of the exam, instead I bought the evening paper and started looking for a job.

This story speaks volumes about the emerging personality of the future businessman and politician – he was a risktaker and quite unafraid, to the point of near recklessness, to take his own path, form his own opinion. It may also be that this decision was the action of a headstrong youth up from the country and slightly resentful of the insider networks that can operate in a big city like Dublin. The feeling of not being in the circle, or not having attended the right school, is a feeling often evinced by country people who arrive in Dublin and go to work in professional occupations. Whatever the case, Reynolds decided to walk, perhaps knowing in his heart that this would not play well back at home in Rooskey with his parents. His mother, in particular, he confessed, was 'devastated'. To add to his difficulties, the friendly bank manager whom she had persuaded to recommend him had written to her to say that Reynolds had done well in the interview and the first exam, and expressed puzzlement as to why he did not go back to sit the second exam. The sense conveyed to Catherine was that her son would have got the job.

What this story illustrates is that Reynolds, even at such a young age, already had the confidence to form his own opinion and the kind of 'take it or leave it' personality that would not make him ideal for the sedentary existence of working in the bank. This steely determination and obstinacy are hallmarks of a good number of entrepreneurs and often make them very successful, allowing them not to shrink from the obvious risks of staking their reputation and money on a project. The education he got in Summerhill, the tentative success in making money in the tuck shop and the supportive family upbringing had clearly given Reynolds a self-confidence beyond any formal qualification he had yet achieved. A more conservative youngster would have sat the exams without trying too hard, thus side-stepping any need for parents to apportion blame or express feelings of being let down by their failure. As Reynolds left the exam building, he would have known that he had burned his bridges on the home front and there would be no easy way back to a financially stretched house, with him, effectively, having thrown his mother's initiative back at her. Whatever his internal feelings, he quite clearly preferred to make his own way by living on his wits.

His first job was in a hardware store located on Pearse Street in Dublin and he managed to find accommodation in nearby Lower Mount Street. His wages were so low that he had very little left after paying his rent. His brother Jim was a qualified carpenter and would put some extra cash his way, but Jim was set to emigrate soon. Whilst the pay was low, however, the experience was valuable in another way. While working in the J.C. McLoughlin hardware store, Reynolds received the following piece of advice:

> I was an office assistant. The old man in charge of the office, Mr Taylor, asked me what I was going to do. At the time I was answering the telephone, doing messages, licking stamps on envelopes and bringing the post down to the local sorting office. Mr Taylor said to me: 'Young man, if you don't think where you are going, you'll be licking stamps for the rest of your life. It is not a question of being someone, but rather choosing to do something, and doing it better than anyone else.'[1]

It was advice that he never forgot.

His rash move not to pursue the job in the bank had left Reynolds on slim earnings. A friend who rented in the same place as him, heard him complain about what he was earning and managed to procure a job for him in the Pye radio factory in Dundrum on nearly double his previous wages, in spite of the fact that Reynolds didn't have the necessary qualifications. His job was to French polish the transistors, so it did not matter, on the surface at least, that he was not a qualified carpenter. However, a vigilant shop steward in the factory discovered that he was not a union man and had got the job only thanks to his friend, so he was soon let go.

Reynolds sat a new set of exams, this time for employment as a clerk with Bord na Mona, the state's turf development board. This job would see him move to Ballydermot in County Kildare, to a huge employment camp set up by the company so that it could extract turf from the biggest bog in Ireland, the Bog of Allen.

The atmosphere in the purpose-built work camp must have been hectic, but it seems that young Reynolds soon began to experience the joys that come with reasonable pay from a big state employer. He and his friends would make regular trips to the nearby Curragh racecourse by bicycle. His love of gambling on the horses started in the most horse-mad county in Ireland: 'It was here I learned to keep my ears open to the racing gossip as we got to know the various riders and trainers and chatted about the chances of the different horses. Instinct and hearsay served me well and I'd often come away with double my weekly wages.' To boost his wages further, he took some turf acreage from his employer and worked the bog for extra money. This had the effect of doubling his income. While in Ballydermot, Reynolds also signed up for an accountancy course by correspondence with a college in Edinburgh.

At this point, he was doing his best to get a formal qualification, still perhaps conscious of the advice proffered by Mr Taylor in the hardware store. Reynolds always said that he had learned and self-developed as he went along. In this respect he was an exemplar of an era when both second- and third-level fees were a heavy burden on a family income. His only choice was to educate himself.

Eighteen months after starting at Ballydermot, he was accepted for a permanent position as a clerical officer (Grade 3) at the state railway company and posted to Dromod station in County Leitrim, a mere two miles from his family home. This was a permanent position and, presumably, he was able to cut his overheads by living at home with the family in Rooskey. Over the next few years, he was moved to different points in the rail network around the midlands.

One particular transfer, to Ballymote in County Sligo, was to prove fateful, as it was there that he met his future wife, Kathleen Coen, a shop assistant in a local drapery store. Reynolds would deliver fabric, which had newly arrived at the station, to the store. 'Some of the girls used to make faces at Albert behind his back, when he was talking to Kathleen. Albert was so shy, and I would come and stand there until he was uncomfortable and then go. But I didn't nip it in the bud,' recalled the owner of the store, Martin McGettrick.[2] Reynolds' landlady of the time remembers him and

Kathleen heading out dancing for their first date, diving into a friend's car to the strains of a singer called Victor Silvester. Reynolds was clearly happy to settle down and the relationship survived his transfer to Longford station, with him making the journey back and forth to Ballymote to visit Kathleen. Not long after they met, her father died of a debilitating illness and Reynolds had to wait a year before proposing marriage to her, as it was the custom of the time for close relatives to mourn a departed loved one for a full year. In addition, Reynolds was not yet in a secure enough financial position to make a proposal.

Living at home in Rooskey, he had taken on the role as secretary to the Rooskey Carnival Committee, an event started by the local parish priest to raise money to pay off a debt incurred by the parish church. Reynolds, with his family's experience of running a dancehall, was the ideal man for the role. After two years, the parish debts were paid off and the local priest said Reynolds could continue the festival in his own right if he wanted to.

When his brother Jim returned from Australia in 1957 with some money, the two of them decided to build a bigger ballroom in their native village. There was a loan from the local branch of the Munster and Leinster Bank, with Albert given responsibility for management, bookkeeping and promotion of the business. His brother was in charge of the construction. The business grew. According to Sam Smyth, then a manager of bands: 'It was a cut-throat business, it was very competitive, it was also – culturally – how boy met girl. From the mid-1950s until sometime into the late '60s that's what young people did, they went to a dance, they met, there was no talk of meeting in lounge bars and cabarets, people went to dance.'[3]

Reynolds hung on to his day job with CIÉ and, in his spare time, booked bands and took his first steps in the music business. Initially, this arrangement worked well. Reynolds' station master was lenient and Reynolds learned to do his job in three hours, thus freeing up time for him to concentrate on his emerging music business activities. When a less favourably disposed station master arrived and insisted he work the full hours, his life became more difficult and he opted to quit the day job.

The prospect of marriage to Kathleen was making Reynolds more ambitious. His relationship with his soon-to-be bride would strongly impact on his subsequent success in business and politics. She was to be a huge lifelong source of emotional and practical support, quite apart from bearing him seven children. They married reasonably young and his family remained a stable foundation for him throughout the ups and downs of his different ventures and careers. In this one aspect of his life he was not a risktaker and, in many ways, it was the stability of his family that allowed him to take on all the other risks for which he was to become so well-known.

CHAPTER THREE

Dancehalls

In November 1961, Kenny Ball and His Jazzmen released a record called 'Midnight in Moscow'; between its release by Pye Records and March 1962, it raced to the no. 2 position in the UK Singles Charts. It stayed in the charts for twenty-one weeks. 'Midnight in Moscow' sold a million copies, reaching no. 1 in Australia, Canada, Sweden and Japan, and was covered by a host of US jazz bands, including those led by Eddie Condon and the trumpeter Teddy Buckner.[1] If this song was good news for Kenny Ball and his band members, it was even better news for Albert Reynolds.

Reynolds who, with Jim, was building his dancehall business, had spotted Ball in advance of the record's success and booked him. By the time his Irish concerts came around, Kenny Ball and His Jazzmen were soaring high in the charts and it guaranteed a big payday for the Reynolds brothers. Albert had booked Ball for ten nights on the trot, taking the risk that he could sell out the ten venues. His luck came good and the money he made from these concerts allowed him to buy a home, Mount Carmel, on the outskirts of Longford town.

At just thirty years of age, Reynolds was flying high. The big dividend from Kenny Ball seemed to justify his decision to throw in the day job with CIÉ. In June 1962, he followed up by marrying Kathleen, the love of his life. There was now a well-appointed address and home where they could live and, of course, eventually raise their children. In July of that year, after the wedding, he and Kathleen had their honeymoon in Majorca. This kind of sun holiday or honeymoon would not have been the norm for most Irish people at the time and indicates the speed with which Reynolds was increasing his income and the profitability of his dancehall business. He had only actually given up the day job at CIÉ in June 1961. So, within a year of quitting his steady job, he was getting married, doing well in business as a music promoter and able to purchase a substantial home for himself without a mortgage. For a man as young as he was that indicated significant success.

That same year, 1962, Reynolds had booked another singer, Acker Bilk, for a sell-out concert in the Royal Ulster Hall; once again, he had spotted and booked him just before a major success. Bilk had a no. 1 in the charts after the booking but before the show. In fairness to the Reynolds brothers, they deserved their success; they were popular people in what was a cut-throat business, often characterised at the time by mean-spirited agents and owners who exploited young bands. Albert appears to have developed a liking for dancing and music from quite a young age, and to have had an ear for talent. Even when at school in Summerhill, he was acknowledged, in the school's annual, to be the resident expert when it came to band music. It was a business he enjoyed, and he kept and maintained the friendships he made during this period for the rest of his life. These contacts became a significant advantage to him when he went on to pursue a career in politics.

The strength and popularity of the Reynolds brothers in this industry are underlined by many who were involved in it. Sam Smyth, who subsequently went on to become an award-winning journalist, was one of their contemporaries in the business:

> They were very successful promoters. They had a very good reputation. They always paid their bills. It would often take a band six to seven hours in travel time to get to a gig and the Reynolds always insisted on a proper dinner at a local hotel for the performers. I ran a chain of ballrooms in the North at the time and I think this approach stood to Albert when he moved on from the business.[2]

This image of Reynolds is further emphasised by the singer Dickie Rock in an interview he gave to Vincent Power for *Send 'em Home Sweatin'*, the definitive account of the showband era: 'He was honest and straightforward with the bands and treated us great.'[3]

'We went from strength to strength with a string of ballrooms: we established Fairyland in Roscommon, Dreamland in Athy, Lakeland in Mullingar, Jetland in Limerick, Barrowland in New Ross, Rockland in Borris-in-Ossory, Borderland in Clones and Moyland in Ballina. I think by the end we owned fourteen ballrooms across the country and we rented even more,' said Reynolds. Some of these venues could cater for up to 3,000 people a night. Operating on this kind of scale, the two brothers could get access to good bands and performers, and offer them multiple venues and concerts. It meant they could also pitch for overseas artists, as it made it worthwhile for bands to fit in a tour in Ireland. They managed to attract some very big names including Roy Orbison, Chubby Checker, Johnny Cash and Jim Reeves.

With the Irish Republican Army (IRA) campaign of the late 1950s over, the early to mid-1960s was a relatively peaceful time in Northern Ireland and the showband phenomenon was big business both north and south of the border. Some of the showbands played multiple venues in the north of Ireland and could find themselves playing the Irish national anthem and 'God Save the Queen' on the same night. With reason to traverse the border often, Reynolds made early business contacts in the North and his friend Sammy Barr, who owned the Flamingo Ballroom in Ballymena, had significant access to local unionist politicians. As a result, Reynolds gained an insight into the unionist community that would serve him well when, as Taoiseach, he focused his attention on bringing about peace on the island.

There were huge numbers of people dancing with the Reynolds brothers when you look at the geographical spread of their venues and the numbers they could cater for. Up to 6,000 people attended a Miss Quinnsworth Final in Cloudland in 1959. Operating on such a scale would only have been possible with a clear business structure and this was achieved with a clean division of labour between the two brothers: Albert worked on the promotion side, while Jim, with his strong building skills, looked after construction and managed the back-office dimension of the business. Albert was not just front of house but would frequently work the ticket desk if a night was busy. Initially, the two men were doing everything themselves, but soon they were appointing managers for each of the venues. Reynolds would, at this stage, have been known to thousands of people up and down the country. In terms of his eventual decision to enter national politics, he had a ready-made network of friends and connections in the business and entertainment scene. This gave an invaluable head start to someone who arrived, in age terms at least, quite late to politics. Sam Smyth, who got to know Reynolds, first as a promoter and later as a senior journalist covering the world of politics, has this to say of him: 'He was a very uncomplicated fellow. He brought the same logic to politics as he did in business. He avoided being ideological in favour of the transactional. He had the business personality, "You give me this and I will give you that."'[4]

What made the Reynolds' dancehall business more remarkable was the fact that none of the venues operated with a bar licence. The returns from the mineral drinks bar would pay for the staff, and the ticket receipts would be split between the promoter and the bands. The profits generated by one venue would fund the building of the next and, according to Reynolds, the brothers had strong support from their bank, which he felt they would not have been able to operate without. There is absolutely no doubt that the business was throwing off huge amounts of cash. Over the years, many believed that it was the cash return from these events that made the Reynolds brothers their fortune. In his autobiography, Albert refers to the fact that, at one point, they came to the attention of the Revenue Commissioners and he was called to a meeting in Athlone with the regional tax inspector. The official, after grilling him, warned that he would get whatever was due, even if he had to follow Reynolds to his deathbed. Reynolds apparently told him that if he left it until then, 'we have a deal'.

In 1961, the two brothers had bought the Longford Arms Hotel on the main street of Longford town. This building was to become the formal office for their music and subsequent property investment companies. The hotel was also offered as an office for one of the local TDs with whom the two brothers were friendly, namely Joe Sheridan. Sheridan was an influential independent deputy who had fallen out with Fine Gael and ran on his own strength. Albert Reynolds would canvass for him and occasionally drive him up to Leinster House in Dublin. Sheridan became significantly important in Irish politics in the 1960s as it was his vote that kept a minority Seán Lemass government in power. This association would have brought Reynolds into political circles. My own father, then a minister, acted as an informal minder for Sheridan to ensure he continued to support the government.

Dessie Hynes, a friend of Reynolds and a shopkeeper in Longford at the time, was well connected in Fianna Fáil. It was Hynes who brought Reynolds closer to Fianna Fáil. Hynes sat on a committee of the party's national executive that mobilised when there was a parliamentary by-election to be held. Given the slight majority available to Seán Lemass, these by-elections would be critical. Neil T. Blaney, the then Minister for Local Government, was the organisational genius behind many by-election victories. People like Dessie Hynes, Eddie Bohan (subsequently a senator) and Albert Reynolds would have cut their electoral teeth in such contests. They were an integral part of the Blaney by-election teams and all from Longford originally, though Hynes and Bohan had moved to Dublin to become influential in the pub business.

In his autobiography, Reynolds states, 'In 1966 I worked on the team to get John O'Leary elected for the first time in South Kerry; in 1967 it was the by-election in Limerick West that first got Gerry Collins elected; and in 1968 I canvassed in the by-election that saw Des O'Malley win his seat for the first time.' By his own admission he learned everything he knew about canvassing and campaigning from the hard task master that was Neil Blaney. The importance of this is not to be underestimated. Blaney was a robust and important figure within Fianna Fáil, and seen by many as a potential leader of the party at this time. He was also a legendary political organiser, with one American political scientist devoting a whole book, *The Donegal Mafia*, to his Donegal political machine. The Blaney approach was 'down to brass tacks' and would certainly have appealed to Reynolds as it was very close to his own business ethic. Blaney, in his role as minister, would have been helpful to the Reynolds brothers when it came to their business and the need to achieve planning permission for various venues.

By 1966, the two Reynolds brothers were going their separate ways. There were, as Albert politely puts it, 'differences' about the direction the business should take: 'He wanted to stay with the ballroom business and expand it: I was convinced changes were coming and it was not worth more investment.' Albert was correct in his assessment. The publicans were fighting back, offering music nights for their customers. Cabaret venues were emerging and, according to Reynolds, the venue operators and bands were beginning to take the audiences for granted. Popular Irish band leaders were getting big money but were cutting down the number of hours they played for in return.

During the splitting up of the business, the relationship between the brothers became acrimonious, and they did not talk to each other for quite a number of years as a result. Albert took umbrage at the way he was being treated and felt he was due much more from the business than was being conceded by his brother. Jim, according to many accounts, was a lot tighter with money than Albert and this seems to have fed into the row. In any event, the younger brother was not going to be pushed around. Much to the shock of his own family and friends at the time, he went straight to a top legal firm in Dublin and initiated a lawsuit against his own brother. This was certainly not the done thing at the time and clearly left its mark on the relationship between the two men. The upshot of the legal action was that Albert left the business with something in the order of £50,000 from an out-of-court settlement. It was a big sum of money then, and those who were friends of both men reckoned that Jim settled because it would have cost him a lot more if the matter had gone to court, where he faced the danger that some of the cash transactions earned from the business might be the subject of hostile scrutiny by the Revenue Commissioners. Albert and Jim only patched up their differences years later, just prior to the former becoming Taoiseach, and only thanks to the women in their families, who persuaded them to start speaking to each other again.

Reynolds' biographer, Tim Ryan, describes the whole incident as 'distasteful' and suggests that the legal action centred on ownership of some of the company's assets, including the Longford Arms Hotel. For many years, Albert's legal action against his own brother was cited by his opponents as evidence of his ruthlessness. However, it must be pointed out that many business families in Ireland have such disputes, and, frequently, these are caused by both family interaction and the attitude taken by those who marry into the family, as well as the inevitable sibling rivalries that can exist. The incident is significant in that it shows the extent to which

Reynolds was motivated to achieve what he regarded as his just rewards. This was a characteristic that stayed with him for life; it resurfaced, to many people's surprise, during his late political career, at which time he chose to pursue legal actions against the media when he felt he had been the subject of an injustice.

Aged thirty-four and out of the ballroom business, Albert Reynolds had more time on his hands and started going to the races more. For a time, he, his friend Dessie Hynes and a few other businessmen became regular racegoers at the Galway races and Ballybunion in County Kerry. Freed from the dancehall business and the family entanglement with Jim, Albert was also now a businessman in his own right and he began to search around for new businesses in which he could invest.

CHAPTER FOUR

Local Paper

Albert Reynolds was a restless and impatient businessman with an energy that many found remarkable. As the 1960s merged into the early 1970s, his entrepreneurial talents were directed at a series of successful businesses that ranged from cabaret, bacon production, hire purchase finance, a cinema, exporting fish and finally taking on the challenge of making one of his local Longford newspapers profitable. During this period, he was also still dabbling in politics, continuing to lend his support to local independent Dáil Deputy Joe Sheridan in his election efforts. Joe Sheridan had the catchy political slogan: 'Vote for Joe – the Man you Know'. Reynolds acted as his director of elections. He was amongst the first to volunteer to help Sheridan when he decided to leave Fine Gael and run as an independent.

Many years later, when he was long retired from active politics, I met Sheridan for a drink in Mullingar. He was a great storyteller and had nothing but respect for Reynolds, who, he confessed, had put a lot of energy into organising for him. Even though Reynolds subsequently left for Fianna Fáil, the independent remained a friend:

> Albert often drove me to Dublin and he spent a lot of time hanging around the Dáil. He was a desperate smoker that time and he always seemed to have loads of cigarettes. But often he would be talking so much on the way to Dublin that he would run out of petrol. But we had great times going up and down.[1]

One of the reasons that Reynolds was making the journey to Dublin was because, following the legal settlement with his brother, he had invested in a bacon business in Dublin's Liberties. Matty Lyons, a friend from Longford, had tipped him off that there was a small bacon factory for sale that needed investment. Lyons and his family were well known in the meat business and Matty was to become Reynolds' main partner subsequently in his petfood manufacturing business. The bacon business, Kehoe's of the Liberties, was run out of the oldest factory in Dublin, having originally been founded in 1742. Reynolds bought the business for £60,000 and reckoned that the property alone might have been worth that sum. He knew little about the business:

> I had put the day to day running of the factory in the hands of two men well known for their expertise in the business, leaving me free to concentrate on the export side of things and on raising productivity. Within a year we had turned the business around from a loss to a profit, employing a steady rota of staff, and it continued as such, until under a government scheme aiming to rationalise the industry, I surrendered my bacon exporting licence.

In spite of the fact that there was a fire at the factory before it closed down, Reynolds subsequently rented it to the Coyle brothers, who took the business forward again. Harry Coyle only had a handshake deal that he could buy the factory and recalled, 'We only had a gentleman's agreement, but he stuck to his word. When we finally bought the factory in 1973, he had been offered a higher price than us, but he never mentioned the fact. He stuck to the deal.'[2] This straightforwardness in Reynolds' character is mentioned again and again in relation to both his business and political career. He was a man who stuck to his word and rarely, if ever, deviated from it.

It was while running the bacon business in the Liberties in Dublin that Reynolds took time to follow the Arms Trial going on in the Four Courts, just a short walk from his business premises. Like the media and everyone else in the country, he was fascinated by the drama that unfolded when two senior cabinet ministers were charged, along with others, with conspiracy to import weapons for nationalists in the North, including members of the IRA. At the centre of these events were one Neil T. Blaney and, of course, Charles

J. Haughey. Though Reynolds didn't know Haughey very well at this stage, Blaney was a very good friend, and both men would be the guiding lights in Reynolds' decision to become involved in politics. When the Arms Trial ended with Haughey's acquittal, Reynolds was there to support him. At this point, Haughey threw down the gauntlet to the then sitting Taoiseach, Jack Lynch, openly challenging him to consider his position. 'Those responsible for this debacle have no option open to them but to take the honourable course ... I think there is some dissatisfaction about the leadership at the moment. The Taoiseach's position is something that will be decided by the parliamentary party', he said, surrounded by supporters, including Reynolds, who had followed him from the Four Courts.[3]

The fact that Reynolds had hooked up with Haughey at this most difficult and traumatic time in his career was a harbinger of things to come. The relationship which began then was to be richly rewarding for Reynolds years later when Haughey became Taoiseach. His strong affiliation with both Blaney and Haughey would place him in the more republican-minded faction of the Fianna Fáil. Yet, apart from this one appearance after the Arms Trial, there is little sense that Reynolds was vocal on either the North or on republican matters. He emerges from this time as a man who is prepared to bide his time and hold his tongue. In time, he would become one of the young men prepared to go out on a limb to push to make Haughey Taoiseach. In the meantime, he had a family to feed and businesses to run, but his fascination with politics had taken root.

Despite the break-up of the ballroom business, Reynolds clearly hankered to be back in the music business. He and Dessie Hynes had identified a few public houses which might offer business opportunities which would make the most of Reynolds' extensive network from his dancehall days, but it was Dessie who found licensed premises to invest in – a small hotel in Malahide. It was originally intended that they would go into business together, but then Reynolds went ahead and invested his own money, raised from the Bank of Ireland, in what became a cabaret venue catering for up to a thousand people. For two years, it seems to have gone well, with Reynolds working behind the bar on occasions when it was busy, while also commuting back and forth to his home in Longford.

The Showboat cabaret opened in the summer of 1968 and burned down in 1970. 'Showboat is a very big and expensive experiment, but I think the time is right for an out-of-town Cabaret Theatre like this,' Reynolds told a music magazine at the time.[4] Years later, he told *Business and Finance* magazine that the place had been underinsured at a figure of £83,000. Quite a bit of refurbishment and building work had gone into the building before it opened for business. It is conceivable that he might have lost money on this venture.

Whatever about the Showboat, Reynolds definitely lost money when he started a business exporting fish. It was blighted by an airstrike in France and an inability to source adequate supplies for markets in Paris and Spain. In his desperation to make the business work, Reynolds purchased an executive de Havilland jet and converted it for cargo purposes so that his lobster and fish could reach the overseas markets, but the cost of the jet and the failure to source supplies rapidly finished the business. In his autobiography, he mused, 'Luckily this had not been the only venture to occupy my time. I now owned a share in the Odeon cinema in Longford, had invested in a hire-purchase company involved in financing the buying of cars and machinery, and, more importantly I was germinating the kernel of an idea that would become my biggest business success.' Reynolds was beginning to research how to get into the petfood sector.

Reynolds had never been idle, in any real sense, since he had left school and taken that fateful decision not to sit the final banking exam. He was a man in an awful hurry. From his marriage to Kathleen in 1962, his business career had followed a steady and improving upward trajectory. Settled in a comfortable home, he had added to his family since his first-born, Miriam, had arrived in 1963. By 1972, he and Kathleen had seven children, with Miriam followed by Phillip (1964), Emer (1966), Leonie (1968), Abbie or Albert junior (1969), Cathy (1971) and Andrea (1972). In his autobiography, Reynolds confesses his disappointment that he was not around for his family as much as he might have liked when they were growing up. In later years, he somewhat made up for this when he bought an apartment in Dublin and was able to be with them when most of them attended university. Yet, for all his regretted absences, he seems to have had a strong relationship with all his children, no mean feat since his busy career in business in the 1960s was soon to run in parallel with his even more time-consuming interest and involvement with politics from the 1970s.

Just three years after the Arms Trial in 1970, Reynolds made his next business acquisition when he bought one of Longford's two local newspapers. In 1973, he purchased the less well-known of the two, the *Longford News*. This investment was to catapult him into the media world and greatly enhance his profile as a local businessman. In the long term, it would also catapult him into national coverage, when he went about standing for election. As Albert explained:

> It was a small-time paper with a small circulation, but I could see the potential for developing it into something to rival other local papers. From my days with the showbands I also knew the value of advertising, and I foresaw that this would become an important part of the future; as towns and commerce modernised and developed, the world of publicity would grow too.

The paper's eccentric prior owner and editor, Vincent Gill, had sold it to Reynolds when he ran into him on the street one day. Gill's mother had been a Reynolds and he got it into his head that he must be related to Albert. Reynolds did not disabuse him of the idea and bought the paper for £5,000.

The first thing Reynolds did on buying the newspaper was to move it to new premises and poach Derek Cobbe, the managing director of the rival newspaper, to head up his operation at the *Longford News*. Cobbe, who was non-political, had gotten to know and become friendly with Reynolds in his capacity as president of the Longford Chamber of Commerce. They hit it off. Cobbe would become a lifelong friend and was involved in Reynolds' petfood business and his election machine. 'The deal he gave me was good. It gave me a good wage, 10 per cent of the company and he bought me a lovely Audi car,' reminisced Cobbe.[5] The car was the first transaction for another Reynolds business venture, a hire purchase company called ABC Finance.

Initially, the newspaper was something of a family affair, with Kathleen and Albert actually distributing the paper to shops around the county. It had a small circulation (*c.* 2,500 copies) compared to its more respected competitor, the *Longford Leader*. Cobbe insists Reynolds did not buy the paper as an investment; rather, he was more worried that the *Leader* would buy it and simply close it down. The *Leader* was a Fine Gael-leaning newspaper and Reynolds, perhaps with an eye on his political future, did not want to be left with just one, politically hostile, paper in his adopted county.

Cobbe states that Reynolds did not involve himself at all with the day-to-day running of the newspaper – he was a great delegator, only showing up for meetings in the office when there were decisions to be taken and his approval had to be given. The circulation climbed and the *Longford News* struck it lucky when its main rival was the target of a debilitating strike, which kept it off the newsstands for over a year. During the strike at the *Leader*, the circulation of the *Longford News* soared to nearly 12,000. It had only been acquired by Reynolds a year or so before this strike. As time went on, the circulation under Reynolds' ownership settled at around 9,000. The newspaper became a training ground for a number of journalists who went on to bigger and better things in the national scene, including John Donlon (the *Star*), Aidan O'Keefe (the *Sunday World*), Liam Collins (the *Sunday Independent*) and the now very well-known crime correspondent and author Paul Williams. This aspect of newspaper ownership was good for Reynolds. It meant that before he even arrived in Leinster House, he was a known and, most likely, welcome figure in media circles. That said, Liam Collins does not think he deliberately set out to court the media but simply had an open and approachable manner.[6]

Eugene McGee of the rival *Longford Leader* provided the following character assessment of Reynolds at this time, prior to his decision to stand for election for the Dáil:

> There are no airs and graces about Albert. He might have driven a £52,000 Jaguar, one of the few concessions he made to his enormous wealth, but he was also capable of stopping the Jaguar when he met a few County Council workers on the road and having a chat as if he was one of their next-door neighbours.[7]

Over the years, the *Longford News* came in for some gentle ribbing from the country's leading satirical TV show, hosted by Frank Hall. As a regular feature, the *Halls Pictorial Weekly* team would have a sardonic review of the local newspapers around the country. Hall was often heard to ask his newspaper reviewer, 'How many photographs of Albert Reynolds in this week's *Longford News*?' It created great laughs but, according to Derek Cobbe, Reynolds was not given overly favourable treatment when it came to coverage. In fact, he points out that since Reynolds was the only TD in Longford when he started out in politics, he would have received equal coverage in the *Longford Leader*. Cobbe, with a sense of humour and in an effort to get back at *Halls Pictorial Weekly*, published over fifty photos of Albert in one edition.

Reynolds, as his political career progressed, was anxious to offload the newspaper. He eventually sold it to Jack Davis of the *Meath Chronicle*, whom he favoured as a buyer because of his Fianna Fáil credentials. Once again, Reynolds had made a big profit on his investment; it fetched somewhere in the region of £95,000. His friend and fellow businessman Noel Hanlon bought the premises from him and leased a portion of it to the *Meath Chronicle*.

The *Longford News* had been fairly kind to Albert Reynolds. It had given him both a national and additional business profile in his constituency. As a local politician from Longford, it also gave him ready access to the national media when he made the big step up to national politics.

CHAPTER FIVE

Petfood

C&D Foods was the business, apart from dancehalls, for which Albert Reynolds was to become best known. It started life in 1969 with a conversation between two friends. Matty Lyons, who had put Albert onto the idea of buying the bacon factory in the Liberties, went into business with Reynolds to establish a new venture in the petfood sector. Reynolds had seen how offal was taken away from the factory in the Liberties and once asked what happened to it. He had been told that it would be frozen and sent to the UK before coming back into Ireland as petfood. The enterprising duo and two smaller investors had started the business with a grant of £45,000 from the Industrial Development Authority (IDA), a state agency, and put no actual money into the venture themselves at its inception; the Munster & Leinster and the Industrial Credit Corporation put up an additional £47,000 in loans. Raising the money was impressive and underpins Reynolds' strong view that bank funding, without personal guarantees, was his preferred option when it came to funding his ventures.

The company came into life prior to Reynolds' entry into public life. It was his longest-lasting venture and, in the end, the one that generated the most profit for him. Following his election to the Dáil, his involvement was to be sporadic. In 1979, his formal ties to the business ended, in executive terms, when he became a minister. But he would turn his attention to the business more at times when his party was sent to the opposition benches, so his next sustained period of involvement came when Fianna Fáil were in opposition between 1983 and 1987. Despite his periods in government, Reynolds always took a keen interest in the company's progress, naturally enough, given that he was the founder and largest shareholder. The company would have been much lower profile were it not for the fact that he was in public life and climbing up the ministerial ladder.

C&D grew, in turnover terms, from the 1970s to the 1990s. It had been grant-assisted or helped by government agencies at key moments in its growth trajectory. Not only did it receive initial funding from the IDA, but there was also to be assistance from the state rescue agency Fóir Teoranta in 1984. This decision was not without controversy since the then Chairman of Fóir Teoranta, Noel Hanlon, was a lifelong friend of Reynolds and an equally prominent businessman in Longford. He would have been appointed to the position in the state body with the help of Reynolds. When questions were asked regarding funding for C&D, Hanlon made it clear that he had absented himself from the boardroom when the decision to assist was taken. In 1981, C&D received funding from FEOGA, an EU funding mechanism for agrifood processing companies in disadvantaged areas. Assistance from this source was also much commented upon, but, although such funding raised eyebrows, it did not become a significant source of controversy. The most controversial assistance given to C&D was significantly later, when Reynolds was Taoiseach; it involved a £1.1 million investment in the company from a Saudi national and businessman.

There was some delay in getting the business off the ground and it was not until 1970 that a site had been acquired in Edgeworthstown and the manufacturing plant built. There had been a launch with a big reception in Dublin but, after a year and a half there, auditors were recommending liquidation on the grounds of insolvency. 'There were many teething problems and difficulties, and customers were hard to win over. We needed them to try our product but we faced a lot of resistance, from British buyers in particular. Sales were not what we hoped for and canning and promotion were costly,' said Reynolds, who, despite the obvious adversity in the business, was determined to keep it going. Lyons wanted out and apparently threw the keys of the factory at Reynolds during one row. Litigation was to follow in the wake of these disagreements, and things were difficult between the two men, particularly since Lyons was the majority shareholder (51 per cent); the balance was held by Reynolds (29 per cent) and two other investors (10 per cent each).

Reynolds threw himself into the business, while Lyons went away to pursue other opportunities. 'Competition was fierce but Albert had employed a very gifted Sales Executive in Norman Spence and in 1974 he was successful in concluding an agreement for the production of the Sainsbury brand. It was this contract that was the key to the future success of the business,' says Bob Cumbers, who acted as an accountant and financial controller with the company until 1979.[1]

Lyons then reappeared on the scene and Cumbers states that Reynolds' biggest business risk was in resisting an attempt by Lyons to take control of the business. Reynolds staged a vote of shareholders, around company resolutions, knowing that, on the basis of a show of hands, of the three shareholders present, he and the other could outvote Matty Lyons. Such a vote should have been on the weight of the actual shares held and Lyons, visibly angry, went straight to the High Court to vindicate his rights as a majority shareholder.

The hearing, in front of Mr Justice Kenny, ended with an unusual result. It ordered that Lyons be bought out by Reynolds at an agreed valuation of the shares and Reynolds be left in charge of the business. According to Reynolds, 'He ruled that while the throwing of the keys by Matty Lyons did not amount to a formal legal agreement, I had nevertheless accepted the responsibility of employing the staff and of servicing the debt, and it was only when Lyons saw the business starting to build up again that he came back and wanted to resume control.' It took two years to resolve the Lyons shareholding issue and it was finally settled by mediation for a sum of around £44,000, according to Reynolds' biographer Tim Ryan. Further litigation was to follow in the years that followed, centred around a 10 per cent promise of shares to Norman Spence. This matter was settled with a payout of £90,000. These legal disputes caused a degree of bitterness and again indicate Reynolds' ruthless side when he took up cudgels against those with whom he had disputes.

The internal fights in the business saw Reynolds consolidate the company's progress and his own shareholding control. As Bob Cumbers remarked, the gamble in the High Court paid off: 'Under Albert's guidance C&D became one of the most successful private label petfood companies in

Europe.' At one point, prior to further customer diversification, Sainsbury's accounted for 60 per cent of the company's turnover. The British retailer had very high standards and demanded a process of continual improvement in companies that it dealt with as suppliers. This very demanding regime put C&D on a very firm manufacturing platform from the outset and gave them the opportunity to chase wider European business and show a strong reference customer with the prestige British retailer. 'It was Albert's management style not to be involved in the day-to-day running of the plant but he insisted on being told of any problems, which might affect our customers. These were reviewed and action agreed during his visits in the evenings,' stated Cumbers. Reynolds would personally contact Sainsbury's at crucial times when the customer had concerns, in order to calm them down and give them assurances about the company's commitment as a supplier. By 1985, C&D had a turnover of £7.4 million, with £4.5 million coming from exports and £2.9 million from the Irish market. Retailers like Quinnsworth, Tesco, Dunnes, Superquinn and Londis were all customers. Reynolds was a significant promoter of his own business in the early years, even claiming to *Business & Finance* magazine that the petfood made by C&D was so good that he had eaten it himself.[2]

Reynolds' enthusiasm for the business never waned. He built up significant employment in the area but was not overly enthusiastic about staff rights and put a quick stop to recommendations for profit-share arrangements for employees. That said, there were trade unions in the factory and the Services, Industrial and Professional and Technical Union (SIPTU) official Bob Brady, who dealt with members in the factory, felt that Albert Reynolds was a fair employer, but there were ongoing problems with wages and conditions. At one time, in the Dáil, Michael McDowell raised the issue of the company pleading its inability to pay a national pay agreement increment to workers at a time when C&D were claiming to be in profit.

In June 1994, the company was plunged into a major controversy that was to unsettle Reynolds as Taoiseach and damage him in the opinion polls. At a time of great tension with his coalition partner, Labour, it emerged that C&D had received a low-interest loan from a Saudi businessman, Mr Masri, who had invested £1.1 million in the business under a state-run passports-for-investment scheme. Two of Reynolds' closest political supporters and friends were involved in flagging up the investment, namely Pádraig Flynn, the then Minister for Justice, and Michael Smith from Tipperary, who was then a minister, too. Suspicions were raised by the fact that the decision around the investment was taken in 1992 in the period after the Progressive Democrats (PDs) had left the coalition government they were in with Fianna Fáil and before the general election had taken place. The media went into overdrive and the Labour Party became very uneasy about the issue.

The PDs, none too pleased about their ejection from government by Reynolds, were not in the mood for holding back on this controversy. Despite protestations of innocence and claims that the decision had been taken at a remove, the Labour Leader Dick Spring investigated the matter personally. Reynolds invited Spring to take a look at the files himself, saying he would get Minister Máire Geoghegan-Quinn to give him access to them in the Department of Justice.

Government press secretary, Seán Duignan, takes up the story: 'Spring, he said, then coolly informed him that he had already done so [looked at the files]. Reynolds told me he could hardly believe Spring had gone ahead without first informing him.' Reynolds confessed to his press secretary, 'I have to admit that, for once, I was speechless.'[3] In any event, having inspected the files, Spring pronounced himself happy that the Taoiseach had not been involved and that the transaction had been carried out on an arms-length basis. McDowell then went on the attack again, stating that Spring was 'morally brain dead.'[4] The whole thing embarrassed Labour greatly, as the controversy had coincided with the introduction of the party's much-heralded new Ethics Bill legislation to cover public representatives. Further embarrassment followed when Reynolds continued to insist in the Dáil that there was no planned legislation to tidy up the passports-for-investment scheme, one of the concessions he had made to Spring to de-escalate the whole controversy.

While C&D had been a great success as a company and brought Albert Reynolds great wealth, its involvement in the passports-for-investment scheme had also caused him a great deal of trouble. The controversy came within a few short weeks of the European elections and two crucial by-elections that would ultimately change the numbers in Leinster House. These became an ominous preview of the results of the controversy that would ultimately bounce Reynolds out of power in 1994.

CHAPTER SIX

Longford

As the 1970s opened up, Albert Reynolds' involvement in politics increased. As we have already seen, he had learned much of his politics during by-election campaigns and in his work with the then acknowledged genius of political campaigning, Neil T. Blaney. This experience had been further enhanced by his organisational role with the local independent TD, Joe Sheridan. Throughout the 1960s and early 1970s, Reynolds appears to have had a huge appetite for learning about politics. He tells us:

> My local political life began to edge forward. I had not only served as the Longford delegate to the Fianna Fáil National Executive from 1971 to 1974, but in 1973 I had also been appointed Director of Elections for Fianna Fáil in Longford. For me a key achievement was when I was selected as President of the Longford Chamber of Commerce in 1972.

The important point here is that Reynolds was becoming even more prominent in the community in Longford and also within the ranks of the Fianna Fáil organisation in the county. His membership of the Fianna Fáil national executive made him significant within the national organisation. This national executive had monthly meetings in the party's headquarters in Dublin, which Reynolds attended, and such meetings were presided over by the party's leader. In addition to those made through his dancehall business, Reynolds was fast acquiring further valuable connections on a countrywide basis.

It was around this time that I became aware of him, less in person, but rather by name. At a very young age, my father brought me over to Longford to have a look at a municipal pool that had been built by Reynolds, Hynes and other local businessmen who had formed a committee, including Reynolds' business partner in C&D, Matty Lyons, and the local Fianna Fáil TD, Frank Carter, who had a shoe business in the town. Neil Blaney had provided a 50 per cent grant for the project from his budget in the Department of Local Government. Carnivals and dances were organised to raise the balance, with the understanding that the community swimming pool would eventually be taken over by the local authority, Longford County Council.

It was a brave project and one that was well ahead of its time. Towns that were considered far wealthier than Longford Town, like nearby Mullingar and Athlone, did not have such a facility. As we drove over to see the pool, my father was very enthusiastic about the project and the businessmen, including Reynolds, who were behind the whole thing. I think I was among the first people to swim in it before it was formally opened. It was a great day out and the committee briefed my father, as the local minister based in the midlands, on their plans. The whole thing appeared very professional to my young mind. Reynolds was a well-known businessman and this project for his town stood out and anchored him firmly in the community where he had chosen to raise his children.

The presence of Frank Carter on the committee underpinned the strong friendship that existed between him and Reynolds at this time. Carter was from a distinguished political family and Carter's father, Tom, had served in the Dáil. The friendship with Carter developed and Reynolds takes up the story:

> In 1974 the local Fianna Fáil organisation, and the long-time sitting TD, Frank Carter, approached me and asked me if I would stand for the local county council, and also if I would start preparing myself to arrange my business in such a way that it would allow me to do politics as well. I was happy to agree.

With the clear backing of the local sitting deputy and his strong community and business profile, Reynolds topped the poll on this, his first electoral outing. He secured just in excess of 900 votes in the town. It was an impressive debut in local politics. The local paper reminded readers of his obvious popularity, stating that a large crowd had gathered outside the Temperance Hall to await the announcement of his victory. At the time, TDs were also allowed to sit on the County Council and Reynolds sat beside his early mentor in politics, Carter, at the council's public meetings. Over time, Reynolds became a sort of right-hand man to Carter, and I remember him being described to me some years later as a sort of 'bag carrier' for him. For a time, the two were inseparable and clearly Reynolds, with his business skills, membership of the national executive and community projects, was useful to Carter.

In his election campaign, Reynolds had stressed the themes of creating more jobs in the county and attracting new industry. This campaigning theme was to be repeated in his subsequent effort to stand for the Dáil and the language clearly chimed with his business profile. The Dáil constituency was a two-county one (Longford–Westmeath) and in the 1973 election, party representation had fallen to just one seat instead of the two it traditionally held, one from Longford and one from Westmeath. My own grandfather, Patrick Lenihan, had been elected from the Athlone area for the constituency back in the 1960s.

Despite having been assisted by Carter as he stood for the first time for election, sometime between the local elections in 1974 and the general election of 1977, relations between Carter and Reynolds began to sour. Perhaps the older man was becoming slightly nervous of the energetic younger man he was supporting. Derek Cobbe, managing director of the Reynolds-owned *Longford News* at the time, believes that Reynolds came to dislike Carter. A story from the time seems to back this up. Jimmy Molloy, who wrote a column for the *Longford News* and owned the *Musical Gazette*, wrote a tongue-in-cheek gossip piece about Carter who, at the time, lived beside the town's graveyard, suggesting he wouldn't need a hearse when he died as he could simply be lowered over the adjacent wall. Carter was annoyed and sued the paper for libel.

It was, according to Cobbe, the only time Reynolds came into the newspaper offices. He was angry, asking whether Cobbe or any of the other staff even read what was going into the paper. Reynolds signed a cheque for £100 for the Vincent de Paul charity by way of a settlement and Carter was meant to receive an apology. However, though annoyed that the piece had been published, at this point Reynolds was clearly tired of Carter. 'I am not apologising to Frank Carter,' he stated. Cobbe found a way around the problem and a clarification rather than an apology was inserted into the paper. Cobbe believes that while the two men kept up appearances, shaking hands with each other when they met, Reynolds, in fact, 'didn't like him at all' by this point.[1]

There is some dispute over what happened next. Frank Carter is said to have signalled to those close to him in Fianna Fáil that he was standing down and would not be a candidate for the party in the 1977 general election when it came. This indication to party activists was the subject of much speculation, but Reynolds appears to have believed that Carter's decision not to run was firm: 'After I was elected to the Council, Frank told me privately he wouldn't be running again.'[2]

It turned out that Carter, having presumably changed his mind, did choose to run again, while, in the meantime, Reynolds had staked out his position with party activists and was also running for the nomination from the local organisation. Many believed that Carter's indication that he was standing down was a simple, frequently played ruse by incumbent Dáil deputies to generate sympathy and support. If he was looking for sympathy and support, however, in electoral terms he was dicing with the wrong man in Albert Reynolds, who decided to stand his ground and push his ambition forward to the party's selection convention. He confessed to journalist Deirdre Purcell of the *Sunday Tribune* that it had been a difficult decision to take on the incumbent deputy; it would have been frowned upon within the party at the time. 'But I was so far down the line, I'd even made management changes so that the business could carry on.'[3] The stage was set for a dramatic confrontation between young and old, master and understudy.

The convention was set for Sunday, 22 May 1977, in the County Hall in Mullingar. The instruction from party headquarters was that there would only be one candidate from Longford. Des O'Malley, then very senior in the party under Jack Lynch, was sent down to chair the convention. Over time, O'Malley would become a sort of nemesis to Reynolds when he finally became Taoiseach; at this stage, however, there was no thought that Reynolds would climb the ladder that far. From this distance, it is hard to know if O'Malley was even aware of Reynolds' wider connections with Neil Blaney (now expelled from Fianna Fáil) and Charles Haughey. Unbeknownst to the then leadership group in the party, Haughey had been assisting his own pledged men to get into positions and win nominations to run in different parts of the country. Reynolds was clearly one of these but had, in typical style, flown sight unseen under the radar.

The result of the convention was truly extraordinary for the time. Reynolds won some 209 votes out of a possible total of 302. Frank Carter, for all his years of Dáil service, could only muster a meagre seventy-seven. In effect, Carter had been deselected, something that rarely, if ever, happened in the party. Carter left the Temperance Hall an angry man. He later lobbied Fianna Fáil's head office to be included or added to the ticket, but they chose instead to add on a younger man, barrister Henry Abbot from Mullingar. It was suggested subsequently that a number of members of the constituency party had tried to persuade Carter to stand down rather than face defeat, but he was not willing to do so.

Some time later, the bitterness Carter felt about the way he had been treated spilled out in an interview he gave to the *Longford Leader*. He claimed he had been the victim of a conspiracy by party headquarters and the parliamentary party. He did not pull his punches when it came to Reynolds either, stating that he would not be backing him, or indeed urging his supporters to do so. Reynolds' simple reply to Carter, when interviewed by the same newspaper, was to tell them: 'But time and tide wait for no man.' It was one of those phrases much used by Reynolds throughout his political life. He was now developing a repertoire of stories, phrases and anecdotes that would carry him forward to the highest office in the land. According to Liam Collins, then a journalist in the *Longford News*, 'he disposed of Frank Carter in a pretty ruthless fashion.'[4] The event in the County Hall in Mullingar was, subsequently, jokingly referred to as the night of the 'short knives' because Reynolds and Carter had sat so close to one another as they waited for the result of the vote.

News of the deselection of Frank Carter travelled fast around the wider party. Though he was not a national figure, Reynolds was already being spoken of as a young gun of the party and being compared to another candidate in Roscommon, Seán Doherty, who together with his running mate, Terry Leydon, had also deselected the sitting TD across the Shannon,

Hugh Gibbons. Reynolds would become an exemplar of the type of pushy, impatient and ruthless new deputies who would win out as a result of Jack Lynch's landslide victory.

Reynolds had not just developed his own repertoire of convenient political phrases but had also adjusted to the political tricks of his new trade. One particular story from the time which exemplifies this relates to the fact that Reynolds had a penchant for big and expensive cars. 'He would park his Blue Daimler car in the Cathedral car park. Because the car was so obviously his, people would think he was around and had in fact attended any funeral taking place there. Reynolds would be elsewhere or in the office,' says Liam Collins.[5]

Another journalist, Kathy Sheridan, gives this glimpse of the election campaign of 1977 and Reynolds' first venture into national politics, clearly indicating that Reynolds had brought a strong element of razzmatazz to the election:

> It was 1977, the general election was in full swing and the one feature that could not be ignored – apart from Fianna Fáil's brazen, vote-buying manifesto – was Albert Reynold's tanned visage. It gleamed out of the full-colour (a first), highly personalised (another first) posters blitzing the entire Longford–Westmeath constituency. The man himself was bounding through both counties, patting babies and pinning the odd fiver beneath a pram hood, trailing a heady air of money, glamour, ferocious energy and US-style razzmatazz. It felt like Hollywood come to Longford.[6]

The campaign was directed from his home, 'Mount Carmel' on the Dublin road. Ensconced there was his business friend Noel Hanlon, lifelong supporter and Councillor Mickey Doherty and Derek Cobbe. 'Mickey Doherty handled all of the relationships with Fianna Fáil in the county, while Hanlon signed the cheques and raised the money. I ran with the leaflets, public relations and publicity,'[7] says Cobbe. The slogan for the contest was 'To get things done, Vote Reynolds 1.' The personalised nature of the campaign and the amount of money being spent raised a few eyebrows. The tradition within the party, up to that point, was for each candidate on the party's ticket to be given equal standing in the literature.

There was also a ban on personalised posters. Reynolds and his team got around this by getting the country singer Larry Cunningham to say they were his posters. Cobbe added the words: 'Issued in support of the candidate by Larry Cunningham, Granard'. It was a neat way of getting around the headquarters ordinance that personalised posters were forbidden. Reynolds was the first candidate in the country to have full-colour posters in a campaign that was designed for impact.

At another level, the campaign was receiving further attention. There was plenty of gossip and rumour being generated behind the scenes. Kathy Sheridan, Joe Sheridan's daughter, noted that Albert's decision to stand created a 'certain frisson between the two men, especially since Albert's brother had sided with Joe, but they remained civilised – in public anyway'.[8] As things turned out, there was no real need to worry, as both Reynolds' old mentor Joe Sheridan and Reynolds himself were elected, with Sheridan heading the poll in the four-seat constituency.[9] Reynolds was bound for Leinster House to take up his place as the new TD for Longford.

The 1977 manifesto that had brought Jack Lynch and Fianna Fáil their whirlwind, landslide election has been well and truly criticised since that event. Many in the party, including my father and Charlie Haughey, were privately opposed to it when it was launched. It is often cited as a prime example of the evils of 'auction' politics. The main promises that stand out now were commitments to get rid of both rates on private dwellings and the car tax. The magnitude of the victory, the promises made and the subsequent poor management by Lynch were to pile problem upon problem on the new Taoiseach. In time, the wolves would begin to circle around Lynch, and Reynolds was to become one of those wolves, more silent than others in the campaign to replace Lynch with Charlie Haughey, but no less lethal than the others involved for the steely determination with which he went about his work. Many years later, Reynolds poured scorn on the 1977 election promises, stating: 'When I was asked my view on that manifesto, I said it was a crime to write it, and an even bigger crime to implement it.' Reynolds was learning the political habit of adjusting your line to suit the times.

CHAPTER SEVEN

Gang of Five

Now ensconced at Leinster House, Albert Reynolds got down to work while continuing to build his business interests. He was one of a group of TDs who came in with the Jack Lynch 1977 intake. Unbeknownst to themselves, this group of Fianna Fáil deputies was to form the backbone of the party's administrations well into the 1990s and beyond. The party's backbenches included people like Reynolds' successor as leader Bertie Ahern, Pádraig Flynn, Máire Geoghegan-Quinn, Charlie McCreevy and many others.

The government relied on people such as Des O'Malley, who had rallied around Lynch in the aftermath of the Arms Trial when the party's previous big personalities, including Blaney, Haughey and Kevin Boland, had been cleared out. Over the next two years, however, the Lynch leadership was shaken to its foundations by its attempts to implement the promises it had made and an economy that had spun out of control. More serious for Jack Lynch was the fact that he and his team were also losing touch with their own parliamentary colleagues. Reynolds and others began pushing for a change of leadership in the party and Charles J. Haughey was the man on behalf of whom they were pushing.

On 30 November 1977, Reynolds made his first speech as a member of Dáil Éireann, during the 2nd Stage debate on the Industrial Development Bill:

> Until the day comes when we develop and process our own raw materials, our factories will never be in a position to pay the prices and give the return to the Irish farmer that he deserves. We are commodity selling abroad and this has been traditional in the beef trade because

that is the easy way out. History has made us a dependent race and we always look to someone else to solve our problems. Down the country they look to Dublin and to this House to solve the unemployment problem and of late people are starting to look to Brussels to solve our problems. The world does not owe us a living.[1]

The speech dealt with a number of issues covering the country's importation of £200 million-worth of agricultural produce and the need for the banks to provide more venture capital to those starting to build their own businesses. Drawing from his expertise in running his petfood manufacturing company, Reynolds bemoaned the fact that so many businesspeople in Ireland did not look further than the domestic market: 'I was not interested in feeding cats and dogs in this country. I was interested in the market abroad.' On the same day as he gave this speech, Reynolds was appointed to the Dáil's most powerful committee – the Public Accounts Committee, which scrutinised in detail all the expenditure by the state. It was another sign that his business background and demonstrable success were putting him on the fast track up the political ladder.

The Albert Reynolds who emerges from this speech is someone anxious to free up opportunities for businesspeople, like himself, to do more. The other thing that strikes you is the tendency on his part to borrow directly from his own experience when making a speech. This pattern would be repeated over the years and, at a very practical level, he tended to speak on topics with which he was comfortable and about which he had knowledge. In this and many other settings, he deployed his own home-spun wisdom on the subjects he was asked to discuss. There are very few high-blown rhetorical flourishes to a Reynolds speech. Journalist John Donlon, who reported on Reynolds during his time in Longford County Council, remarks, 'In fairness to Albert, he always cut to the point.'[2]

During this period, Charles Haughey was Minister for Health and was assiduous in the attention he gave to his parliamentary colleagues. He brought in a civil servant, whom he had worked with over the years, as a Special Advisor; his name was Brendan O'Donnell. O'Donnell briefed and kept in contact with the Fianna Fáil backbenches. This was a new level of service from a minister and the new intake, including Reynolds, could not but be impressed. Haughey became the most accessible of the ministerial team under Lynch and for many of the newer TDs he was the one they related to most. Many of the new TDs were simply 'unknowns' to the group gathered around Lynch and, in some cases, Lynch's men would have struggled to remember their names. Not so Haughey.

When the government started to run into difficulties, it came as a surprise to the Lynch group, but these newer deputies, and especially Reynolds, were much more impatient than their predecessors. Reynolds and many others were not content to hang around, obediently, until their time had come:

> Lynch should not have been surprised. Even in the first flush of victory in June 1977 he recognised that the scale of his win would become a problem. He remarked on television on the night of the election count that he would have preferred a smaller majority. In a remarkably short time he was proved right. Very early on discipline in the party began to break down.[3]

The Lynch leadership of Fianna Fáil had been something of an electoral fairy-tale. Put into the role of party leader in 1966, with the help of both Blaney and Haughey, he won the election in 1969, establishing himself as a popular phenomenon in his own right and less the compromise candidate he had been presented as. However, the party had been in power for too long and, after the Arms Trial of 1970, it started to suffer because of this, losing out in the 1973 general election that led to a Labour/Fine Gael coalition government.

In the wake of the landslide electoral success of 1977, Lynch's government was soon derailed by a spate of industrial unrest, in particular a five-month postal dispute. A badly handled attempt to task farmers' incomes by his Finance Minister (and heir apparent), George Colley, led to a backlash amongst his own deputies when the farmers and, ultimately, ordinary taxpayers in the PAYE category hit the streets in anger that their tax burden was being ignored. The local and European elections in mid-1979 saw Lynch's party secure their worst result for fifty years. Fianna Fáil lost two by-elections in Cork, Lynch's native county and electoral heartland. These realities, combined with sniping from his own backbenches about security co-operation with the British over Northern Ireland, became a giant nail in the Lynch coffin.

A strong push against Lynch's leadership began with Jackie Fahey, a TD for Waterford, and Tom McEllistrim, a TD for Kerry. Both were unhappy about how the government was faring, McEllistrim all the more so because he came from a strong republican background. Around this time, a lot of the party's rural TDs, like McEllistrim and Fahey, would stay in Jury's Hotel in Dublin's Ballsbridge. The hotel gave a good rate for TDs up in Dublin for the Dáil's three-day sittings and, as a result, the hotel became the focal point for a number of deputies plotting to change the leadership of Fianna Fáil and install Charlie Haughey. According to Vincent Brown in *Magill* magazine, the Fahey and McEllistrim thought that 'Of the other TDs staying in Jury's on a regular basis, they had good reason to believe that two of them, Albert Reynolds of Longford–Westmeath and Seán Doherty of Roscommon–Leitrim, shared their disenchantment with what was going on.'[4] On an approach from the two men, Reynolds stepped into the beating heart of the conspiracy to get rid of Lynch. Mark Killilea of the Galway East constituency was next to be enlisted in their efforts. This brought their number to five, hence the description of them as the 'Gang of Five' once the heave against Lynch was over.

The presence of Mark Killilea was important because he shared a house and a friendship with Ray McSharry, who became one of the crucial, behind-the-scenes movers in the Haughey campaign. McSharry had to be guarded in the way he went about things as he was a Minister of State in the government serving under George Colley in the Department of Finance. From Sligo, McSharry had attended the same Summerhill boarding school as Albert Reynolds. The two got on well and were determined to keep their role in the plot that was to unfold as discreet as possible. Both men had a background in business and knew how to proceed with their plans in a confidential manner.

The Gang of Five got down to work and made contact with others whom they knew were disgruntled. All of this contact work had to be done under the radar and under the nose of the established leadership of the party. The first meeting of the Gang of Five was held in the Coffee Dock restaurant in Jury's Hotel. All five of them agreed that they wanted a change of leadership and that the replacement should be Charlie Haughey. They decided to keep their preferred choice for a new leader to themselves while they focused on first removing Lynch. Their first initiative was to stake out some ground and stage a meeting for TDs who were their colleagues in the party; in line with the American custom, this was referred to as a caucus. The 'caucus' meeting had to be carefully arranged so as not to draw attention or suspicion from the top element of the party. In the autumn of 1979, the five went around the corridors of Leinster House surreptitiously mentioning to those they believed shared their discontent that a meeting was planned to discuss the party's predicament. This was not an official gathering of party deputies, so if news got out, it would get people into trouble. Yet, to the surprise of the Gang of Five, some thirty colleague deputies showed up. Jackie Fahey was informally appointed to chair the meeting. He ruled out any attempt to raise the leadership issue, confining the discussions to sources of discontent.

Such was the success of the meeting that the five decided it was too risky to stage another one. Despite the 'cloak and dagger' aspect to the way the meeting had been arranged, the leadership had found out about it after the fact. At the next gathering of the parliamentary party, the top brass were 'furious'. Not knowing who was at the caucus meeting, nor even who the ringleaders were, Jack Lynch demanded that his TDs state who had attended. According to Vincent Brown, he was met by a 'wall of silence' from his colleagues.

As time went by, those who were discontented paid informal visits to other hotels where TDs were staying, such as the Wicklow Hotel and Power's Hotel. The epicentre of the plot remained at Jury's, however, and, over time, many more TDs started turning up. It had a sociability to it that they all enjoyed.

Whilst all of this was going on, Reynolds was starting to be noticed more widely in political circles. One valuable insight into his character as a backbencher at around this time comes from Finn McCool, a Department of Finance official, who acted as an assistant private secretary to Ray

McSharry in the late 1970s. He needed a guest speaker for a business dinner down in the West of Ireland. Senator Eoin Ryan had asked for a minister to attend and address a gathering of influential businesspeople. Ryan was both a senator and a key figure in the Fianna Fáil party's fundraising efforts with industry. McCool was not able to book Minister for Finance Colley and his Minister of State was having a medical procedure, so he pulled out the *Nealon's Guide* to the members of the Dáil in desperation to see if he could find a suitable speaker. His eyes landed on Albert Reynolds and, encouraged by his business background, he decided he would be a suitable candidate to deliver the speech which would cover budgetary and economic matters. He called over to the Dáil to meet Reynolds, who was delighted to take up the speaking engagement. McCool informed him that the request had come from McSharry.

Reynolds agreed to meet McCool the next morning at his office to discuss the matter further and look at the possible speech. McCool was stunned when Reynolds was there waiting at reception at 9 a.m. Most departments did not open, in those days, until 9.15 a.m. Reynolds took the script, attended the event and, by all subsequent accounts, impressed the audience of senior businesspeople. Ryan, who was very influential, was more than impressed, having initially expressed disappointment to McCool that a minister could not be found to perform the task. Reynolds delivered his speech, without notes, and the story illustrates his determination to get on and impress people.[5] He was becoming a past master in the art of making friends and influencing people.

Following their success with the caucus meeting, the Gang of Five conferred amongst themselves again and decided to escalate things further. They were now not only promoting discontent, but agitating for Lynch to be replaced by Haughey. Jackie Fahey befriended another new deputy, Síle de Valera, a granddaughter of the party's founder. She spoke out against Lynch in relation to the government's policy on Northern Ireland. Then, while Lynch was on a visit to the United States, Clare TD Dr Bill Loughnane called him a 'liar' in relation to statements and agreements made with the British Prime Minister Margaret Thatcher about security co-operation along the border with the North. George Colley, minding things for the Taoiseach while he was abroad, stepped into the controversy and insisted on a motion to expel Loughnane from the parliamentary party over his outburst. When Colley put the motion to the party's deputies, they were hostile to it. The move against Loughnane was seen to be heavy-handed, in particular because Jim Gibbons, a member of the cabinet, had recently defied the whip to vote against his own government and got away with it without punishment.

The meeting of party deputies was adjourned for lunch in a bid to calm things down. 'Albert Reynolds went to Colley and told him his motion had no chance of succeeding but the Tánaiste was adamant.'[6] Colley may have viewed the Reynolds approach as helpful, as, like many of his ministerial colleagues, he was probably unaware of the Longford TD's agitation in the background. Reynolds, like his friend McSharry, was playing his cards close to his chest. Closer to the contest, both of these men were known to be on the Haughey bandwagon, but despite this, right up to the eve of the leadership vote George Colley mistakenly believed that both of them were supporters of his. 'At one stage during the campaign Colley actually believed that Albert Reynolds, one of the Gang of Five, was actually out there canvassing for him. He had never spoken to Reynolds about leadership and neither had any of his canvassers.'[7]

Lynch had intended to resign, but the pressure that had built up had, in the end, forced him to retire earlier than he might have expected. Feeding into his decision to retire was the fact that he believed Colley's assessment that if he, Lynch, went early, then Colley would win the contest to take over as leader. They had not reckoned on the determination of Haughey, or, more importantly, that of the Gang of Five, McSharry, Flynn and a whole host of others. Reynolds, in his affable and inoffensive way, participated behind the scenes and, unknown to his own party leadership, was a significant player in one of the greatest backbench revolts in the country's political history.

On 5 December 1979, Jack Lynch stood down and a hurried contest to replace him was held in a matter of days. Haughey beat Colley by a narrow margin (forty-four votes to thirty-eight) but had managed to persuade only one of the incumbent cabinet (Michael O'Kennedy) to publicly endorse him in advance. Reynolds, for his part, had been tucked in nicely behind the winner for quite some time. He had observed Haughey at close quarters in his hour of turmoil in the Arms Trial. He had kept in contact with him subsequently. In October 1979, Haughey had come to Longford to deliver twenty acute beds for a local nursing home in Edgeworthstown. After the event, he had dined at the Reynolds home. At that stage, Reynolds was actively canvassing support for Haughey as the next leader of the party. Haughey liked Reynolds; he was a self-made businessman and a high achiever. Reynolds' direct approach to life must have suited Haughey, who would show his appreciation in due course, when he sat down to form his first cabinet as Taoiseach.

Just over two years after making his first speech in Leinster House, Reynolds was about to be appointed as a minister. By any yardstick, he had made swift progress through the ranks and was now set up for a twenty-five-year career in politics. His money was made, his family well on their way to being reared and his bank balance full enough to be able to withstand a succession of elections between 1979 and 1982. He had carefully learned the lessons and techniques of the Neil Blaney machine. He had won even more votes in the Longford County Council election of 1979 than in previous elections. The experienced journalist and Longford man John Donlon says there was always an 'excitement about him'.[8] He, Donlon, never believed that Longford County Council was the apex of Reynolds' ambition and formed the view that he was going to head on to higher things. The fact that he had remained unnoticed as a Haughey supporter for so long was testament to his cunning and ability to operate in the murky world of politics while disguising his true intentions.

CHAPTER EIGHT

Minister

The earliest public indication of the Fianna Fáil earthquake, on the election of Charles Haughey, was the new leader's first press conference, where he was flanked by backbenchers with hardly a cabinet minister in sight. In short order, Haughey started to frame his new cabinet, making a flurried set of telephone calls to people about what he should do next. My father, based at home, gave him advice. Most of it was to the effect that he needed to heal the divisions exposed by the leadership contest itself. Albert Reynolds was appointed Minister for Posts and Telegraphs and, in his memoirs, he talks of his surprise at being given a ministerial position:

> I hadn't been expecting anything let alone a cabinet post – after all, I was a fairly new boy in politics, only two years on the back benches – so I was delighted to be given, as I thought, a position in a junior ministry and accepted. It wasn't until someone explained the situation that it dawned on me that it was a full cabinet post.

Haughey had explained to him that it was 'a right bastard of a job' when giving it to him. The country's telephone and postal services were ramshackle and prone to debilitating industrial unrest. Reynolds quickly rang his wife and summoned his family up to Dublin to witness his formal appointment before a full Dáil session.

Alone out of the fabled Gang of Five, Reynolds had been rewarded with a full cabinet ministry. The other four were appointed to junior portfolios, along with other key Haughey supporters like Pádraig Flynn. To the rather more aloof Colley faction, the losers in the contest, these backbench ringleaders were regarded as 'wild men' and disdainfully considered unsuitable to hold ministerial positions. The bitterness of the faction which remained loyal to Lynch, then Colley, and later Des O'Malley, was unquenched, and they would continue to be a source of significant opposition to Haughey. It had been a very close voting result in the leadership contest and bitterness was to characterise the continued feuding until Haughey put down the final revolt of three in 1983.

For his part, for most of his ministerial career, Reynolds was managing political instability within his own party, trying to resuscitate a fragile business environment and focusing on the revival of a heavily indebted macro economy. In the early part of his ministerial and front bench career, he was juggling competing demands and the pressure of three general elections over a short period of time from June 1981 to November 1982. It was a shock immersion in politics at a senior level, but his local constituency machine never failed him. He had taken the precaution of modelling himself on his mentor, Neil Blaney, and copper-fastened stability at a local or constituency level. This allowed him to focus his energies on his national governmental and party obligations.

In keeping with the confidence Haughey entrusted in him as a serious businessman, Reynolds was, shortly after his appointment, given the additional responsibility of Transport, giving him a workforce of 52,000 people across CIÉ, P&T and, separately, the state broadcaster RTÉ. It was more than enough for one man, but my own father, who served at the same cabinet table, assessed him to be one of the most effective ministers he had seen at that stage. According to Reynolds himself, 'The unions were very strong at that time and industrial relations were not at all good. The system was antiquated and disorganised, with mail, even that posted locally, sometimes taking weeks to be delivered.' The challenges were daunting.

'The system Reynolds inherited was more like a patchwork quilt than a communications network. Consecutive governments had failed to plan even one year into the future and had persisted in regarding the P&T as a convenient money-raiser. Throughout the sixties the telephone service had been starved of funds and largely ignored once it continued to return profits.'[1] The poor telephone service, prior to Reynolds' arrival, was a significant blockage to industrial development and those running the IDA were also tearing their hair out because it was cited as a reason for why big companies would not come and invest in Ireland.

Reynolds did not waste time. He did his homework and, before his first cabinet meeting, he had prepared a pitch to his own colleagues. He reckoned he might meet with resistance amongst the more established cabinet colleagues as a new boy on the block coming up with an ambitious plan. Reynolds wrote in his autobiography:

> I told the rest of them in no uncertain terms that if we didn't invest in modern communications and technology the country would lose out, and that if we didn't have a modern phone system we would have no business and without business there would be no jobs. I had a five year plan, I told them, to turn the Posts and Telegraphs system around and I needed Ir£1.1 billion to do it. There was a stunned silence of disbelief, I remember.

Few around the table seemed to believe he would be able to spend such an enormous amount of money. However, he got the support he asked for, most significantly from the Taoiseach and the Department of Finance. It was all predicated on the money coming back to Finance if it was not spent. Reynolds, with his ever-impatient approach, had thought big, gambled and done his research. Much praise followed as he got to grips with the dire communications situation across the country. My father, as a constituency TD, was bedevilled in his constituency work with people asking him to get them an all too scarce telephone. Significant targets for new telephone installation were set and met. Reynolds, never one to miss an opportunity for his Longford constituency, persuaded the company to locate a £1 million Telecom Engineering Headquarters in his home town, an investment that bolstered his credibility on home turf.

Reynolds' achievement in the area of telephones was significant and, according to Patrick Banks, then on the management side of the Industrial Relations machinery at the department of Posts and Telegraphs:

He took the whole thing by the scruff of the neck. Civil servants were sceptical of ministers at the time. Conor Cruise O'Brien had started the modernisation but was too preoccupied by Northern Ireland to focus on it. Reynolds gave the whole system a huge boost. He knew his own mind and made sure things were implemented. It really made his reputation both at a political as well as a publicity level.[2]

Reynolds was helped at the time by a formidable senior civil servant, Ita Meehan, a significant force within the department. She came up with the legislation, accelerating and driving through the telecommunications plan. While Conor Cruise O'Brien had made a start, he had been unable to mobilise his colleagues behind a big capital investment plan. Reynolds succeeded in this and derived huge political credit for what he had done. He also managed to attract two of the country's best-known businessmen to take positions on the interim boards of what were to be two new commercial state bodies to manage the telephone and postal services. These were Michael Smurfit and retailer Feargal Quinn. In the process, Reynolds had to move 30,000 employees from the civil service and into these more commercially focused bodies. The two services employed about half of the then 60,000 strong civil service. The whole process would take years of negotiation and would finally be completed after he had left the ministry.

Other projects that Reynolds pushed during his ministerial career, before his elevation to the role of Minister for Finance, were to include the delivery of the Cork to Dublin gas pipeline, the DART rail system, and the early development of aviation activity at Knock airport, at the time being championed by his old rival from the dancehall era, the charismatic local priest in County Mayo, Monsignor Father Horan. This last project was hugely controversial and depicted by a hostile, largely Dublin-based set of commentators as a costly white elephant that was a waste of taxpayers' money. It emerged as nothing of the sort and came to represent a significant infrastructure development in the west of Ireland's drive to attract tourists and investment. The Cork to Dublin pipeline demonstrated Reynolds' sharp business skills. It was a hugely expensive capital project that was delivered within budget and on time. This was a very hard ask in the context of the time, when every landowner along the route had a huge expectation of generous compensation payments, and there was the prospect of onerous legal delays. The hands-on approach taken by Reynolds to delivering, monitoring and ensuring no cost over-run impressed the people who worked with him on the project.

The former Department of Finance official, Finn McCool, was moved over to the Posts and Telegraphs Department to oversee a reorganisation of the post office services. From 1979, a process began which involved responsibility for the postal service being moved away from the department and established as a state-sponsored commercial company or semi state, as they were known. McCool describes Reynolds as 'decisive and interested' and very impressive in his role as minister. It was clear he wanted to get things done and had assembled a good team of civil service advisors around him.[3]

In his role as Minister for Industry and Energy, Reynolds frequently flew out of the country on promotional trade and investment trips to the United States and elsewhere. He was considered by senior officials of the IDA as a good minister to work for and his business knowledge added to his credibility with big companies considering making an investment in Ireland. This was difficult in the context of his ministerial role in the early 1980s but became much easier when he found himself in the same role in the late 1980s as the Haughey government got to grips with public spending and economic expansion plans. In the early 1980s, however, Haughey's controversial opposition to Mrs Thatcher's intervention in the Falklands War ruined viable prospects for further investment from the UK, something which was criticised heavily by Peter Hanley. Hanley, a significant businessman, was a key Fianna Fáil party fundraiser and Reynolds' backer. It is likely that Reynolds would have lined up with this view held by his Rooskey friend.

While Minister for Transport, Reynolds was confronted by a crisis that few would expect in a small country like Ireland. An Irish monk hijacked an Aer Lingus flight as it was waiting at a French airport. Haughey ordered Reynolds to France to deal with the situation and liaise with French security people on the ground. Reynolds rushed to the scene and took in all of the attendant publicity of being photographed by the domestic and international media gathered for the hostage crisis. He patiently began negotiations with the hijacker, working alongside the security people to resolve the situation. The hijacker had a bizarre request; he was demanding the 3rd Secret of Fatima from the Pope in exchange for releasing the passengers. It was late at night and Reynolds, with the French, devised a plan to get an Irish newspaper to run a story the following day to the effect that the Pope had released the Secret as per the hijacker's demand. Michael Hand, then a news editor with the *Sunday Independent*, and a friend of Reynolds from his music days, facilitated the ruse and Reynolds climbed the steps of the plane to talk with the hijacker. Simultaneously, a special forces crew climbed into the plane. Reynolds distracted the hijacker while they entered. The whole episode unfolded in full view of the world's media and Reynolds travelled home to Ireland something of a hero, in the company of passengers who had previously been hostages.

While Reynolds was carrying out his ministerial job, he and my father were also becoming key strategists in the endless rift within Fianna Fáil between the pro- and anti-Haughey factions. Both men entertained reservations about Haughey's performance in government, in areas ranging from the economy to the Falklands War, and his negative response to the FitzGerald government's groundbreaking Anglo-Irish Agreement of 1985. Despite these private reservations, both opted to stay in the Haughey faction. For my father, it was a matter of party discipline and the need to maintain it while the party was in government. For Reynolds, it was the case that his first sponsor in politics was Charlie Haughey and he had achieved a significant jump up thanks to his appointment to full cabinet rank in 1979.

The significant team of Reynolds, my father and Ray McSharry fought off three separate challenges to Haughey's leadership between 1982 and 1983. The first one failed and did not even crystalise into a motion because of the incompetence and poor organisation of those opposing him. Reynolds appears to have been ingenious, at this particular point in his career, in providing a willing 'listening ear' to TDs in the different factions. This role was probably facilitated to a great extent by his friendship with Charlie McCreevy, an early Haughey dissenter and sponsor of a motion against him.

There was a strong drinking culture at that time in Irish politics, which lasted into the 1990s but then rapidly died out due to changing societal attitudes and also the more demanding work rate in the political profession. But Reynolds was a teetotaller and a night owl, and he could keep later hours more than most and still maintain his discipline in both mental and physical terms. His non-drinker status probably helped him through exhausting late-night meetings listening to the unfolding plots.

This ability to be part of the crowd and keep long hours has been commented on by many who watched his career. Kathy Sheridan, the journalist and daughter of Joe Sheridan, the independent deputy for Longford–Westmeath back in 1961, was one of Reynolds' first political friends. She testified to Reynolds' staying power and his teetotalism: 'To many observers of that hard-drinking culture, his ability to weather boring drunks into the dawn while stone-cold sober, verged on the miraculous. A useful talent in the early hours, observed others, for a keen listener and memory man when in the company of important people whose tongues are loosened by alcohol.'4 Reynolds was very adept at picking up on whatever issues were being talked about by TDs disposed to blurt things out over a drink. In fact, he was so good at mixing in this kind of setting that many were actually surprised when they discovered he was a non-drinker. He had an ability to connect with anyone he spent time with. This skill of cultivating people, gossip and sensitive information was to serve him well through the endless party infighting and, again, when he took on the role of Taoiseach and became involved in the peace process. His only vice at this stage appears to have been cigarettes and a particular taste for Mars bars to recharge his batteries. He put in the late nights but still preserved his reputation as a family man and solid businessman.

Reynolds was also assiduous in cultivating the media as he fought for the Haughey faction in the internal party feuds against his rivals, first Gorge Colley, then, of course, Des O'Malley. It is possible to believe that the mutual antipathy that emerged between Reynolds and O'Malley had its roots in these faction fights. Neil Blaney, Reynolds' early mentor, also had a poor regard for O'Malley's talents, so it may be that this opinion was shared by Reynolds.

Having cultivated his journalist contacts, we have seen that Reynolds was not shy when it came to promoting himself. One such opportunity for self-promotion presented itself with *Aspect* magazine in 1982. It is noteworthy and worth quoting since, at that point anyhow, few if any Fianna Fáilers viewed Reynolds as a potential leader of the party:

> Translated into political life, that business acumen has led him, despite his public espousal of the Haughey faction, to leave lines of communication open into the other camp … There is no doubt that Reynolds considers himself a serious contender in the power struggle and there is a possibility that he could emerge as the man to bridge the gap if he can get over his image problem.[5]

Whatever about his image problem, Reynolds, or a supporter of his, was keen to make the media aware that he was a person of substance and had significant ambition. This article appeared in September 1982, well before O'Malley left the party, and presents the notion that Reynolds could be a compromise leader between the two factions. The line deployed in *Aspect* magazine was never really taken up in the more mainstream media commentary about him, but the analysis, viewed from a distance, was prophetic. However, in one sense it was quite wrong. Reynolds would never emerge as a compromise candidate; in fact, quite the opposite.

I remember some discussion around this article at the time, and the suggestion of him as a compromise between Haughey and O'Malley lacked serious credibility, although it, along with Reynolds' openness to listening to both sides, may have set warning bells ringing with Haughey and his erstwhile advisors. But while the article does rate as a serious indicator of his personal ambition at this very early stage, there were bigger political beasts on the block and so the extent of this ambition was probably both underestimated and not taken too seriously.

Notwithstanding the above, by 1987 Reynolds had become a formidable player. If his leadership ambitions were not taken seriously in the 1980s, they were to catapult him to prominence in the 1990s as Haughey stumbled from crisis to crisis, out of touch and financially tarnished as well. It is a sign of Reynolds' growing self confidence that, in the aftermath of the 1983 heave against Haughey, he was unafraid to inform him to his face that while he had backed him again, this was the last time he would do so. Many at this stage, maybe even Haughey himself, had begun to believe that the Fianna Fáil leader was invincible. Many of those who surrounded Haughey were also, quite frankly, afraid of him. Not so Albert Reynolds.

When Haughey framed his cabinet in 1987, Reynolds' clear preference was to return to the Department of Industry and Commerce to resume his work promoting industry and investment. Haughey called him to his office and offered him a position that involved forestry and promoting tourism. It was a worthy ministry but not what Reynolds wanted. He refused the position, stating, 'I've got better things to do with my time. I've a factory being built.' He walked out of the office, but not before he had asked who was getting the Industry and Commerce brief. Ray Burke was the man being favoured for the position and this may well have rankled with Reynolds. Burke had been far less loyal to Haughey, having wavered in at least one of the internal heaves. However, he was now ensconced as a major Haughey loyalist. In the event, things did not play out as expected and Burke was not appointed. Reynolds' cool rebuttal of Haughey's offer had led to Haughey changing his mind and backing down. Reynolds was appointed to the Department of Industry and Commerce. Few, if any others, were able to stand up to Haughey like this.

Apart from the above incident, there were some episodes which would have implications for Reynolds's future career as Taoiseach. He had clearly become an enemy of Des O'Malley and this poor relationship would cause difficulties down the line when Reynolds had to steer a coalition government which included O'Malley. As Minister for Industry and Commerce, Albert Reynolds, by many people's calculations, was far too generous with export credit funding for major and influential Irish beef processors. The decision made around this would come back to haunt him during the Beef Tribunal (discussed in detail in Chapter 16). While Minister for Posts and Telegraphs, he had succumbed to a media invitation to appear on a light entertainment show and croon a song called 'Put your sweet lips a little closer to the phone'. He was all decked out in a Stetson and cowboy gear. For many critics it made for cringeworthy television. More importantly it was a potent weapon later used by Haughey to discredit him. When he became a threat to Haughey, a smear appeared about him to the effect that he was some sort of country bumpkin and that the group which he led was a sort of 'Country & Western Alliance'. Haughey could be lethal when it came to enemies, but so, too, could Reynolds. The other bone of contention left over from his ministerial days was the anger that Ray Burke must have felt towards him. This chicken was also to come home to roost when he got into trouble in the Beef Tribunal.

CHAPTER NINE

Finance

Reynolds' arrival at the number two position in the government was neither predicted nor accompanied by any particular hang-ups on his part about how budgetary policy should be shaped. He admitted as much one year into the job, in an interview with the *Financial Times*, when asked did he see himself as a future Prime Minister: 'I'm ambitious. Everyone is in politics but I must admit I never expected to be Minister for Finance.' As always, at this stage in his career, Reynolds was a pragmatic individual who based his decisions on experience from his business background. His reputation, in ministerial terms, was as a safe pair of hands and as someone who got things done, not a prisoner to history nor hidebound by ideology.

The 1987–89 government is seen as having been one of the most successful governments Haughey ran, although the election had been a personal disappointment to him and he was forced to form a minority administration. My father and Ray McSharry were the two individuals who bolstered his confidence post-election, urging him to rule as if he had a majority and daring a divided opposition to pull his government down. Haughey had seen off his adversary Garret FitzGerald, but the elusive majority, so beloved by his party, had evaded him.

The new government was faced with the difficult work of cutting public spending in a very serious way and contradicting their own election promises. Initially McSharry became Minister for Finance and, as discussed in the previous chapter, his friend Reynolds became Minister for Industry and Commerce. Then McSharry, seen by many as the clear favourite to succeed Haughey, was appointed a European Commissioner in 1988, leaving the post of Finance Minister for the taking. Few had anticipated this, least of all Reynolds.

As the word went out that McSharry was going to be leaving the domestic political stage, a fevered race between ambitious ministers ensued to become the next Minister for Finance. Haughey dithered over the appointment, but both the internal and external word was that Pádraig Flynn was the front-runner for the position. Flynn, then Minister for the Environment, was, at this stage, a very close confidant of the Taoiseach and had been priming himself for the Finance position. Haughey would have trusted Flynn much more than Reynolds. Reynolds' blatant promotion of himself as a potential compromise to replace Haughey earlier in the 1980s had not gone unnoticed and had led to a kind of cooling between the two men.

Speculation about who would fill the position initially put Reynolds as an outsider. Yet my father, then Minister for Foreign Affairs, and Peter Hanley, a supporter of both men, felt that the job should be given to him and pushed hard for his appointment. Their concern was that Flynn had no real credibility or experience with the business community. In the end, Haughey was swayed by this; after all, the country was only just emerging from draconian cuts, and the growth in the economy was fragile, with significant public indebtedness. The choice of Reynolds would reassure the markets and investors – still nervous about Ireland's financial stability. As it happens, the economist Colm McCarthy, then with the economic advisors DKM, saw it that way, too: 'He will be taken seriously. Of all the guys available Albert Reynolds would command the most confidence as Minister for Finance.'[1] McCarthy had been invited to advise the government on the kind of public spending cuts that should be delivered in the hard medicine that was to be given to the economy.

A profile in *The Sunday Business Post* commented favourably on Reynolds, stating, 'Unquestionably his forte is tackling economic issues. He views issues, even the most complicated, in an uncluttered manner, hence his high rating with the business community. Two of his most ardent admirers are Michael Smurfit and Tony O'Reilly.'[2] Like his own leader, Haughey, Reynolds was acquiring friends in high places. At the time of his climb to Finance, O'Reilly and Smurfit would have been the two most admired businesspeople in the country. O'Reilly, through his ownership of the Irish Independent media group, was extremely influential, while Smurfit had achieved significant impact via his chairmanship of the state-owned telephone company. Both were influential employers and businessmen.

Strong as his advocates were, Reynolds still faced a significant challenge in the new portfolio he held when appointed in 1988. However, he did not have to go through with the kind of austerity cuts implemented by his predecessor. McSharry had earned the nickname 'Mack the Knife' for his determination to cut public spending in a sharp way. In contrast, a buoyant international economy made it easier for Reynolds to balance the demands of continued spending control and address the separate issue of building on the popularity of the government. He had been lucky that this was the context for his elevation to the second most important job in government. Reynolds came into the Department of Finance just as the wheel of fortune was about to turn. From 1987 onwards, his party had been able to cut spending and reduce the general burden of taxes on citizens. Ireland was undergoing a metamorphosis from a predominantly agricultural-based economy to a knowledge-based economy. Between 1985 and 2002 private sector jobs increased by 59 per cent. Massive investment by the Intel Corporation in a new facility at Leixlip in County Kildare came just one year into Reynolds' appointment. This investment became symbolic of the transition that was about to re-shape the country.

There was an easy, homespun, wisdom about everything Reynolds said and the theme for his first budget was going to be 'steady as she goes'. The sense that he had got the job by luck and was expected to underpin further stability in the economy seems to have influenced him greatly as he stepped into his new role. It was as if he had been preparing for the role; some observers noticed that he had ditched his flashy ties of previous years and was now dressing in sober, darker-toned suits. His friend, and later Minister for Foreign Affairs, David Andrews remarked around the time of his appointment to Finance, 'He has grown in stature in the last two years. Up to that he has been seen as a promoted dancehall owner.'[3]

Reynolds' budgets were, more often than not, leaked in advance. He was somewhat dismissive of the whole notion and culture of secrecy that used to surround budget day announcements. His old friend from the *Longford News*, Liam Collins, remembers Reynolds facilitating him with an early copy of the key details because he had a very tight deadline for the *Evening Herald* in Dublin. My own impression, as a journalist covering him at the time, was that he was more than willing to facilitate the media in terms of access. Previous ministers had been slightly less willing and more interested in the remote sense of gravitas that the position of Minister for Finance conferred. Reynolds was one of the first to begin this habit of leaking out the details of the budget day announcements well in advance. In effect, this allowed him to monopolise the business coverage of the budget for weeks in advance of the big day. From a political perspective, it also allowed him to manage the expectations around the budget better and prevent either a build-up of disappointment, or huge dissatisfaction on budget day itself.

At the time, the local radio station I worked for in Dublin had a networked news service, which we fed to all of the private FM stations that had sprung up around the country. We were a minnow competitor to RTÉ in the news stakes and had nothing like the resources they could deploy. However, we tried, and succeeded, to get news out on air before them. Reynolds was one of the few politicians who understood our importance in terms of the local stations we were feeding. Often, I would come to his office in advance of a major announcement and pre-record an interview that would go out on the hour while the official press conference was still finishing.

This was the period when I really got to know Reynolds well. When the officials left the room, he would chat with me over tea, discussing the latest political developments. He made charming and very candid conversation, and frequently peppered his sentences with curses of one kind or another. For all his supposed ruthlessness, he had a ready demeanour and openness that allowed him to talk with virtually anybody. Yet Reynolds was much more a listener than a talker. He could spend hours of his time listening to people, seemingly contributing to a conversation, but in fact saying very little. He took in the person, the background and almost everything that was being said.

Reynolds' budget of 1990 marked a distinct departure from the past. Up to that point, austerity and the further cutting of the country's massive borrowing requirement had been the order of the day. But in 1990, he introduced a mildly expansionary budget. In a timely exercise, he set out new, medium-term objectives for fiscal and budgetary policy that allowed a certainty and predictability. At the core of these objectives was the aim to bring the current budget deficit into balance for the first time in twenty-one years and to bring the country's crippling debt to GDP ratio down to 100 per cent. This ratio stood at 130 per cent back in 1986, and in 1990 it was at 118 per cent. The idea was to try and achieve the cut without having to introduce further damaging public-spending cutbacks.

A post-budget assessment by Davy's Stockbrokers of the 1990 Reynolds' budget felt that even robust advocates of fiscal rectitude could hardly object to an exchequer borrowing requirement that was just 2 per cent of GDP compared to the 16 per cent of GDP it stood at back in 1986. The Davy's report went on to say that:

> ... because progress in restoring order to the public finances has been so dramatic in the last three years, and more particularly, because such progress has been a good deal more rapid than was thought possible, or planned for that matter, it was always likely that 1990 would see somewhat less emphasis placed on cutting the EBR further and rather more attention paid to the other objectives of economic management.[4]

Reynolds was able to open up a bit on public spending, as well as taking the standard rate of individual tax down 2 per cent from 32 per cent to 30 per cent. The higher rate of tax fell from 56 per cent to 53 per cent. In response to agreements with the trade unions, social welfare rates were increased more than the then rate of inflation. Reynolds was now identified with the turning of the tide in Irish economic fortunes and, in a political sense, would clearly benefit from this.

Reynolds' 1991 budget marked another move away from fiscal rectitude, with Davy's Stockbrokers report this time warning about the prospect that financial commitments under the Programme for Economic and Social Progress (PESP) may have to be adjusted or suspended to maintain the government's fiscal objectives.

Speaking in relation to that time, Don Bergin, a Finance official who became friendly with Reynolds on a personal basis through his work, said, 'I think that Albert became a conventional Minister for Finance. There was no room for new initiatives. Things were run on an even keel. All of the big decisions around spending had been made by McSharry.' Bergin was responsible for the shareholdings in the state companies and, at the time, the government was selling these, not so much to bring in money but more because the state was not prepared to re-invest in them. Bergin wrote speeches for Reynolds, but said he was much better when he put the official script to one side. Scripts made Reynolds seem wooden and he was a much more engaging speaker when delivering his message *ex tempore*.[5] Something of the flavour of Reynolds' thinking on budgetary policy is given in his autobiography:

> Financing government borrowing was still a huge drain on our economy, and only by getting our economy moving could we service the interest on the mountain of debt that burdened us every year. And the way to get things moving had to be through the tax system; tax relief for manufacturing companies, cutting corporation tax, making our country highly competitive with low tax rates for foreign investors and, at the other end of the scale, lower personal taxes and special investment tax assistance for the more impoverished sector of the population.

Ray McSharry, Reynolds' predecessor in Finance, suggests that:

> ... there were those who believed that Albert had lifted his foot off the pedal, in terms of public spending, but that was against a background where it was perceived I had put the pedal down too hard on spending. The reality was there was more money coming in with the interest rate burden on mortgage holders declining from a high of around 22 per cent in 1987. I had no issue with him releasing a bit on the public spending.[6]

McSharry believes that Reynolds managed Finance with much the same conservative approach he took with his business and family finances. Reynolds only believed in increasing borrowing for productive purposes. One suggestion which had been put to McSharry had not been taken up by him, most probably because of time constraints. This was the creation of a new agency to manage the national debt using a more efficient, market-based approach. Michael Somers, a Finance official on the debt management side, proposed the idea and it was Reynolds who implemented it. Reynolds said:

> At that time management of the debt had become so complex and sophisticated that it became apparent we had to introduce an independent office which, with flexible management structures and suitably qualified personnel, could fully exploit the potential for savings. To this end I announced in my 1990 budget speech the introduction of a Bill to provide for the establishment of a new office to be called the National Treasury Management Agency.

This was a huge initiative in relation to the management of the national debt and Reynolds had faced considerable resistance from the higher echelons of his own department about this move. The National Treasury Management Agency (NTMA) went on to perform excellent work, not just on debt, but on state financing schemes, for quite a few years to come. It also allowed Ireland to attract private sector professionals and specialists at rates of pay that were outside the normal civil service grades. 'It was so successful that it led to savings of more than IR£1 billion to the Irish taxpayer over five years – and continues today as one of the key agencies with the cash and the know-how to help Ireland out of the current recession,' said Reynolds.

In early 1991, there were public arguments between Reynolds and Michael McDowell, then Chairman of the Progressive Democrats (PDs), who, though not a member of the PDs' ministerial or parliamentary team, was maintaining a high profile for himself by publicly commenting on matters of government policy. This was a source of great annoyance to Fianna Fáil ministers but a source of great copy for the media. McDowell was pushing for sharper tax cuts and Reynolds shot back at him to spell out what services he wanted pared back in order to achieve these further tax cuts and reforms. Reynolds, at this time, shared the PDs' agenda in cabinet of shedding state-owned companies, but, essentially, he was pragmatic about both this and the need for tax cuts. In typical Minister for Finance terms,

Reynolds was insisting that tax cuts, wherever they were to come, had to be paid for.

While juggling his responsibilities as Minister for Finance, Reynolds was also laying down markers, in a very public way, that he had the ambition to become Taoiseach. One very telling indicator of this was a speech made in Fermoy in September 1991, during which he said, 'You can take it that whenever a vacancy occurs, my name will be there. At present there is none, but if one arises, I will be interested.' As a working journalist at the time, I was struck by this kind of random, very open, acknowledgement of intent, which was not the norm in the period when Charles Haughey was Taoiseach. This, effectively, set the ball rolling in terms of an internal leadership contest.

In private, government spokespersons and those around Haughey were becoming increasingly disparaging about Reynolds. In the Irish fashion, there was a word here and there being shared. It was a delicate time. Reynolds was becoming more open in his commentary and, on economic policy, he opened up a public rift between himself and the Taoiseach. The PESP had been agreed between the government, trade unions, employers and farmers. The agreed measures, including incremental wage rates, were part and parcel of the agreement. In an interview, Reynolds told RTÉ that the probability was that these generous pay awards could not be paid in full. During the formal negotiations of these increases, Reynolds, as Minister for Finance, had fought against the pay awards. So much so that a leading trade unionist voiced his concerns to me at the time, suspecting that Reynolds was not just doing this for the familiar Department of Finance reasons, but rather because of a power play with Haughey within the government. Normally this kind of background dispute on a policy issue does not get canvassed in public. The interview given by Reynolds was very quickly attributed by the government press secretary, P.J. Mara, to 'the usual Department of Finance rhetoric'.[7] This very public put-down would not have played very well with Reynolds and would only have added to the existing anxieties in the Haughey camp about Reynolds' leadership ambitions.

CHAPTER TEN

Haughey

On the week Albert Reynolds was elevated to the position of Minister for Finance, the *Sunday Tribune* newspaper ran a profile of him, complete with cartoon drawing, bearing the headline 'The Heir Apparent'. It was hardly the kind of headline that would endear him to an already suspicious boss in the shape of Charles J. Haughey. Unknown to Haughey, and within a short period of four years, he was to be wracked with scandal, and fatally undermined by his own misjudgements and an unforgiving parliamentary party anxious to move him towards retirement.

Reynolds was acquiring status, respect and was now in pole position to replace him. He sat patiently in the Department of Finance, enhancing his credibility and burnishing his image in what was a collegiate, as well as a harmonious, government. Haughey delighted in the favourable media and opinion poll support for the government he led. Not generally a man for the majesty of grand state visits abroad, he went on one to Japan, which he enjoyed greatly. However, the formality and deference to authority that the Japanese had extended to him had the effect of inducing hubris in Haughey.

Back home in Dublin, he was reminded how precarious his position in parliament was, with a defeat on a vote on a health cost measure. There was no need to take the defeat too seriously, but Haughey did. Urged on by cabinet members like Ray Burke and Pádraig Flynn, arch loyalists at this stage, he decided, in the light of the favourable opinion polls, to call a snap election. Reynolds and my father argued against such a move. Both were ignored and Haughey was left with an electorate that blamed him for plunging the country into an unnecessary general election. The results of the 1989 general election were not good for Haughey and arguably would have consequences for his survival chances.

With post-election numbers looking bad, Haughey could only credibly form an administration by going into an uncomfortable coalition with his oldest and most vociferous adversaries, the PDs led by Des O'Malley. Given that the PDs had been founded, primarily, out of a dislike for Haughey and his politics, a coalition with them was never going to make for a pretty spectacle. Reynolds, as Minister for Finance, was appointed to the negotiating team to discuss terms of governing with the PDs. Reynolds and Bertie Ahern were to negotiate with Bobby Molloy and Pat Cox of the PDs, while O'Malley and Haughey were supposed to await the outcome. Ahern takes up the story:

> We felt we were making real progress in getting a good deal for Fianna Fáil. That's why we were so aggrieved when it became obvious that Haughey had gone behind our backs in dealing directly with the PD leader, Des O'Malley. Talking to O'Malley was Haughey's prerogative as leader. Failing to tell us was not. Albert and I only learnt that Haughey was prepared to concede two cabinet seats to the PDs when we heard it on the radio.[1]

Both men felt they had been made to look like idiots in the negotiation. They would have expected, as a matter of courtesy, that Haughey would have kept them in the loop. Ahern tells us that he got over it, but Reynolds did not. The two men told Haughey that he should stick with the mantra that only one seat at the cabinet table was to be conceded to the PDs. Haughey was raging at their, as he would have seen it, insubordination on this issue. As it turns out, Haughey cut the deal and the PDs got their two seats at the cabinet, but neither Reynolds nor Ahern were prepared to be fall-guys for Haughey by taking the blame for this two-seat concession. It was a clear humiliation for both men, but they got on with their jobs in the new government. If these two negotiators were angry, then the ordinary rank-and-file members of Fianna Fáil were likely to be even angrier.

Reynolds moved into overdrive and started taking on, as Minister for Finance, constituency speaking engagements, not something most Ministers for Finance are able or willing to do. He was clocking up 85,000 miles a year going from function to function at the invitation of party TDs who were well-disposed towards him. It was a fast-paced and quicker version of what Haughey himself had done in his wilderness years. The difference, of course, was that Reynolds was not in the wilderness but at the very centre of power in his ministry. He was now becoming the hot draw for party fundraisers up and down the country with people prepared to pay up to £75 a head to hear him speak, while close friends denied that this significant series of speaking engagements was, in effect, a leadership tour. In early 1990, Reynolds was, according to Liam Collins, his old friend from the *Longford News*, 'a bundle of energy' since he gave up the fags.[2]

Around this time, Reynolds arrived for a key speech before 400 seated supporters at the Duhallow Lodge in County Cork, five miles outside the town of Kanturk. Most of these party members and supporters were already seething about the Coalition with the PDs when Reynolds told them in his after-dinner speech: 'I hope the temporary little arrangement which we have with our junior partners won't be there very long.' The place erupted in cheers and the speech itself was given the title 'The Kanturk Declaration'. To anyone who cared to analyse what he had said, it was a declaration of his own determination to wrest the leadership from Haughey. Reynolds had, again, made clear his intentions, while keeping within the rules and proprieties of politics in not stating his ambition outright. A journalist from the local radio station, John O'Connor, got himself a scoop and dismissed the idea that it was an off-the-cuff remark from Reynolds: 'there was no attempt to back-track and the speech got rapturous applause, it went down very well.'[3]

The Albert Reynolds campaign was now well underway and the battle for the party's nomination to run in the presidential election would be a good opportunity for him to build some support amongst his parliamentary colleagues. Reynolds, quietly and behind the scenes, gave his backing to John Wilson, an experienced minister and classical scholar with an avuncular disposition. My father, as it turned out, won the nomination and went on to run in a scandal-hit election which ended up with him being sacked from his position as Tánaiste and Minister for Defence by his 'old friend of thirty years', Haughey.

My father, brother and a campaign manager left Haughey's Kinsealy Mansion by helicopter having just been given a draft resignation statement by the Taoiseach. We were bound for Longford to campaign in the Midlands. Reynolds sped his way from Government Buildings to hook up with us as we campaigned in his constituency. Despite the crisis that had now gripped my father's campaign, Reynolds was as cool as a breeze. He abandoned his state car and ministerial driver, and sat himself down beside me on the campaign bus. It was the first time I had spent concentrated time with him and I was impressed. He was straightforward and, though Haughey might not have liked to hear what he said, his advice was simple: 'Don't let your father resign. There is no need to do it. Let Haughey face down the PDs.' My father had no intention of doing so anyway, but I believe Reynolds was being sincere, both in his support and his belief that there was no sense in giving in to their demands.

As we went from stop to stop, Reynolds would bound off the bus, into some hall where activists were gathered, and make an impromptu speech in support of my father. It made for good politics for him to support a popular midlands man, like himself, in this way. The only problem for him was that Haughey would get to hear of it and Haughey was trying to get my father to resign. But the reaction from the activists seemed to embolden Reynolds further. Back on the bus, he threw his eyes up to heaven at Haughey's efforts to get my father to resign. On this subject, Reynolds would write in his autobiography: 'This episode was to have severe consequences for Haughey in the future. His lack of support for his friend, and his readiness to bend to the wishes of the opposition, signalled his overriding ambition and a willingness to do anything in his power to hold on to his leadership. This served only to damage his reputation.'

It seemed to me, at that time, that Reynolds had already moved far beyond fear of Haughey and fear of consequences on this issue. This was a hallmark of his personality and he was clearly ready to take on Haughey at any level. Whatever about some misgivings of opportunism on his part, I for one was impressed with his approach. It was entirely no-nonsense. When Haughey went on to sack my father, the party activists, already seething about the PDs, were ready to remove him in a way that they hadn't been before. Reynolds simply waited until the time was right to make his move.

As 1990 turned into 1991, Haughey became painfully aware that his Minister for Finance was positioning himself to take the job of Taoiseach from him. One sign of Haughey's weakness at this time was his continued postponement of a promised ministerial reshuffle. He knew it would be easier to keep his ambitious deputies in line with the promise of jobs to fill, rather than creating the inevitable disappointment that came with filling positions and not giving jobs to those on whom he did not look favourably. Clearly the stealth campaign against him was getting to him and, at a European Commission (EC) summit in Rome, with Reynolds present at the press conference, Haughey chose to publicly humiliate him in answer to a question about British economic policy: 'We all know that Chancellors of the Exchequer and Ministers for Finance are neurotic and exotic creatures whose political judgement is not always the best.'[4] While there was praise for his predecessor, Reynolds and his 'Country & Western' supporters would soon come in for a degree of unattributed smears and rubbishing. The remarks about Reynolds were all the more incredible given that Haughey himself was a former Minister for Finance.

Over the summer of 1991, Pádraig Flynn toured the country talking to TDs to get support for Reynolds, whom he was now supporting, having declared himself of the view that not going into coalitions was a core Fianna Fáil value. Reynolds was on good terms with Bertie Ahern from their experience in the negotiations to form a government, and rumours began to spread that the two of them had a mutual support pact in relation to the leadership – Reynolds would go first and then reciprocate support for Ahern as his successor.

From the autumn of 1991, Haughey and his administration were rocked by a series of financial and other scandals which carried the strong whiff of aggrandisement and insider dealing on his part. There were so many that it led to allegations in the Dáil that there was an insider group in both business and politics made up, in effect, of a 'Golden Circle' enriching themselves at public expense. Haughey had become toxic and his time in leadership was becoming past tense. The most damaging controversy came during a botched effort at a reshuffle, when Jim McDaid, a young deputy from

Donegal, was to be promoted to cabinet; this appointment was blocked by Des O'Malley and the PDs as it emerged that McDaid had given witness evidence on behalf of an IRA man who had been before the courts. In a sense, McDaid was morally obliged to give evidence, but that did not matter to the PDs. McDaid's nomination as minister had to be withdrawn, in a move that echoed the PD role in the sacking of my father.

After another controversy, it was decided, at an informal level, that my father and Dr John O'Connell TD should be the people to advise Haughey when it was time to retire. This plan, willingly entered into by Haughey, soon unravelled in a maelstrom of further controversy. The group around Reynolds never believed Haughey would go of his own volition and a restive group of younger deputies was also becoming impatient. Haughey had apparently pleaded to be allowed to go in his own way, begging not to be 'humiliated'. The group circling around him now, however, led by Reynolds, was not in a mood to let him go in peace. They also believed he was surreptitiously trying to promote a younger alternative to Reynolds in the form of Bertie Ahern. The clock was ticking on Haughey's survival and it was Reynolds who was setting that clock.

In the midst of all this, there was a further negotiation with the PDs in the form of a mid-term review of the policy commitments made under the coalition government. Reynolds, as Minister for Finance, was on the negotiation team, but Haughey believed that he was trying to be difficult and hold up an agreement to bolster his own leadership ambitions. Haughey told Ahern to go in and wrap up the negotiations, which he duly did. Reynolds had won plaudits from the Fianna Fáil organisation and TDs for standing up to the PDs during the negotiations. When the discussions concluded, Haughey pointed at Ahern, in front of political correspondents, stating, 'He's the best, the most skilful, the most devious and the most cunning of them all.'[5] The quote went viral via the media and many interpreted it as a sign that Haughey was now backing Bertie Ahern as his official, endorsed successor.

Reynolds and his team were, at this stage, meeting at his apartment on a regular basis. They now had a strong imperative to push ahead swiftly against Haughey. The dilemma for Reynolds was to find the right reason to do so. There was a conventional view at the time that the person who moved against an incumbent leader would suffer in the subsequent leadership contest. Reynolds was certainly of this view, but circumstances were about to force him to make a choice. In November 1991, Seán Power, a younger deputy from Kildare, put forward a motion of No Confidence in Haughey. Reynolds' stealth campaign was about to come to an end. He would have to get off the fence.

CHAPTER ELEVEN

Leader

The series of scandals that occurred in 1991 had made everyone jittery, not least Albert Reynolds. The whole air of instability at a political level added to the anxiety. From his perch in Finance and within the party, Reynolds was clearly stoking controversy. Younger backbenchers were on edge. The long-delayed reshuffle and botched appointments by Haughey had fed impatience amongst those who wanted a ministerial promotion. Reynolds had now assembled a significant crew of ministerial colleagues who were ready to support him. Haughey was damaged, there was blood in the water, and the sharks were circling; his denials of involvement in any of the public scandals were the stuff of satire.

In the context of the deep disbelief in the Reynolds faction that Haughey would go of his own volition, Ahern paid a visit to Kinsealy, Haughey's home, at the end of summer 1991. As Haughey set out his plans up to the following Easter, Ahern formed the view that he was intending to stand down but, in his assessment, 'the problem was that Albert wouldn't wait'. Ahern was urging Reynolds to be patient, but the latter was restive. The following passage from Ahern's autobiography is telling:

'Just wait,' I told him. 'Charlie's going soon.'
He wanted specifics.
'When?'
'Early next year.'
'He told you that?'
'No, but that's when he will go. He's near the end now.'[1]

After this conversation, Power's No Confidence motion moved forward. It is absolutely clear that Reynolds was not prepared to believe Haughey. He felt that the Taoiseach would do anything to stall things further. Moreover, Reynolds' supporters distrusted Ahern's claims of being an honest broker in the whole Haughey retirement plan. Ahern, for his part, did want to ease Haughey out and knew that he had his own informal pact with Reynolds, but this would be torn to tatters in the events that followed, namely the No Confidence motion and the subsequent leadership contest. If Reynolds had held off, as Ahern had urged him to, then he might have enjoyed a smoother transition to leadership. The motion meant that Ahern was less certain about his own position, in the aftermath of a Haughey departure. Both Reynolds and Ahern were playing for high stakes.

The No Confidence motion had been set for 9 November. With some drama, Reynolds announced he was supporting the motion since, in his own words, 'for some time now there has been considerable political instability which has led to an erosion of confidence in our democratic institutions. This uncertainty must not be allowed to continue.' The instability was only set to continue as Reynolds decided to defy Haughey by refusing to resign when asked, thus forcing Haughey to sack him.

To add to the drama of it all, the Reynolds faction had prearranged a series of announcements, at intervals, in the run-up to the actual vote. Pádraig Flynn, Máire Geoghegan-Quinn, Michael Smith and Noel Treacy all forced Haughey to sack them. In all, two cabinet and three junior ministers were fired. It left a gaping hole in the Haughey government and a lot of frenzied speculation in the corridors of power. The sheer drama of these forced sackings led the media to believe that Haughey's time might be at an end. As a reporter covering these events, like other reporters, I overestimated the number of supporters behind Reynolds and, even at this late stage, Haughey had the numbers; an open roll-call (or public show of hands) gave him 55 votes to 22 for the Reynolds faction. An earlier vote on whether to hold an open ballot was won by 44 to 33. My father, despite his treatment by Haughey, had supported his leader in line with his previous track-record of supporting the party leadership when confronted by such motions. The Reynolds faction let it be known, in the aftermath of the vote, that their true numbers were higher and that some of their supporters had chosen not to show themselves in the context of the open vote.

Things settled down as the country faced into Christmas and the quiet period into the new year of 1992. Reynolds, for his part was not idle; he was simply marking time. Freed of the trappings of ministerial office, he had more time on his hands and became more available for meetings with journalists both in and around Leinster House, and outside its precincts. He had not lost his confidence with his loss of office and journalists like myself were grateful to have better access to him. He was charming company and would informally join us over coffee in the Dáil restaurant, the visitors' bar, or wherever he found us. It was in these idle hours of chat that people, in particular journalists, really got to know him. He could be the life and soul of the company, but, on close observation, his conversational technique was intriguing. He would nod patiently at any insight you offered, but when you examined the discussion afterwards, you would realise that he had not, in fact, contributed a great deal to the conversation. He had this impeccable body language of empathy, nodding and seemingly agreeing with what you said. This was how he absorbed information and insights. It was a rare attribute in Ireland, given how much time people, in particular in the media and political circles, spend listening to their own voices rather than those of others.

Haughey's respite over Christmas did not last long. Gone was the informal deal with my father and Dr John O'Connell about a reasonable departure time. Most believed it was inevitable, despite the vote victory, that he would go. It was only a matter of time. But Reynolds and his crew were not leaving things to chance. Seán Doherty was silently spoiling for a confrontation with Haughey. Some time before, it had come out that he had authorised the bugging of two journalists' phones and he had lived under a cloud since that incident had been exposed, even though most who analysed the controversy suspected all along that Haughey had ordered the bugging. Now, Doherty gave a TV interview and then a formal press conference stating, for the first time, that the bugging had not just been known about by Haughey but approved by him back in 1982. He confirmed that he had actually handed the taped recordings of the conversations of the two journalists directly to Haughey. This allegation was magnified by the fact that the RTÉ newsroom was on strike at the time and the entire Doherty press conference was fed live into the main evening news bulletin.

Even at this stage, few were prepared to formally write Haughey off, but the PDs were not prepared to continue to support him and their formal statement in the aftermath of Doherty's revelation was menacing, if not explicit. They did not attend the next day's cabinet meeting. Haughey's denials of involvement in the bugging counted for nothing. There was a chasm of disbelief around statements of denial from him at this point in his career. Then, in a press conference, he suggested it was a plot by the 'Country & Western Alliance' against him.

The late Veronica Guerin suggested an elaborate conspiracy, based on the idea that a group of businesspeople including Reynolds had been involved in bringing the Doherty revelation back to life. She was a good friend of mine and met me, as a working journalist at the time, to discuss it. She had been a member of Ógra Fianna Fáil when I was in it and had subsequently worked for Haughey in the New Ireland Peace Forum. Neither of us could find further evidence for this supposed plot, which suggested that Doherty had received money for his efforts. However, there does appear to have been advance knowledge of the content and potential impact of the Doherty allegations amongst those agitating for a Reynolds accession to power. My own view is that Doherty had motive enough for making his revelations and that he hardly needed help in terms of how he should go about it, even though he must have known that Reynolds would be the chief beneficiary. The leadership race to become leader of Fianna Fáil and Taoiseach was finally on.

Reynolds started fast and, using his impressive media operation, began to put about speculative figures indicating his actual level of support. He had started his own campaign earlier than anyone else and had a solid core of support among the ministers who had left the government and those whose favour he had cultivated over the years. However, doubts about his ability to win the contest surfaced as the old Haughey rump began to promote the possibility that Bertie Ahern, who had replaced Reynolds in Finance and introduced his first budget, might be a suitable candidate. This possibility of

Ahern becoming an opponent was a real threat. A certain degree of panic started creeping into the Reynolds bandwagon. Ahern was a much younger man and could easily depend on support from the Haughey faction. At another level, he could appeal to wavering deputies and those who were slightly discomfited by the manner in which Haughey was being bundled off stage. The chance that Ahern might run also undermined the carefully developed public message that Reynolds and Ahern were, in effect, a 'dream team' working together in the Haughey succession stakes. Although there was certainty in the Reynolds camp about his candidacy, Ahern never fully declared that he was entering the race, though speculation was rife that he was counting the numbers before making a decision. My own father, who admired Ahern a great deal, went so far as to announce on radio that Ahern was going to be a candidate, and he also believed that Ahern had the numbers to win the race.

Amidst the feverish speculation about Ahern, the Reynolds campaign decided to take matters into its own hands. Ahern's private life was complicated because he was separated from his wife and in a new relationship. Michael Smith, a leading Reynolds supporter, was quoted in his local paper vocalising the issue of Ahern's suitability given his unclear marital arrangements. This made the Ahern campaign furious; it was seen as a dirty trick by the Reynolds camp. The blatant way the Reynolds' campaign had dragged Ahern's private life into the public limelight showed a degree of ruthlessness previously unseen in Irish politics. There is no doubt this tactic spooked Ahern and, shortly afterwards, he decided to meet with Reynolds the weekend before the formal vote so that they could check on each other's intentions. Ahern, still not a declared candidate, had totted up the numbers and the potential personal consequences for himself, and he had decided to step away from the fray.

'I had agreed to meet Albert that weekend. We didn't want the press watching us arrive, so each of us came up in a service lift from the basement of the hotel. He was already in the room when I arrived, sitting at a table doing some work.'[2] Reynolds opened the conversation in this crucial meeting. He immediately apologised for the Michael Smith remark, claiming that Smith had not meant it in the way it was taken.

'He did mean it all right,' Ahern replied, indicating a strong annoyance about what had happened.

Reynolds pressed on, stating that the comment attributed to him, Reynolds, was made by someone else, not him. He said he would not be around for long as Taoiseach and that Ahern would be his successor. The deal struck then between the two men would ensure Reynolds would become Taoiseach.

While Reynolds was now certain to be Taoiseach, the legacy issue with regard to the high-profile comments about Ahern's personal life may have made Ahern a lot more ruthless in his dealings with Reynolds from this point on, despite the outward appearances of a professional working relationship. There were also consequences resulting from this Reynolds–Ahern power meeting. Word trickled out that both he and Reynolds, including their supporters, had swapped notes on their respective supporters. The most interesting thing that emerged was that several of the party's TDs had given promises of support to both men when the lists were tallied. Interestingly, one person who appeared on both lists was a young deputy from Cork, Micheál Martin.

For now, Reynolds and Ahern were to become, in David Andrew's words, the 'dream ticket' for the party leadership. The Haughey rump, upset at Ahern's failure to stand, were initially reluctant to get behind Reynolds, but Ahern patiently worked on winning them over. Reynolds focused on the impending vote, which he won easily with sixty-one votes compared to ten for the Haughey veteran Michael Woods and six for my aunt, Mary O'Rourke. It was a decisive victory and left him with a party mandate of a significant kind.

Reynolds' victory in the party leadership election swept through the corridors of Leinster House as a rumour of a landslide before the numbers were formally announced. There were supporters and friends all over the house, but it was 6 February and about 3.30 p.m. in the afternoon when the results became clear. Reynolds slipped out of Leinster House and went back to his apartment in Ballsbridge, where his wife, Kathleen, close friends and family were waiting. It had been a harrowing time for Reynolds, and more so for Kathleen. In fact, politics was the last thing on either of their minds as

Kathleen had been struggling to recover from a cancer diagnosis for some months prior to all of this. It is testament to Reynolds' inner toughness that he had been able to conduct himself as busy Minister for Finance, leadership candidate and husband during the months leading up to this point.

Reynolds then travelled the short distance from his apartment to Jury's Hotel to hold his first press conference as leader of Fianna Fáil and Taoiseach-in-waiting. He would become Taoiseach in the Dáil on 11 February 1992, when Haughey formally stood down. He set out his priorities, namely Northern Ireland, the economy, reducing unemployment and emigration. In his own words:

> People were surprised, shocked even; they had expected me to talk about the economy, but not my concerns for Northern Ireland. True, apart from the position I had taken over the Anglo-Irish Agreement in 1985, I had never commented on the problems of Northern Ireland – but that was normal procedure: in government it was always understood and accepted that only the Taoiseach spoke on Northern Ireland affairs.

In his short period as Taoiseach from 1992–94, Albert Reynolds would demonstrate very ably just how well he could deal with things in Northern Ireland. Most of his early activity was conducted in the background, mobilising his networks of influence, friends, media and an array of intermediaries, all in his effort to achieve a momentous result.

CHAPTER TWELVE

Taoiseach

Tuesday, 11 February 1992 is a day etched on the memory of political correspondents and all observers of the goings-on at Leinster House. Albert Reynolds was voted in as Taoiseach and promptly moved for the adjournment of the Dáil, as is customary, to depart for The Phoenix Park to collect his seal of office from the then President, Mary Robinson. It was to be an extraordinary day in politics. The changes Reynolds made in his first cabinet were considered a 'massacre'. A full eight of the old Haughey cabinet were dispensed with and Reynolds followed up by firing nine of the twelve Ministers of State from the ancient regime.

As political correspondents, including myself, gathered at the Dáil, they looked on dumbfounded as household names sheepishly took their seats on the backbenches. Some of the dismissed ministers were smiling, but inwardly they were fuming. Many of them had spent most of their careers as ministers. The introduction by Reynolds of a hire and fire culture in the appointment of people to public office was a new thing for the political system to cope with. It underlined for everyone that there was a new broom and he was sweeping the boards clean. The ruthlessness of what Reynolds had done was lost on nobody that day in Leinster House. Accustomed to using mafia metaphors when referring to Fianna Fáil, some newspapers labelled it the 'St Valentine's Week Massacre'. Other commentators depicted him as 'The Longford Slasher', a nod to the Longford GAA club, the 'Slashers'.

Out went Gerry Collins, Michael O'Kennedy, Ray Burke, Mary O'Rourke, Rory O'Hanlon, Vincent Brady, Noel Davern and Brendan Daly from Clare. Most of them had a significant presence in the party and would surely lie in the long grass nurturing the prospect of political revenge against Reynolds.

It was a bold political risk on Reynolds' part and seemed to underline something he had privately told Ahern in his final talk with him before the party leadership contest. Reynolds had decided he was not likely to be in power too long and he was determined to gather his own team around him. The justification for doing this, I was informed by Tom Savage, his PR advisor, was to create a clear line between his own, new administration and all of the controversy and scandal that had been so much a feature of Haughey's last spell in office. A new era of open government was being promised rather than the tired old scene of cloak and dagger that seemed to define Haughey's time. However, this new, more ruthless, approach to running the government was to be severely put to the test over the next few years as the two Reynolds-led coalitions went into premature collapse.

Seán Duignan, the newly appointed press secretary, takes up the story of that first day:

> I was fascinated by how he went about it. Before leaving for Áras an Uachtaráin to receive his seal of office, he informed staff he wanted to see most of the above upon his return. He was reminded that by then he would have not much more than a half hour to spare before leading his new ministerial team into the Dáil. That, he assured everybody, would give him plenty of time.[1]

It took him a mere fifteen minutes to dispense with all of the experienced ministers, although two (Mary O'Rourke and Dermot Ahern) argued with him over what was being done. Reynolds told Dermot Ahern, 'Nothing personal – you just backed the wrong horse.'[2] There was now the inevitability of a Haughey rump forming on the backbenches and it was to get even with Reynolds some years later when he sought the party's nomination to run for president. It also gave Reynolds little scope for making mistakes and meant that his time as Taoiseach would be competitive, with a strong dissenting faction within the party from the outset.

Back into government came Pádraig Flynn, Michael Smith and Máire Geoghegan-Quinn, who had been fired from government in the power struggle with Haughey. Four of the new Reynolds' entries to the cabinet table were people who had sided against Haughey in the earlier heaves of the 1980s – Joe Walsh, David Andrews, Séamus Brennan and Charlie McCreevy. Dr John O'Connell, once in the Labour Party and now in Fianna Fáil, was made Minister for Health, something of a long-term ambition for him. Brian Cowen, a future Taoiseach, and Noel Dempsey, from the younger ranks of the parliamentary party, were new additions to the line-up.

The Dáil debate on Reynolds' nomination as Taoiseach was devoid of particular drama. It was as if the political system were heaving a collective sigh of relief that the scandal and controversy of the Haughey era were over and the system itself would get a well-deserved rest. The leader of the opposition, John Bruton, made much of the 270,000 unemployed people in the country, as did a number of other speakers. The Labour leader, Dick Spring, noted that 'Deputy Reynolds' views on Northern Ireland had not been forcefully expressed in the past. 'There is no reason to believe he is encumbered by any of the myths and shibboleths that have dominated the past.'[3] Fine Gael's Austin Deasy, striking a note of optimism, said, 'I hope the Taoiseach's acquaintance with the British Prime Minister, Mr Major, will be of assistance to us, personal relationships such as that can be enormously helpful.'[4] There was no hint from this debate that the first Reynolds administration was to be short-lived and filled with further controversy.

Tom Savage, his personal PR advisor, had plans to make Reynolds a much more open figure than his predecessor. In fact, John Bruton had welcomed this commitment to a more open approach. Government Buildings, including the Taoiseach's office, were to be opened to visitors and, more contentiously, so was the Taoiseach himself. Reynolds agreed to giving the political correspondents, based at Leinster House, open, on-the-record briefings on a regular basis. The opportunity was well-exploited by journalists and it soon became a source of regular controversy itself. Journalism in Leinster House had become sharp-edged and investigative, with a media pack that had become used to asking more probing questions than in previous times, thanks, in large part, to the scandals that had dominated Haughey's final years.

Seán Duignan's appointment as government press secretary was a surprise. Duignan had been the political correspondent with RTÉ TV and greatly respected in that role over many years. Tom Savage, who had been advising Reynolds on his leadership ambitions, had reached out to the RTÉ man to ask him to take up the position. Duignan quickly immersed himself in his new role and 'was soon to learn that Albert Reynolds consistently played for high stakes, was prepared to back his hunch to the limit, and preferred to bet on the nose rather than each way. This made for a precarious existence; it left little margin for error, and, when the chips were down, no margin at all for the unexpected.'[5] As ever, the unexpected was about to happen.

For years and years, figures like Charles Haughey and Garret FitzGerald had tried to ignore the issue of abortion. Lay Catholic activists forced their hands by proposing the 8th Amendment to the Constitution, which was designed to prevent abortion being introduced without a public referendum – in other words so that it could not be legislated for by parliament. Successive political leaders since then had adjudged it safer not to go near the outright confrontation that would be certain to arise between the forces of secularism and the Catholic Church if the issue were raised. Both FitzGerald and Haughey had left a ticking time bomb in the pro-life amendment to the constitution, which affirmed the equal right to life of the unborn child and the mother. Peter Sutherland, the Attorney General at the time, had warned that the ambiguity of the wording could mean that, over time, the clash between the two equal rights could be resolved in favour of the mother to the point where the amendment would act as an unwitting article that could, in fact, lead to the introduction of abortion via the courts.

In 1992, only a matter of days after Reynolds took office, abortion was back on the front pages and promising to be one of the biggest issues to confront him in his first administration. A 14-year-old girl (Miss X) had been the victim of rape and her parents had reported the matter to gardaí, prior to taking her away to the UK for an abortion. The gardaí, aware of the ban on abortion in the constitution, had notified the Director of Public Prosecutions about the matter. He had referred the matter onward to the Attorney General, Harry Whelehan. Whelehan took the decision, in his own independent role as law officer, to apply for an injunction to prevent the parents and the girl from travelling to Britain. The High Court granted the injunction. The Supreme Court, in due course, reversed the High Court's decision, stating that the child and her parents were entitled to travel to the UK, given that there was, in the court's view, a substantial threat to the life of the mother, citing the probability, based on evidence, of a threat of suicide. The diary entry in Sean Duignan's *One Spin on the Merry-go-round* reads:

> They're all pointing the finger at Harry. Calling him a right-wing Catholic and Opus Dei type. But he tells me he is not Opus Dei and I believe him. He just seems to me the kind of guy who calls it as he sees it in strict legal terms, ie a dangerous man. A guy like that can cause all kinds of mayhem. You gotta think political Harry.[6]

The X Case was to become an incendiary issue and already there were half-baked rumours on the go that the Attorney General took the action he did because of some inherent, conservative position on his part. The perception raised by this controversy about Whelehan were set to follow him continuously, up to his failed attempt at appointment to the High Court and the consequential departure from office of Reynolds in 1994 during yet another legal controversy.

Duignan contacted Reynolds with the Supreme Court decision as his motorcade swept its way into central London for a meeting with British Prime Minister John Major at Number 10 Downing Street – 'Albert says something to the effect that this puts us right up to our necks in it, also that it means we'll be attacked on all fronts.'[7] Reynolds had taken care to define his new role as Taoiseach as being primarily about the economy and Northern Ireland. He was now about to be immersed in the moral minefield of abortion rights, and complicated legal and constitutional issues, as well as being sandwiched between the twin demons of liberal and conservative opinion.

'What has been done to this Irish Republic, what kind of State has it become that in 1992, its full panoply of authority, its police, its law officers, its courts are mobilised to condemn a fourteen-year-old girl to the ordeal of pregnancy and childbirth after rape at the hands of a "depraved and evil man"?' read the editorial in *The Irish Times*.[8] There was a great deal of outrage everywhere. In the aftermath of this, one day I was sitting in Leinster House, covering the Dáil and chatting to my colleagues in the visitors' bar. P.J. Mara, the former government press secretary, came in and introduced us to singer Sinéad O'Connor. She was very animated over the abortion issue and had agreed to do an interview with any journalist or broadcaster she could find in the precincts. It made for a memorable break from the tedium of life at Leinster House. P.J. ushered her up towards the Taoiseach's office, confirming that Reynolds had agreed to meet with her. This made for even more headlines on the issue. It is not every day that a celebrity rock star arrives at Leinster House to lobby the Taoiseach. The Derry-based socialist republican, Eamonn McCann was part of her entourage.

As Reynolds remembers it in his autobiography:

> Passions were raised and criticism poured down on the government even from Catholics within our own party. The pressure from the bishops was immense – they were vociferous in their disapproval – but it wasn't just the establishment hierarchy who joined in: there were liberals and women journalists allowed on the pro-liberal wing, the pro-choice as well as the pro-life, traditional Catholics – even some of my own deputies joined in the tirade against me and what I was doing. I took them all on.

For a devout Catholic and father of seven children, it must have been a difficult time for Reynolds. His rather direct style of address in the Dáil on these issues was not always appreciated. The forces which were ranged against and unhappy with him must have infuriated him. My own impression from covering him at this time was that he seemed uncomfortable – it was not his natural style to proclaim on this type of issue. His career to date had seen him assigned to ministries with an economic focus. In his parliamentary trajectory up the political ladder, he had been happy to confine himself to the topic he knew best, namely business.

The issue was soon to be further complicated, however. A new European Union (EU) treaty, called the Maastricht Treaty, was due to be voted on by referendum over the summer. It was an important treaty conferring significant sovereignty on Brussels, as well as paving the way for a new European currency. However, the EU was becoming tired of constant efforts by Irish governments to seek explicit reassurance that they would not interfere in an area that was outside of their competence – namely how Ireland regulated abortion – which was delaying their negotiations. Reynolds was, as he had anticipated, coming under significant attack from every direction, not least his erstwhile adversary and coalition partner, Des O'Malley. The PDs had dug themselves in on the media-led belief that it would be better to have a referendum on abortion before holding one on the Maastricht issue. Reynolds disagreed and this difference of opinion with O'Malley became public very quickly. Reynolds faced the PDs down in cabinet, insisting that the two issues be separated out and the European matter be dealt with first. Effectively, Reynolds told them to like it or lump it. The PDs did lump it, but they were not happy about it, mostly, one suspects, because it involved facing down the orthodox wisdom of the mainstream media on the issue – which was that Maastricht should follow an abortion referendum. Even the then President of the European Commission, Jacques Delors, was panicked by Reynolds' strong view that the European referendum should precede anything relating to abortion. The people of Denmark had already rejected the treaty by way of referendum, and Delors was now wary that his brave new plans for the EU were also going to go up in flames in Ireland. But Reynolds was determined to push ahead. In private, to his press secretary, Reynolds admitted something that he would never say in public in the context of the campaign itself: 'They'll see that I'm right. The people won't let abortion get muddled up with Maastricht. The Irish keep their money and their morals separate. They know precisely where their bread is buttered. Mark my words.'[9] While Reynolds' decision annoyed his coalition partners, his judgement was ultimately proved correct – the public voted by a margin of 69 to 31 per cent in favour of the Maastricht Treaty.

The referendum vote was set for 18 June, but there was plenty of high-wire excitement between the decision to go ahead and the actual voting day. The Church had geared itself up for a power-play with the government. The conference of Bishops had issued a tough and critical statement about the government and the referendum in relation to abortion rights. It looked like they were prepared to recommend a No vote. Reynolds was furious and rang some of them directly to indicate his displeasure. I remember talking to him around this time. He was cursing and unforgiving about the stupidity of the Church's position.

Reynolds, in the midst of his row with the Church, was thrown a lifeline in the form of a huge public scandal involving the Bishop of Galway, Dr Eamon Casey. Casey had a penchant for fast cars, speeding fines and liberal causes. In fairness, he had also done much to raise awareness of the plight of the Irish in Britain and the challenges facing the developing world in Africa and elsewhere. He was a frequent guest on *The Late, Late Show* with Gay Byrne. Now Byrne was interviewing the Bishop's long-term lover, Annie Murphy, about their affair and the child they had together. There was also some suggestion that Church money had been used to support the situation. Annie Murphy had first appeared on *Morning Ireland* to tell her story. You could hear a pin drop all over the country. The story itself brought down the roof on Catholic power in Ireland. As I drove to work that morning, I and everyone else knew it would be the last time that an elderly, male group of bishops would be lecturing anybody about faith and morals in Ireland. The eminent bishops, from their base in Maynooth, quietly modified their position on the Maastricht referendum or, as Reynolds put it, 'In other words, they now accepted that ratification of Maastricht did not equate with the introduction of abortion in Ireland.'

This episode was the proverbial 'baptism of fire' for Reynolds on taking up his position as Taoiseach. He had gambled on setting out on his own and, as far as his ministerial shake up and the Maastricht referendum were concerned, his approach had been the right one. The biggest issue for him now was whether his coalition partner would find his fire too hot. The PDs' Mary Harney seemed to be hinting that they would not jeopardise the government's stability over the abortion issue, but there would be plenty of wrangles between them and Reynolds before the year was out.

Unfortunately, it was Fianna Fáil itself that had lit the match under the tinderbox of the PDs. The PDs were now painfully aware of the disdain in which they were held by Reynolds and the new faction within Fianna Fáil.

Back at the party's Ard Fheis in March 1992, Brian Cowen, a protegé of Reynolds, had asked the rhetorical question: 'What about the PDs?' There was a tremendous roar from appreciative party activists when he simply replied to his own question – 'If in doubt, leave them out.'

At the same Ard Fheis, Reynolds himself threw caution to the wind, boldly declaring that 'Fianna Fáil does not need another party to keep it on the right track, or act as its conscience.' It was tough talk, but by year's end the party would run up against the determined obstinacy of Desmond O'Malley and his evidence before the Beef Tribunal. The 'fighting talk' was evidence, if ever it was needed, that Reynolds' vision for his party in the future did not include the PDs. The statements from both Reynolds and Cowen were symptomatic of a party that was still not comfortable with the whole notion of coalition. It was part of Reynolds' ploy to advance his own ambitions to hint at his own opposition to coalition. However, as events were to prove, he had no trouble going into government with another party when his own neck might have been on the line. Viewed with hindsight, the rhetoric about the PDs may seem to have been ill-advised. But, from Reynolds' point of view, he was giving them an early warning of his intentions.

CHAPTER THIRTEEN

John Major

In November 1990, John Major became Prime Minister of Britain. He was cut from a different cloth to his predecessor, Margaret Thatcher. While Thatcher had led a process of rapprochement with Dublin, culminating in the 1985 Anglo-Irish Agreement, later in life she expressed regret at having done so. Her refusal to back down in response to the hunger strikers in the early 1980s had effectively led to a renewal of Sinn Féin under the leadership of Gerry Adams and Martin McGuinness. Two of Thatcher's best friends, Airey Neave MP (1979) and Ian Gow MP (1990), were assassinated by the IRA. In 1984, Thatcher herself was a target, while attending her party conference in Brighton; she was very nearly killed.

John Major sat at the cabinet table and wrote down his priorities as Prime Minister: 'They were a mixed bag. Inflation. Public services. Northern Ireland. Unemployment.'[1] The choice of Northern Ireland was curious, but in line with a contemporary frustration at the level of continued violence being perpetrated by the IRA and the absence of any kind of political settlement or agreement on shared power structures within Northern Ireland. Major and Reynolds had become quite friendly when the former served as British Chancellor of the Exchequer. The relationship between the two men grew into one of great mutual respect when Reynolds led the gathering of Finance Ministers during the Irish Presidency of the European Union in the first half of 1990. Both men and their wives socialised together around some of these occasions. The Majors, according to Kathleen Reynolds, 'are a very natural couple'. After the couples met at an EU Finance Ministers' gathering in Ashford Castle, Major and his wife, Norma, returned the hospitality with an invite to their country residence. 'They show us pictures of their kids and we show them our lot,' said Kathleen.[2]

This informal friendship was to prove critical as the peace process began to gather pace. Major wrote in his autobiography, 'I liked Albert a lot, and I thought we could move things forward together. I invited him over for supper a fortnight after his election as Taoiseach.'[3] In the past an Irish taoiseach might have to wait months before any kind of formal meeting could be arranged with a British prime minister. 'The trust and understanding between us, that neither would see the other short, was a very good starting point. We agreed at that first meeting to do everything possible not to condemn another generation in Northern Ireland to sectarian killing,' said Reynolds about their first supper meeting.

Up to the onset of the modern peace process, the relationship between the two heads of government had been strong. Thatcher and Haughey got on well but, as with FitzGerald and Thatcher, it would be hard to describe it as a relationship of equals. Common membership of the European Union had done a lot to dissipate tension but had not conspired to produce a solution about the divided nature of Northern Irish society. Neither John Major nor Albert Reynolds could have been predicted as the two key individuals who would kickstart the peace process. In truth, it was probably a surprise to themselves.

There were, nonetheless, some straws in the wind that were to advantage both Major and Reynolds. From March to September 1988, John Hume of the Social Democratic and Labour Party (SDLP) in the North conducted talks with Gerry Adams. News of these behind-the-scenes talks broke publicly and led to widespread condemnation of Hume for having engaged with Adams. One of the most trenchant critics was former Taoiseach Garret FitzGerald who favoured further marginalisation of Sinn Féin and was firmly against any efforts to woo them into mainstream politics. While the talks had 'ended in failure, with the SDLP refusing to contemplate a common strategy while the IRA campaign continued', the key point was that the two men agreed to continue their dialogue.[4] This development initiated by Hume was critical to the unfolding peace process.

When these talks were taking place, I was the *Irish News* correspondent at Westminster and would regularly dine with Hume when he attended the House of Commons. Despite the condemnation of his contact with Adams, Hume was adamant that he would continue to engage when and if necessary. This determination on his part convinced me that there was something quite big on its way. Hume was becoming disillusioned about the idea of all-party talks and an internal solution to the problems of Northern Ireland, which gave the British a starting point. Simultaneous to his talks with Hume, Gerry Adams was carrying out discussions with Fianna Fáil, which had been authorised by the then Taoiseach, Charles Haughey. Martin Mansergh, a special advisor to Haughey, was the key interlocutor on the Fianna Fáil side. Reynolds, when he became Taoiseach, wisely decided to retain Mansergh as his advisor on Northern Ireland, even though many expected, at the time, that he would depart with Haughey. It proved to be a wise decision.

The first sign that the British government was changing its approach to Northern Ireland came with a carefully choreographed speech by the Northern Secretary, Peter Brooke, prior to John Major's arrival on the stage. In this speech, Brooke indicated that the British government 'has no selfish, strategic or economic interest in Northern Ireland: our role is to help, enable and encourage'.[5] This came out of the blue and was like a bright flare in the middle of the night. According to Jonathan Powell, 'The speech was designed to be heard by the leadership of the IRA and as limited a British audience as possible, and Brooke therefore delivered it to the Association of Canned Food Importers. His speeches were met by matching responses from Gerry Adams and Martin McGuinness indicating their interest in the ideas put forward'.[6] Powell, subsequently a key civil service advisor to Tony Blair, makes the point that these speeches by Brooke were continued by Sir Patrick Mayhew, appointed by Major as Secretary of State for Northern Ireland, and led to the re-opening of a secret channel of contact between the British government and the IRA. The man appointed to keep this channel open was a regular visitor to Martin McGuinness' home, and the latter once told me he became so familiar that he would be sitting there having a cup of tea made for him by McGuinness' wife, Bernadette, when McGuinness would come back to his house. The existence and extent of this secret channel to the IRA was to become a burning source of controversy when it became public during the peace process. The Irish government, including Reynolds, had not been told of it by Major.

The point, I suppose, is that neither Reynolds nor Major were fully aware of the private contact both of them were having with the IRA through intermediaries of one sort or the other. The extent and duration of contact between the three sets of parties, prior to the formal peace process itself, came as a surprise to many. Fr Alex Reid, a Redemptorist priest, based at the Clonard Monastery in West Belfast, was the key person who brought Adams into play with the various interlocutors. McGuinness kept the contact with the British government.

At their first meeting Reynolds, for his part, had informed Major that he was pursuing his own unconventional ways of arriving at a settlement. Haughey had been unwilling to allow Mansergh to get into direct talks with Sinn Féin, but when Reynolds came in he gave the go-ahead to Mansergh immediately so that, from the middle of 1992, a series of meetings with Adams took place. There is no doubt that Haughey was unwilling to take on the same level of risk and responsibility, if the contact leaked out, that Reynolds was willing to take. A quote from Seán Duignan, made while he was still unaware that Reynolds had given the green light for discussions to go ahead, shows just how secretive these talks were: 'Soon after that first Reynolds–Major meeting at No. 10, I was struck by the words of two former Presbyterian Church Moderators, Dr Jack Weir and Dr Godfrey Brown, who had just held much criticised talks with Sinn Féin. "Somebody has to start talking to them."'[7]

Later on, as the peace process progressed, Reynolds co-opted me into his network of intermediaries. At this stage, I was a reporter covering Leinster House, so it was easy to talk with him. He would frequently ask me to his office to chat. On one occasion, I was invited up to the Taoiseach's office, but our discussion was interrupted by a call on his 'black phone', a scrambled phone on which calls to foreign leaders were often made. I stayed there listening to what was being said but signalled to him to see if he wanted me to leave the room. I got a definitive 'No!' by way of a response. Reynolds was cursing and shouting at whoever was on the other end of the line. It was only when I began to piece together that it was a discussion about the peace process that it finally dawned on me who he was talking to. Reynolds calmly put the telephone back on its cradle with a big smile saying, 'That's John Major, a nice guy.' Major and Reynolds got on very well and their relationship was clearly able to withstand bad-tempered exchanges such as the one that I had witnessed. This relationship between the pair was one of the reasons why Reynolds was able to take huge risks for peace.

On a grey and dismal February afternoon in 1993, John Major sat at the cabinet table again, this time poring over papers, when he was handed a message, delivered to him via an intelligence link to the Provisional IRA. The contents, if true, were to become both contentious and explosive:

> The conflict is over but we need your advice on how to bring it to a close. We wish to have an unannounced ceasefire in order to hold a dialogue leading to peace. We cannot announce such a move as it will lead to confusion to the volunteers, because the press will misinterpret it as a surrender. We cannot meet the Secretary of State's public renunciation of violence, but it would be given privately as long as we were sure that we were not being tricked.[8]

The letter and confirmation of its authenticity from their own intelligence services set John Major and his ministers to thinking about their response. Major, with his Secretary of State and friend Sir Patrick Mayhew, decided it was time to pursue the matter. The phrase 'the conflict is over but we need your advice on how to bring it to a close' was to prove controversial and a source of much dispute. By the end of 1993, everyone in the world was to learn that the British government does talk to terrorists, regularly and often, despite the very public denials. Albert Reynolds had also denied contacts with the IRA, other than those through community people in the North, of course. In these shifting circumstances, with the reality sometimes hard to glean, Reynolds, with his friend Major, had kicked off a process that had been bubbling under the surface for quite a while.

It was the fact that neither of these men carried any baggage with them in terms of previous or prior commitments on Northern Ireland that made them suitable to carry this process forward. Major had risen, almost without trace in the Tory party, until he was propelled to prominence as a leadership candidate when Thatcher unexpectedly lost an internal party vote. Reynolds, for his part, had been much more visible throughout his contest with Haughey. That said, he had made few if any parliamentary interventions or speeches on Northern Ireland prior to his arrival in power. Both men had worked under leaders who were considered to have towered above them – Haughey and Thatcher. By way of further coincidence, both men had left school and not gone on to university. The ordinary-man appeal of both of them was plain to see.

Former Taoiseach John Bruton found Major to be 'a person easy to get on with. If he had a problem he would tell you and not hide the fact. He never stood on his British dignity if you like. He had these people around him in the system who made these unattributable briefings in a Perfidious Albion way.' The fact that Major was reliant on Unionist MPs for support at Westminster did, of course, inhibit him, and Bruton believes 'he came to be in a progressively weaker position as time went on'.[9] Throughout the peace process, Major was hamstrung by his dependence on Unionist votes at Westminster and significant right-wing MPs in his own party who were opposed to his policy on Europe. There was a series of well-publicised parliamentary revolts over votes for the Maastricht Treaty. The MPs who opposed Major at this point were unlikely to have welcomed any dealings with the IRA and would probably have reacted against any radical moves by him on the Irish issue.

One of the key persons involved in Major and the British government's direct contacts with the IRA was a man called Michael Oatley, an MI6 officer. Oatley had been undertaking his back-channel role of facilitating such contact for the best part of twenty years. His contact with the IRA in Derry was a Catholic businessman called Brendan Duddy. Then, at Christmas 1991, Oatley went to the home of Noel Gallagher, another long-term contact of the British government in the IRA. Gallagher had received instruction from the IRA's Army Council to co-ordinate and link up with Duddy. He was warned to listen but not to compromise on any operational matters raised in discussions. On the visit that Oatley made to Gallagher that Christmas, the former stated that a ceasefire from the IRA would be responded to, within minutes, by the British government.

Gallagher had known Martin McGuinness since the latter was a child, and he also knew Albert Reynolds from his days owning the bacon factory in Dublin's Liberties. Thanks to this friendship with Reynolds, Gallagher was to become a critical link as the peace process unfolded. The first meeting between Reynolds, McGuinness and Adams happened in his home, well before the IRA declared their ceasefire.[10]

CHAPTER FOURTEEN

Irish America

In his first ministerial portfolio of Posts and Telegraphs, Albert Reynolds had led a vast investment programme to upgrade what was a very ramshackle telephone service in the 1970s. Businesspeople lobbied TDs, in a frantic way, trying to get a telephone connection. Ordinary citizens faced a long wait before they had telephones installed. As part of his push to raise investment in the telephone service, Reynolds paid a visit to the United States. In his own words:

> I didn't know anything about modern telecommunications at that time, but I did know that AT&T, the big telecommunications company in America, were making major developments and that I needed to talk to them. I planned to attend a convention in New York, and decided to set off a bit earlier and combine it with a family holiday in Hyanis Port. While we were there we were invited to the home of Senator Edward Kennedy, where we were warmly welcomed by his family. His mother was being cared for by a young Irish nurse from Ballymahon, County Longford, and there was a young girl working there too who happened to be from our own home town of Longford.

Reynolds chose the occasion to press Senator Kennedy for an introduction to senior executives at AT&T. A meeting of its board of directors was taking place in New York at around the time of the convention Reynolds was attending. Reynolds, with his business acumen, realised that he would get higher-level access to AT&T through an introduction from Kennedy. At this time, Kennedy was the doyen of Irish-American politics, along with

Senators Daniel Patrick Moynihan and Tip O'Neill, who would later become Speaker of the House during the Reagan era. For Reynolds, this Kennedy connection was to prove a valuable one and was to be of great use when he began his efforts to further the peace process. According to Conor O'Clery, the veteran *Irish Times* journalist:

> Edward Kennedy was already a strong supporter of all things Irish and his influence was a vital ingredient in the fight against violence. According to Reynolds as far back as 1977 Senator Kennedy, together with John Hume, had worked to set up a group of high-powered Irish-Americans that became known as the 'Four Horsemen', whose aim was to help break down the traditional reluctance of certain other Irish-American Democrats to condemn Republican violence and to encourage instead constitutional Nationalism as a viable alternative.[1]

US support for the Anglo-Irish Agreement of 1985, signed by Garret FitzGerald and Maggie Thatcher, also proved important. The then Irish ambassador in Washington, Seán Donlon, had put a huge amount of work into cultivating Irish-Americans in the Senate and Congress.

Then, in April 1992, Bill Clinton, a little-known governor from Arkansas running for the Democratic nomination for president, accepted an invitation to attend a meeting in the Sheraton Hotel in Manhattan in a bid to win over the influential Irish-American voting bloc. At the meeting were luminaries from the New York-based Irish-American community: Martin Galvin of NORAID, a fundraising front for the IRA; Mayor Ray Flynn of Boston; Ray O'Hara; Niall O'Dowd, editor of the *Irish Voice*; Paul O'Dwyer, a well-known human rights lawyer, and Peter King, then comptroller of Nassau County, but subsequently a highly influential Republican congressman in the city of New York. Conor O'Clery was present to cover the event. 'Clinton said that sometimes America was too reluctant to engage in a positive way with Northern Ireland because of our long-standing special relationship with Great Britain and also because it seems such a thorny problem.'[2] Clinton came across as knowledgeable on the issues and, in answer to a question from Galvin, indicated he would, if elected, appoint an envoy to Northern Ireland.

After the meeting O'Clery chased up Clinton to ask if he was aware who Martin Galvin was. He received the following reply: 'Give me a break. I am doing my best.' The audience of Irish-Americans were left 'starry-eyed' by Clinton, who was extremely well briefed on the issues. 'I never heard a candidate who knew more about Ireland,' said Paul O'Dwyer to O'Clery.[3] The Clinton enthusiasm for Irish America was only added to when it emerged that the British Tory administration had somehow assisted his Republican opponents in their attempts to dig up some political dirt on Clinton from his period as a Rhodes Scholar at Oxford. 'They even, at the request of the Bush administration, went so far as to investigate his passport files, in an attempt to detect whether or not he had tried to change his nationality in order to avoid the Vietnam draft. This was to cause deep resentment in the future,' according to Reynolds.

Clinton, as American politicians go, was quite well informed about Ireland. He told O'Clery that, during his time at Oxford, he had watched the development of the civil rights movement in Northern Ireland and had been impressed by Bernadette Devlin. It is also believed that two very prominent Irish-Americans made significant donations to the Clinton campaign when it was engulfed in controversy because of Clinton's fling with Jennifer Flowers, a singer, actress and model. The Clinton friendship with Irish America and the group's support for him was to prove hugely important in the story of the peace process.

Reynolds, when installed in the job as Taoiseach, had not been idle in his attentions to Irish America. In the summer of 1992, after discussions with the then Ambassador to Washington, Dermot Gallagher, Reynolds established a new Ireland-America Economic Advisory Board. According to Gallagher, it brought together 'a group of fifteen to eighteen Irish-American businesspeople who were invited to be members of a special board set up by the Taoiseach. He would then meet them twice a year in the US and brief them on economic developments in Ireland and in return get their thinking on global economic developments.'[4] Reynolds had always been conscious of promoting Ireland from an investment perspective. Those appointed to the board were heavy hitters from corporate America including Dan Tully of Merrill Lynch, Don Keough of Coca-Cola, Jack

Welch of General Electric, Tony O'Reilly, and billionaire Chuck Feeney. Feeney, along with other members of this body, would become a key driver in the unfolding peace process. Along with Feeney, Bill Flynn of Mutual of America was also regularly briefed by Reynolds on developments in the peace process.

Reynolds was very much of the view that the violence in Northern Ireland had had a very bad impact on the opportunity to entice US investment to the Republic of Ireland. He was also savvy enough to know that when people looked at the latest act of violence on their TV screens, internationally, they did not always distinguish between what was going on in the North and what was happening south of the border. Reynolds often spoke passionately about this in private. He was very conscious of the high cost the Troubles were imposing on the southern economy. It was one of his key motivations and reasons for the speed and aggression he deployed in the peace process.

The first meeting between Reynolds and the now President Clinton was to be an important one. Clinton hosted a huge dinner in the White House with guests invited from the world of Hollywood, the administration and Irish America. After the dinner and earlier meeting with Reynolds, O'Clery, the *Irish Times* correspondent to Washington, ran into Clinton. Clinton confided to him that he liked Reynolds' 'straight business talk'.[5] In their discussions of earlier that day, Clinton had reluctantly agreed to temporarily stall his election promise of sending a peace envoy to Ireland. The appointment at that time would have sent both the British government and the unionists around the bend. Reynolds, according to O'Clery, had confided in Clinton that he was working quietly with British Prime Minister John Major on 'unconventional ways to stop the violence'. Clinton was impressed and decided to take the inevitable flak he would receive from Irish-Americans by backing down on the issue of an envoy. In his interview for O'Clery's book *The Greening of the White House*, Reynolds told Clinton that the last thing he wanted was failure: '... put it on the shelf. If you send an envoy nobody will talk to him. I will be back later with something else.'[6] Much later, once the IRA ceasefire had been delivered, Clinton would appoint George Mitchell as an economic envoy.

Reynolds proved to be astute and, in a subsequent phone call from Major, was thanked for his part in stopping the appointment of an envoy. Reynolds had accurately calculated the negative impact a US envoy appointment would have had at this point and used the meeting with Clinton to build up further credit with Major.

In addition, Reynolds did not leave the White House empty-handed. The most significant announcement from his St Patrick's Day visit was the appointment of Jean Kennedy-Smith as the next US Ambassador to Dublin. Kennedy-Smith was, of course, sister to Reynolds' old friend Senator Edward Kennedy, and the appointment as ambassador was to have not just symbolic importance back in Ireland but also to be of huge practical help as the peace process unfolded. Often US appointees to the ambassadorship in Dublin do not have ready or immediate access to the president or administration. This was not to be the case with Kennedy-Smith, who, through her own efforts (and, of course, those of her brother) had a fast-track to the powers that be back in Washington.

Another person who played a significant role in the peace process as a background player was Tim Pat Coogan, author and former editor of *The Irish Press*. Coogan was very well connected to Gerry Adams and the Belfast membership of the IRA. He was introduced to Ambassador Kennedy-Smith soon after her appointment. Coogan hosted a lunch in his house in Glenageary that was attended by Fr Alex Reid from the Clonard Monastery in Belfast, who was the key interlocutor between the SDLP, the IRA and Dublin. According to Coogan, who had written a groundbreaking book on the IRA, this early immersion with someone who was at the heart of the process 'made Jean Kennedy-Smith central to it. Alex Reid told her that Adams was to be trusted. It was a genuine steer from Reid and Kennedy-Smith was a Catholic at heart and whatever about me saying the same thing she would have taken it better from a priest of Reid's standing.'[7]

The efforts being made by Kennedy-Smith were frequently opposed by people in the State Department, as well as her colleague Raymond Seitz, the US Ambassador in London. Perhaps absorbing the paranoia of some quarters of British officialdom, Ambassador Seitz, in his book of memoirs, accused Kennedy-Smith of being 'an ardent IRA apologist' and of acting as 'a promotion agent for Gerry Adams'.[8] At two key junctures in the peace process, Kennedy-Smith intervened to ensure that both Adams and veteran IRA man Joe Cahill were given visas to visit the United States. Cahill's visa, as well as the earlier one for Adams, were vital in terms of opening up and locking the IRA itself into the process. The influence exerted by the US administration had a telling effect. Ambassador Kennedy-Smith was, during this period, a regular guest at the Taoiseach Albert Reynolds' home.

There were also many others from Irish America at work in the peace process. Perhaps one of the most influential was Niall O'Dowd, editor of the *Irish Voice*, a publication aimed at the Irish-American community. He had teamed up with philanthropist Chuck Feeney and brought delegations across the Atlantic to visit Belfast. Bruce Morrison, a Congressman, was also a key member of the O'Dowd group and enjoyed a high reputation in Ireland because of his championing of the Immigration Reform Act of 1990, which meant more visas were available for the Irish. Morrison was, critically, trusted in Dublin as well as having been a friend of Bill Clinton from his time at Yale University.

Many of the members of the O'Dowd delegations were impressed by Reynolds. They were taken into the Taoiseach's confidence, sometimes before, but often after, returning home from visits where they met key figures in the North. In the twelve months prior to the IRA ceasefire, Morrison paid for three trips to meet with key figures north and south of the border. Such was the credibility of these visiting delegations that the IRA acceded to a request from O'Dowd that they would have an 'unannounced ceasefire, for the period of which our delegation will be in Ireland. We will inform the White House in advance of that ceasefire as an example of your good faith.'[9]

This Irish-American dimension to the peace process was both nurtured and welcomed by Reynolds. He was very assiduous in keeping the links open. O'Dowd, for his part, was in touch with 'Edward Kennedy's Foreign Policy Adviser, Triona Vargo, who in turn briefed Nancy Sodeberg of Clinton's National Security Agency'.[10] Equally, Reynolds was not averse to picking up the phone and ringing these and other key people in the administration to get his point of view across. Dermot Gallagher, the then Ambassador to the

United States, was impressed with the support he got from Reynolds in his role:

> It was obvious that Albert clearly saw that the US was going to be core, was going to be central to breaking down the Northern logjam, and he had this date every St Patrick's Day in the President's diary and he was going to use it at prime ministerial level. That way, too, knowing that they were going to meet on an ongoing basis he could establish a relationship and that was critical.[11]

Reynolds' use of Irish America is testament to his lifelong networking skills honed by exposure to both the world of business and politics. As in many other areas of his life, in harnessing Irish-America to his needs, Reynolds was careful not to let an opportunity pass. In Clinton's words, 'When Albert visited the White House in 1993 for our first meeting, I liked his easy manner, quick wit, and his clear conviction that we needed to work together to end the violence in Northern Ireland. He knows I agreed with him and he was determined not to let me off the hook. I liked that.'[12] Reynolds, as will become apparent later in this book, was not someone who allowed people to get away with not honouring a promise if they had given him a commitment. Even in my own dealings with him, he was quick to follow up if I had agreed to take on a particular task. The single great achievement of the period of the run-up to that first IRA ceasefire was that Ireland, for the first time in its history, had the edge over Britain when it came to influencing the White House.

CHAPTER FIFTEEN

Progressive Democrats

The Fianna Fáil–Progressive Democrat government was never destined for success. Reynolds resented the way the coalition pact was put together and many of the party's rank-and-file members were hugely hostile to the PDs. Pádraig Flynn, a key Reynolds confidant, had stated that opposition to coalition government was a 'core value' for the party. Reynolds, while in the coalition, described it as a 'temporary little arrangement'. This undoubtedly made him popular with the wider Fianna Fáil membership and support base but clearly would not have pleased the PDs. Equally, they would not have been impressed with Brian Cowen, Reynolds' protegé, stating at the Fianna Fáil Ard Fheis: 'If in doubt, leave them out', with regard to the party. Cowen, and later Reynolds as well, was speaking to the wider Fianna Fáil constituency, with its pent-up annoyance at the perceived 'Moral Watchdog' role played by the PDs in relation to Fianna Fáil. The idea that the PDs stood on some higher moral ground and were, in effect, 'keeping Fianna Fáil honest' in government was deeply resented.

If the mood between the two parties was not good, it appeared to be the case that the personal relationship between Reynolds and Des O'Malley was also poor. This is hardly a surprise. For the most part, from 1979, on his appointment as minister, right up to 1983, Reynolds had been a steadfast defender of Charles Haughey in the bitter internal party feuds over the latter's leadership. On all three occasions when there was an actual motion to remove Haughey from the leadership, Reynolds had been active in supporting the man who had first appointed him to cabinet. This would have set him against O'Malley who, up until the point at which he decided to leave the party to found and lead the PDs, was the primary leadership contender or challenger, a position worsened by Reynolds' growing interest from 1982 in potentially becoming leader of the party. Moreover, Reynolds was the businessman pursuing appointments in the economic or business ministries, something that was also a priority for O'Malley, who cherished the position of Minister for Industry and Commerce. O'Malley was a lawyer by profession, whereas Reynolds was a self-made businessman. Not only would they have been positioned differently in party rows but, temperamentally, they were quite different as individuals, in terms of their life experiences. In a very real sense, the departure of O'Malley from Fianna Fáil helped Reynolds up the ladder.

Bertie Ahern, the Minister for Finance in that first Reynolds government, later noted:

Albert was not a man who could rise above personal dislikes. O'Malley irritated him and he let that show. It would often become clear during cabinet meetings that Albert had not briefed Dessie on matters coming up for decision. There was no trust there at all. Unfortunately their personal dislike became very public. O'Malley had given his evidence to the Beef Tribunal that summer [1992], when he described decisions made by Reynolds as 'grossly unwise, reckless and foolish.' Albert was furious but he wasn't due to give evidence before the tribunal until the autumn.[1]

Ahern formed the view that summer that the coalition with the PDs was not going to last long. Haughey had been very attentive to the PD leader, notwithstanding his own dislike of him, mainly because his political survival depended on him. But there was simply no relationship between O'Malley and Reynolds.

Charlie McCreevy, who served in cabinet, confirms that neither man really ever saw eye to eye. 'They didn't get on. Des is not an easy man to get on with. He was very difficult. He would cause a row in an empty house and I told that to Des himself once,' stated McCreevy.[2] Charlie sees it as ironic that Haughey and O'Malley did not have the same level of antipathy towards each other, once in cabinet, that Reynolds and O'Malley had. But Haughey saw the personal benefit of developing a relationship with O'Malley in order to maintain himself in office, despite the years of feuding with him, whereas Reynolds saw no great need to do so. It appeared to be his political mission to downsize the PDs rather than give them fresh victories around the cabinet table.

The controversy over abortion in the X Case had engulfed Reynolds' new government within days of him taking office. It soon became obvious that the terms of the Supreme Court's judgement on the case would have to be followed up with referendum on the matter. The timing of this was the source of additional aggravation between Reynolds and O'Malley. Reynolds was pragmatic and, in a private sense, Catholic. In contrast, O'Malley and his party were on the liberal side of social issues. As we have seen, O'Malley and the PDs pushed for the abortion issue to be dealt with before the referendum on passing the Maastricht Treaty. However, Reynolds was determined to go ahead with the Maastricht referendum first. Most observers, at the time, seemed to think it was critical to separate the two issues from each other, including members of Reynolds' own ministerial team. 'The PDs put their oar in, siding with the liberals and claiming the amendment was dangerous for women. For a time the issue threatened the stability of the government, but ultimately O'Malley backed away and argued that to plunge the country into an election on the abortion issue would be unforgiveable.'[3]

The manner in which the PDs vocalised their opposition via media would have annoyed Reynolds and he chose to outvote them at cabinet. His government press secretary, Seán Duignan, said, 'I thought it ominous ... that Mary Harney said afterwards that the abortion row would not bring down the government. She seemed to be insinuating that the break-up was on its way, but on a different issue.'[4]

There was another unseemly clash between Reynolds and O'Malley towards the middle of the year, involving the all-party talks that were underway in relation to the North of Ireland. On one occasion neither of the PD cabinet ministers, O'Malley and Bobby Molloy, were able to attend the talks. They proposed that Mary Harney, a junior minister, attend instead. Reynolds vetoed this, insisting it was only open to cabinet ministers. There was no malice on Reynolds' part, but he was determined to keep the talks process involving Dublin, London and parties in the North on an even keel. The PDs had a view of the North that was different to that of Fianna Fáil and closer to that of the main opposition party, Fine Gael. Reynolds wanted to preserve a unified voice on the Irish government side during these sensitive discussions. Privately, Reynolds also believed the official talks were going nowhere, a view echoed by John Hume. Both Reynolds and Hume were pursuing, unknown to everyone, the option of opening up communications in private with Sinn Féin. The PDs would have been dead set against any such thing had they discovered it, so Reynolds made sure they heard nothing of it. These contacts meant that the cabinet team at the all-party talks, which excluded Sinn Féin, was holding the line that no changes in relation to Articles 2 and 3 of the Irish constitution (which express the view that the island of Ireland should be united) could be given as a concession in these talks. Reynolds was holding the reins tight in this sense. The PDs, if given the chance, would be glad to signal their different approach.

Even with the public spats with his coalition colleagues, by the summer of 1992, Reynolds' popularity was strong among the general public. One opinion poll at this time showed Fianna Fáil on 50 per cent and the PDs on a paltry 4 per cent. 'These figures lulled Reynolds and other senior Fianna Fáil people into the false belief that the PDs would have to avoid an election at any cost, no matter what the provocation from Fianna Fáil,'[5] wrote Stephen Collins, a political commentator. This complacency on the part of Fianna Fáil was foolish. The poll rating for the party and Reynolds was probably more reflective of the fact that the electorate were relieved that Haughey, along with much of the controversy that accompanied him, had gone. Most voters were ready to support Reynolds once he was running things smoothly and there was a quieter life for all. John Major was gaining from the same effect in the UK – at its simplest, he was not Thatcher and the drama around the Iron Lady had dissolved. Often the electorate like a period of quiet after a charismatic leader has led them through a series of controversies.

Reynolds had moved at a blistering pace since he became Taoiseach. The X Case had ensured there was no grace period or honeymoon for him. He was operating an exhausting schedule and appeared to have no time to relax. Furthermore, in the years just prior to him taking charge, there had been a significant change in the media landscape in Ireland with the creation of the new local FM stations up and down the country. Reynolds now had to confront a much bigger forest of microphones wherever he went as Taoiseach. He was media friendly and John Major, amongst others, observed that he often found it difficult to pass a microphone without giving some form of comment. The then opposition leader, John Bruton, believes that Reynolds was, in many ways, overactive for his age. 'It may have been a strength in one context and a weakness in others. He was not getting enough sleep. He made mistakes. His earlier life as a ballroom proprietor made him, of necessity, keep late hours, but it would not have suited him in the role as Taoiseach.'[6] This is a significant point. His predecessor Haughey never kept late hours and was mostly in bed by around 10 p.m. Reynolds, on the other hand, was a bit of a night owl and there are multiple accounts of him making late-night telephone calls and staying up with others into the early hours. At sixty years of age when he took over as Taoiseach, Reynolds may not have realised the full toll the wear and tear of the years in politics would take.

On the surface, things looked good for Reynolds in this his first year as Taoiseach, but ominous storm clouds were gathering. The 'grossly unwise, reckless and foolish' statement made about him by O'Malley in evidence to the Beef Tribunal in the summer of 1992 had set him brooding for revenge. O'Malley had also staked out his strong reservations about both Haughey and Reynolds' apparent favouritism towards beef producer Larry Goodman. Reynolds was tetchy about his reputation, particularly in relation to the question of whether export credit guarantees had been distributed fairly to Goodman's companies when Reynolds had been Minister for Industry and Commerce. In his last period in office, Haughey had begun shifting the blame for the controversy over this matter onto Reynolds. This had the effect of piling the pressure on Reynolds and there were plenty of rumours in the background that he had been far too generous to the beef baron.

One of the weaknesses in Reynolds' position early on in his leadership was that he had a relatively inexperienced ministerial team. On the positive side, he had carefully picked people like David Andrews, Seamus Brennan,

Charlie McCreevy and Joe Walsh to become cabinet ministers. All four of these had been very close to O'Malley when he was opposing Haughey within Fianna Fáil and some of them were believed to have been close to defecting to the PDs. It is all the more surprising, given their friendship with O'Malley, that none of them appeared able to significantly influence Reynolds or O'Malley to tone things down while in government. Benny Reid from Reynolds' Longford constituency, and a seasoned observer of his, believes the massacre of ministers on his first day was a mistake: 'He was absolutely stupid to ditch someone like Gerry Collins. If he had kept Collins in his cabinet he wouldn't have made the mistakes that he did. Whatever else Collins was, he was streetwise.'[7] Collins had significant cabinet experience and knew O'Malley very well as a fellow Limerickman and cabinet minister.

Along with Reynolds' difficulties with the PDs, he was compounding his troubles by his tendency to sue media outlets which he felt had sought to damage his reputation:

> He had adopted a strategy of taking legal action against newspapers he believed had libelled him and this soured his relations with a number of media people. Even before he took over the Taoiseach's office he was involved in a legal action against the *Irish Times* over an article by anti-EU campaigner Raymond Crotty who had accused him of attempting to use his position as a minister to secure European funding for his family pet-food firm.[8]

A number of other media outlets were also the subject of legal action. Reynolds told Duignan that he wasn't taking this sort of thing 'lying down'. Whatever about the motivation for taking this approach, it was not designed to ensure continued friendly coverage from the media. News travelled quickly around media circles about his habit of instigating litigation. It did not please people and may have made them more wary of him. During this, his first government, which lasted for a period of just ten months, there were media operators who were more than willing to find fault with him and pick holes in his arguments. Despite his obvious familiarity with the media, some of this bred a sort of contempt.

Fintan O'Toole of *The Irish Times* was to become something of a nemesis for Albert Reynolds, in particular, during his appearance before the Beef Tribunal. This liberal or left-wing commentator once wrote of Reynolds: 'When Mary Robinson said, "Come dance with me in Ireland", and the people accepted the invitation, knowing what would fill a ballroom on a wet Tuesday night in Rooskey was not part of the equation.'[9] This kind of slighting prose about Reynolds was not unusual and can hardly have endeared the media to him.

CHAPTER SIXTEEN

Beef Tribunal

In June 1991, on the first day of the Beef Tribunal, based at Dublin Castle, there was a short break. The judge, Mr Justice Liam Hamilton, adjourned the proceedings and went into a room to his right. On the way there, he signalled to myself and another journalist, John Kelly of *The Sunday Press*. We both followed him inside. It was a cigarette break for the judge and for us, the reporters covering the proceedings, and he had communicated with us in this way before while covering court cases in the Four Courts. As he pulled on his cigarette, Hamilton seemed uneasy at even being there. When asked what the whole thing was about, he said it was 'a political ball of smoke', though I don't think he realised just how big a political ball of smoke the Tribunal was going to become as we sat, puffing our cigarettes, on tea chests packed to the brim with documents and evidence of all sorts.

The Tribunal became so big it would dominate politics and media coverage for the next few years of its existence. Barristers down in the Law Library were salivating at the fees that could be earned and were competing to represent one or other of the witnesses who would inevitably be called. Some of the best-known barristers in the country were rubbing their hands in glee at the prospect. The whole thing had come about because of an ITV programme aired in 1991 and allegations of illegal activities, fraud and malpractice in the beef processing industry, centred on the country's biggest beef processing company owned by Larry Goodman. At the heart of the parliamentary allegations was the suggestion that under Mr Haughey's government, Goodman's company had enjoyed 'favoured' status and had been on the winning side of every dealing it had with the state. Haughey agreed to set up the Tribunal as a result of pressure from his coalition colleagues, the PDs, and because Haughey was involved, there were also rumours not just of favouritism, but of money changing hands and backhanders from businessmen.

A big 'legal circus' sprang into action, with the only obvious beneficiaries being the lawyers and, to a lesser extent, the journalists covering it, like myself, as fresh news rolled out every day that could be fed into broadcast news or newspapers. Apart from the beef industry, all the big figures of the political world were, at one stage or another, called on to give evidence. Since Haughey had been forced to retire, Reynolds became the big target whose evidence people wanted to hear. Back in 1987, Reynolds had, as Minister for Industry and Commerce, been very generous in the amount of taxpayers' money he had given to the Goodman companies for their meat contracts in Iraq. He had been so generous, in fact, that rivals of Goodman and certain political figures claimed that Goodman had monopolised the export insurance cover to the detriment of others. In the summer prior to Reynolds giving his evidence, Des O'Malley, Reynolds' coalition partner and nemesis, had already described his decisions as 'unwise, reckless and foolish'. The media began to speculate about a big showdown between the two men when Reynolds took the stand to defend himself in October 1992. Even those most immediately around Reynolds felt he would be looking to settle his score with O'Malley and get his version out.

The tribunal dragged on for two long years after Reynolds gave his evidence before the Dáil finally got around to debating the final report produced by Mr Justice Liam Hamilton. A lot of things had happened in the meantime and Reynolds was still Taoiseach. The debate happened the day after the announcement of the groundbreaking IRA ceasefire of August 1994. Much of what was said and written about the Tribunal debate in the Dáil was overshadowed by that bigger story. The then leader of the opposition, John Bruton, set out his argument on the issue in a carefully constructed speech. Amongst other things, he said that Reynolds, as minister, had broken all the terms of a cabinet decision about export credit insurance and had done so within hours of the actual cabinet decision. He had done so in a private meeting, without officials present, and given the valuable credit to two meat industry businessmen – Oliver Murphy and Pascal Phelan had been allocated £10 million each in cover without even having contracts to sell meat in Iraq. The same cabinet decision 'was to give a straight and needless gift of £274 million to the Goodman organisation,' according to Bruton.[1] Bruton drew a distinction in his speech between Reynolds' personal as opposed to his political integrity and concluded that his conduct meant he did not have the requisite trustworthiness to hold political office.

Now a former Taoiseach, Bruton believes ministers should not have meetings without officials present when major decisions are being made about the allocation of taxpayers' money. He says of Reynolds, 'Hunches and private meetings are not legitimate when significant state resources are being put at risk – as with export credit guarantees. I have nothing wrong with the government picking and backing industrial champions but the decisions have to be made in a transparent way. It is inherently risky. My feeling is that he was less than careful.'[2]

Reynolds, despite this and other conclusions insisted that the report of the Tribunal had vindicated him and his personal integrity. When he gave his evidence to the Beef Tribunal it was, probably, the most dramatic day of the proceedings, as it led directly to the collapse of Reynolds' government and a general election. Sometime later, he conceded to Duignan, 'Looking back on it from a political point of view, and I stress the word political, I was badly advised.'[3] How badly advised we shall now see.

The day of Albert Reynolds' appearance at the Beef Tribunal had come. The room in Dublin Castle was packed to capacity. The key exchange was to be the one between Reynolds and the senior barrister for Des O'Malley. Adrian Hardiman was acknowledged as one of the foremost barristers of his time. He subsequently went on to become the first barrister appointed straight into a position in the Supreme Court. In University College Dublin (UCD) he had been auditor of the L&H debating society and a student of Pure History, under the direction of another legend, Robin Dudley Edwards, a man who tested his students so much that it represented a form of psychological torture for some. Hardiman was a friend of mine. His cross-examination of Reynolds was riveting stuff. Sitting in the press reporters' bench, the contrast was stark – intellectual lawyer versus self-made millionaire politician. Hardiman had tried and failed to make it in politics – Reynolds had brought his entrepreneurial talents to politics and made it his life's business.

Reynolds did not make a good witness. Observing him, at a distance of about twelve to fifteen feet, it was obvious to me that he was uncomfortable and, in a sense, was not hiding the fact that he did not want to be there. His body language changed, from edgy and uneasy to solemn and then casual. He rarely looked Hardiman in the eye, preferring instead to take in the judge and address his remarks to him. This alone gave an appearance of disdain for the cross-examination process. He was giving his evidence off the cuff. The sheer detail of the rival figures being thrown around about the export credit allocations seemed to bore him. His approach was home-spun but not appropriate in a legal setting. Reynolds' argument was that O'Malley had misrepresented and used incorrect figures with regard to the export credit insurance allocations. However, the problem was that the figures presented by the state at the Tribunal were also wrong.

In his evidence, Reynolds basically accused O'Malley of deliberately exaggerating: 'He puffed up Goodman's claims for what I regard as cheap political gain. He was reckless, irresponsible and dishonest to do that here in the Tribunal.'[4] Hardiman conflated the word dishonest as being an accusation by Reynolds that O'Malley had committed perjury. There was a tetchy exchange between the two which was dragged out, back and forth, with Reynolds stating, 'Perjury is your word, dishonesty is my word.' There was an awkwardness to the whole thing and neither man seemed prepared to let it rest. The impact of these words in a room full of watching analysts, political and Tribunal reporters was greatly magnified, all the more so because those who had received briefings from government sources in the run-up to the event were given a soothing message that there would not be unnecessary hostility between Reynolds and O'Malley – an impression had been given that things would be calm.

Comparing Reynolds to Haughey, in terms of the latter's appearance at the Beef Tribunal, Labour's Fergus Finlay made the following point:

Nobody expected Albert Reynolds to adopt the same demeanour [as Haughey] when he took the stand. He had developed a series of mantras to describe himself – 'I am what I am, what you see is what you get, like it or lump it, good bad or indifferent' – and these could come tumbling out, often in the same sentence, whenever he was under any questioning, in the Dáil or in the media. His style was plain, no nonsense, and matter-of-fact. This would be a more down-to-earth performance. But still, as Taoiseach, he would have to be careful. It wouldn't, we thought, be likely that he would be offering any controversial evidence.[5]

Seán Duignan felt surprised by the coverage given to Reynolds' testimony. The depiction of Reynolds in the media as coarse, insolent, petulant and bullying began to get to both Reynolds and his family. Duignan, in his book, gives vent to the desperation many of his supporters felt as they saw the prospect of a general election looming. People were willing Reynolds to soften the accusation against O'Malley. Hardiman, in a key part of the evidence, offered Reynolds the opportunity to state that his client, O'Malley, was merely incorrect as distinct from 'dishonest'. It was a singular moment and it seemed Reynolds understood what was being asked. Reynolds made a one-word reply – 'dishonest'. Hardiman had cornered Reynolds a number of times while he was giving evidence, but this was the moment when everyone assumed that the PDs would walk and the government collapse. In Fergus Finlay's view, there was no way Hardiman could have gone after Reynolds the way he did without explicit instructions from O'Malley to do so.

When Reynolds had finished giving evidence, there were half a dozen or more ministerial Mercedes waiting in the yard of Dublin Castle. The light had gone and the ministers scurried back to Leinster House. It was clear they had attended the Tribunal, when Reynolds was giving evidence, not just to support their Taoiseach but to see if they would continue to hold their jobs. After filing my report for the radio, I dropped into the Clarence Hotel for a drink. By coincidence, Adrian Hardiman happened to be there. His lawyer friends were cock-a-hoop in a quiet bar to the rear. They regarded his cross-examination as a great triumph, glasses were raised in his honour and the words 'iron man' were uttered in an impromptu toast. It was clear to them at least that their man had got the better of the Taoiseach.

In a matter of days and amid much recrimination, Albert Reynolds was in Áras an Uachtaráin seeking to dissolve the Dáil and call an election. Up in the Áras, I observed a sense of desperation about the whole thing. The President was abroad and the Presidential Commission was there instead. It was a cold November night as I waited outside. Nobody was going to welcome an election at this time of year. There was a hunted look about Reynolds. This was the election that he had not planned for. It would be the first and only general election he would fight from the position of taoiseach. There was no plan. He was a hostage to fortune due to the evidence he had given.

In the election itself things would rapidly go from bad to worse. The first opinion poll showed his personal popularity rating had collapsed. According to Noel Dempsey, his chief whip, 'The election was a nightmare. The campaign was all over the place. There was very little planning for it. The media were going after him. Most of his ministers ran back to their constituencies avoiding media engagements on the national campaign.'[6] The PDs had delayed their decision to formally pull the plug on the government for a couple of days and used that time to spin negative messages about Reynolds via the public media. In the first week of campaigning down in Killarney, there were precious few Fianna Fáil activists out to meet the Taoiseach and the accompanying media got wind of it.

In a crucial radio interview with RTÉ's *This Week* programme, Reynolds made a few verbal gaffes. Instead of stating he wanted to humanise the social welfare system, he used the word 'dehumanise' several times. In a slip of the tongue, he also called the main opposition leader, John Bruton, 'John Unionist'. These slips were compounded in another interview where he had dismissed something as 'Crap. Total crap.' The media depicted it as a crude utterance and an inappropriate phrase for a taoiseach to use. The reaction was over-blown but, along with the verbal gaffes, it gave the impression of a man stumbling from bad performance to bad performance.

An interview given by Kathleen Reynolds sought sympathy: 'I can't believe what's happened over the past few days. I can't recognise the man I married in what's being said about him. In three weeks, he's gone from being the best man around to someone none of us recognise.'[7] The reaction to the radio interview with the gaffes seemed to totally dishearten Reynolds. He put the bad performance down to exhaustion, telling Kathleen: 'it's just that I'm so tired.'[8]

Duignan, who was with the Taoiseach most of the time, felt it was impossible, at this stage, to re-invent Reynolds' persona in some other way. The only solace for Fianna Fáil and Reynolds was that it was equally apparent that their main rivals, Fine Gael under Bruton, were not capturing the public imagination either. This was to be Labour's election with a surge in support for the party led by Dick Spring. Once the results were in, their seat gains had climbed to an all-time high of thirty-three in what came to be known as the 'Spring tide'. Dick Spring, for a period of two years prior to the election, had outshone Bruton in his formal speeches in Leinster House on the controversies that affected Haughey and then Reynolds.

Reynolds had, on the advice of John Major it seems, invited in the assistance of political consultants from the London-based Saatchi & Saatchi advertising firm. They had contributed in a big way to the Tory party's campaign. News of their involvement in Ireland with Reynolds, however, was greatly scoffed at. It did not turn out to be such a good idea after all. One of their techniques was the 'negative campaigning' that seemed to work well in the UK. This same approach, in the Irish setting, however, backfired and probably led to Labour winning more votes. It smacked of desperation and came too late in the campaign. My father, now a backbencher, had actually spoken publicly to advocate giving preferences to Labour, realising they were going to do well. In a book he had written about his experience in the presidential election, he had come out strongly in favour of forming a future coalition with Labour. His election statement, to the same effect, did not endear him to Fianna Fáil headquarters, given the negative campaigning they were engaged in against Labour. However, the numbers and election results quickly demonstrated the wisdom of his approach. In the election itself, Fianna Fáil's level of support dropped below 40 per cent for the first time since 1927. Fine Gael also dropped seats.

Throughout the campaign there had been a gathering storm around the EU Exchange Rate Mechanism with destabilising trading in European currencies. Ireland was standing against speculators pushing for a devaluation of the Irish pound. One of Reynolds' election organisers had spoken in an inopportune way about the currency crisis to fend off journalists who were asking when the Taoiseach was going to arrive at his Longford constituency count. The off-the-cuff comment was carried internationally and knocked a few pfennigs off the German mark. Meanwhile, Reynolds had taken to bed in his apartment home in Dublin for a much-needed rest.

The election triggered in November 1992 by Reynolds' testimony to the Beef Tribunal had exacted a terrible price for the incumbent Taoiseach. It now looked to his opponents, as well as impartial commentators, as if Reynolds would go down as the shortest-serving Taoiseach in the country's history. When the fog of war dissipated, it seemed likely that his own party would come for him with knives. The way he had ruthlessly culled the Haughey cabinet would probably have won him few friends and even his own cabinet appointees had run for cover during the campaign. He who lives by the sword, dies by it. His obstinate response at the Tribunal in answer to Des O'Malley's evidence had brought him to the brink and beyond; Reynolds had played a very bad hand of poker and had lost big time.

To everyone's surprise, however, in the post-election game, Reynolds had a few more cards to play that would astonish his sternest critics and friends alike. A career that appeared in ruins was about to emerge triumphant from the ashes of defeat. The best of Albert Reynolds was yet to come.

CHAPTER SEVENTEEN

Europe

In the week or so immediately after his defeat in the 1992 general election campaign, Albert Reynolds was, in many respects, a broken man. The intense speculation in media circles related to how John Bruton and Dick Spring would form a 'Rainbow' coalition. This idea, floated during the campaign by Bruton, without reference to Labour, had taken off once the election was over. Fianna Fáil was going out of power and merited no attention. In the absence of a new Taoiseach, however, Reynolds was still in charge. His appearances in the office were rare and he seemed cocooned in his luxury apartment in Ballsbridge, sight unseen. Operating from Leinster House I was reporting dutifully on the inevitability of a Fianna Fáil departure from office. Things were so quiet in the aftermath of the election that I would occasionally walk over from Leinster House by the link bridge to visit Seán Duignan in his office. He and I got on well on a professional level. We would break out a bottle of whiskey and toast the old times. There was an eerie silence in the Taoiseach's office – an air of bereavement about the place. There were no media requests or queries for the Taoiseach.

On the run-up to this and since his heart-rending defeat in the presidential election campaign, my father had not been idle. He had written a book and in it, he publicly aired his preference for a future Labour coalition. He had also, sometime in the previous year, attended the launch of the Tom Johnson Institute, a Labour think-tank, to which he had been invited by some of his Labour party friends. During the election campaign, he had put a few calls in to Labour party people suggesting they might consider a Fianna Fáil coalition once it was over. It was optimistic on his part, but he had read the electoral numbers well. After the campaign, more phone calls

Albert Reynolds and Derek Cobbe (right) pictured outside the *Longford News* office with Jack Davis of the *Meath Chronicle* when the paper was sold to the Navan publisher. (© Derek Cobbe Collection)

Outside Longford Courthouse, Albert Reynolds introduces Fianna Fáil leader Jack Lynch to a packed Main Street during the 1977 general election campaign.
(© Derek Cobbe Collection)

The three Fianna Fáil candidates in the Longford/Westmeath constituency for the 1981 general election – Sean Fallon, Albert Reynolds and Seán Keegan – pictured in the Longford election headquarters. (© Derek Cobbe Collection)

During Albert Reynolds' tenure as Minister for Posts and Telegraphs, many towns and villages went from manual local exchanges to automatic. Reynolds is pictured here with Fianna Fáil party colleagues Mary O'Rourke (then a member of Athlone UDC and Westmeath County Council) and Councillor Stephen Price at Athlone Telephone Exchange. (© Derek Cobbe Collection)

Albert and Kathleen Reynolds relaxing with four of their seven children at Mount Carmel House, their Longford home. (© Derek Cobbe Collection)

A Longford/Westmeath constituency canvass card from the 1987 general election. All three Fianna Fáil candidates – Albert Reynolds, Mary O'Rourke and Henry Abbott – were elected. (© Derek Cobbe Collection)

Albert Reynolds at the Fianna Fáil Ard Fheis, 7 March 1992. (© Independent News and Media/Getty Images).

Albert Reynolds with President Bill Clinton, Senator Ted Kennedy and Jean Kennedy-Smith, 17 March 1993. During his speech, Clinton named Kennedy-Smith as US Ambassador to Ireland. (© Martin H. Simon/Pool via CNP / Alamy Stock Photo)

Secretary of State Patrick Mayhew, Foreign Secretary Douglas Hurd, Prime Minister John Major, Taoiseach Albert Reynolds, Foreign Minister Dick Spring and Minister for Justice Máire Geoghegan-Quinn at Dublin Castle, 3 December 1993. (© PA Images / Alamy Stock Photo)

Gerry Adams, Albert Reynolds and John Hume shake hands outside Government Buildings in Dublin, 6 September 1994. (© PA Images / Alamy Stock Photo)

Albert Reynolds waits in vain for Boris Yeltsin to disembark at Shannon Airport on 30 September 1994. (© REUTERS / Alamy Stock Photo)

Martin McGuinness, Albert Reynolds and Gerry Adams in Belfast outside Féile an Phobail, 10 August 1995. (© PA Images / Alamy Stock Photo)

Albert Reynolds leaves the High Court in central London with his daughters Miriam (left) and Leonie in July 1998 after winning the right to a new libel trial against *The Sunday Times*. (© REUTERS / Alamy Stock Photo)

Albert Reynolds with Northern Ireland's First Minister Ian Paisley in November 2007. (© PA Images / Alamy Stock Photo)

Albert Reynolds with former Taoiseach John Bruton at the requiem mass for Cardinal Cahal Daly in Armagh, 5 January 2010. (© Stephen Barnes/Religion / Alamy Stock Photo)

Irish politicians pay their respects at the State Funeral of Albert Reynolds, 26 August 2014. (© PA Images / Alamy Stock Photo)

were made. He met with Ruairi Quinn, the deputy leader of the Labour Party, and a few others.

Back in government buildings, when I suggested to Duignan that a Labour coalition might be on the cards, if only a remote possibility, he looked at me with total disbelief and poured me another whiskey. Reynolds himself, when I saw him at the office, looked out of place. He would be well-dressed as ever but occasionally was unshaven. For a man who was so punctilious about his personal appearance, there was a hint of neglect. To outward appearances, his cause was a lost one.

The first meeting between John Bruton and Dick Spring had not gone well, however. It had been depicted in the media as something of a stand-up row. Fergus Finlay, Spring's press man, was as present as ever in providing me and media colleagues with excellent background briefings. There was apparently previous form between the two men dating back to the Fine Gael–Labour coalition between 1973 and 1977. Bruton wanted to make up the numbers by including the PDs, whereas Spring wanted the inclusion of the Democratic Left, a rival party on his left flank. Despite this initial, hostile encounter, the conventional media wisdom was still that the two would stitch together a coalition deal.

At around this time, Reynolds was due at the Edinburgh summit of European leaders, but prior to his departure, he was approached by his advisor, Martin Mansergh, about the possibility of forming a coalition with Labour. Mansergh had done his homework. Reynolds instructed him to work up a policy document to put to Labour – Mansergh was already working on one. Labour had invited all parties to send them proposals in relation to possible coalition partnerships, but the decision to include Fianna Fáil was a mere token effort. Labour's advisor Fergus Finlay was surprised when he received the Fianna Fáil response: 'It was all there, in the document we received. A third banking force, reform of confessional legislation, significant investment in social services. Anything we were likely to find contentious in their policy position was simply dropped.'[1] On foot of this document, Reynolds set up a meeting with the Labour leader, Dick Spring, the following Sunday, on the afternoon he returned from Edinburgh.

The summit in Edinburgh would involve a significant negotiation on structural funds for Ireland in the years ahead. 'With Labour "watching for a sign", as Bertie Ahern put it to him, it was now literally a matter of political life and death.'[2] Newspapers and analysts were sceptical of Reynolds' opening bid at the summit; he was looking for £6 billion in funding in the years ahead. His pitch was depicted as unwise and optimistic. The summit was being hosted by Reynolds' friend John Major, with dinners and events around the location. 'After hours of tough haggling we reached a deal which saw the Community budget increased from £52 billion in 1992 to £64 billion in 1999.'[3] This meant that there was £12 billion available in additional funding through this budget. Reynolds had already staked his claim on a good portion of this large pot of money. The Commission President, Jacques Delors, was, to some extent, already in debt to Reynolds because of the latter's determination to go ahead with the Maastricht referendum and win it despite the jitters on Delors' part that it might all fall apart. Delors had phoned Reynolds on the day of the Maastricht victory in the referendum to express his gratitude. 'Jacques will get every chance to show how grateful he is,' had been Reynolds' cryptic comment after the call, to his press secretary.[4] As well as backing from Major for the Irish bid for funds, Reynolds had also secured support from the German Chancellor Helmut Kohl. Kohl, at this stage, was the most influential political leader around the European table. Reynolds, in the midst of his election travails, had met with Kohl. The discussion had been about the IRA. Reynolds said of the meeting:

> He had a problem, he informed me and he needed it solved. British troops stationed in Germany were being attacked, he said. Was there anything I could do to help the situation? Kohl and Major were obviously very concerned and embarrassed that so far they had not been able to stop these attacks; I think that during their discussions John Major had inferred that as I was in the process of trying to negotiate peace in Northern Ireland, and as I seemed to have connections in the North, maybe there was a chance I could get a message through to the right people.

Kohl said he would support Reynolds with the allocation of funds, 'if you can give us any help with this'. It was after this exchange that attacks by the IRA had either petered out or been ordered to a stop. Reynolds, while at the Edinburgh summit, had put in a call to his old friend Noel Gallagher who, by coincidence, was six miles away buying horses. Gallagher had been in contact with a Lutheran clergyman, Eberhard Spiecker, who had arranged meetings in Duisburg in Germany between leading nationalist and unionist figures back in 1988. Fr Alec Reid had attended the talks as a go-between for Sinn Féin. Reynolds brought Gallagher to his meeting with Helmut Kohl. 'It was Kohl who convinced Albert that he should look for £8 billion. Albert was only looking for £6 billion.' Kohl, according to Gallagher, said, 'I'll guarantee it.'[5]

Writing about Helmut Kohl, the host at Edinburgh, John Major, said, 'He was always hugely interested in what Albert and I were trying to do for Ireland and his influence in those meetings was always good, but there was a case for a better deal for Ireland. I was attracted to a better deal for Ireland on its merits and for wider reasons and Helmut was supportive.'[6]

Even with this type of money coming to the table, there was an atmosphere of despair amongst the Irish delegation at Edinburgh. The night before a decision was taken on funding, Seán Duignan had thrown a party for the Irish journalists covering the summit. To all intents and purposes all present knew the government was finished. 'It was like the last supper,' said RTÉ journalist Tommy Gorman, who covered the event. According to him, 'that money was the game changer. If that hadn't happened Albert Reynolds was finished. It was a huge boost for Ireland. It was as if we had won the jackpot.'[7]

An article written by the Dublin correspondent of the London *Independent*, Alan Murdoch said, 'Albert Reynolds' success in returning from Edinburgh with more than he had ever hoped for in EC aid could provide the kiss of life for his threatened leadership of the Fianna Fáil party.' Murdoch noted that Reynolds looked deeply alarmed when an overall agreement on the EC budget was getting beyond reach. He declared the final deal 'the single greatest achievement of his period in office'. The article in the London *Independent* acknowledged that the knives were out amongst his political colleagues prior to the summit.[8]

Reynolds arrived back in Dublin at 2 a.m. after the summit and the next day he was scheduled to meet with the Labour Leader Dick Spring in the Berkeley Court Hotel in Dublin 4. Fergus Finlay observed the meeting between Reynolds and Spring:

> The first revelation was how bright and breezy he [Reynolds] was, like a man without a care in the world. He had just arrived back from Edinburgh, where he had astonished everyone by announcing that he had secured £8 billion in structural funds over the next few years. He had gone there expressing determination that they would be doubled which would have yielded a figure of £6 billion. Either it was a negotiating triumph, or he had considerably exaggerated his success. But why would he do that, since he was on his way out of office?[9]

Reynolds, however, had other ideas and he was about to make Labour an offer they could not refuse. He knew he had to get a deal with Labour. He shared with Dick Spring the details of his private, behind-the-scenes efforts to achieve peace in the North. It made quite an impact on Spring, not least because Reynolds had told him that this work had not been shared in any respect with his previous coalition partners nor indeed with Des O'Malley. Dick Spring had assembled his team of inner advisors in another room in the hotel. They were to spend hours there considering whether to go in with Fianna Fáil. 'At the end of the discussion, Dick asked each of us to express a view, for or against opening discussions with Fianna Fáil. In my recollection, Ruairi, Brendan, Pat Magner, Greg Sparks and James Wrynn, voted for. Barry Desmond, Donal Spring, William Scally, John Rogers and I voted against', remembered Fergus Finlay on the five-all vote.[10] Spring was left for a day or two to think the thing out for himself. As a precaution he put in a phone call to John Bruton to test him on whether he would accept the notion of a rotating Taoiseach arrangement and accept the inclusion of the Democratic Left in any coalition. Bruton was negative on both suggestions and this appears to have been the motive for Spring to then action the negotiations for government with Fianna Fáil.

The negotiations to form the coalition with Fianna Fáil dragged on until Christmas and into the new year. During that period, Spring had to give evidence to the Beef Tribunal. Fortunately Spring did not make any allegations about Reynolds' role in relation to export credit guarantees when he served as minister. A controversy did rear its head, though, concerning a contretemps between rival barristers who had appeared in the Beef Tribunal. The controversy centred on a gathering of barristers at Dublin's Shelbourne Hotel, in its famous Horseshoe Bar. An allegation had surfaced from a meeting between Spring and Des O'Malley. The allegation was that some legal documents prepared by the state side in the Beef Tribunal had found their way to Fianna Fáil headquarters. Spring took the matter directly to Reynolds. The Attorney General was asked to investigate the matter and reported back that nothing untoward had happened. The episode made for lurid headlines but did not deter Spring from pressing ahead with Reynolds.

In the space of less than a year, Reynolds was forming his second coalition as Taoiseach. He had gambled and lost in an election but shown his adept negotiating skills in leveraging a result from an electoral disaster. If the point of politics is survival, then Reynolds had most certainly proved his tenacity. His patient negotiation of £8 billion for Ireland from Europe was a fitting tribute to his steely calm at the time of the Maastricht referendum, despite the obvious panic that had been in the air. He had pressed ahead with the vote and got the result on the European issue. His standing in Europe was high, not least because of this, but also because he had cultivated contacts and made friends with both Major and Kohl. One way or the other, he had put an end to the IRA attacks on the continent. While this was not known publicly, the people who needed to know, most pointedly Kohl, did know and were grateful.

Everything Reynolds had done since he became Taoiseach had been something of a high-wire act, but he was showing the nerves of steel required to deal with the problems of violence on the island of Ireland. With the PDs out of the way, he was now going to head up a coalition government with a very large majority. It may not have been a coalition of his choosing – he needed Labour rather than Labour needing him – but with his poker player's habit, he had made them a compelling offer and won out in the end.

CHAPTER EIGHTEEN

Labour Coalition

The Fianna Fáil–Labour coalition was launched amid much, albeit private, euphoria. There was a strong belief that with its significant parliamentary majority, it was an arrangement that was anything but temporary and that it had the potential to last for at least two elections. My own father was an enthusiastic supporter and felt that Labour would be a far more reliable and stable partner than the PDs. One of the funnier insights he offered me into the whole business of forming the coalition with Labour was the speed and determination with which the Labour side made it clear that their first demand was that Reynolds' close confidant Pádraig Flynn be taken off the pitch. Labour did not want him in the coalition cabinet and the message was passed on by my father to Reynolds. Faster than he might have expected, Flynn was appointed as the country's nominee for a top job in the European Commission.

Despite the strong working majority for the coalition in parliament, the arrangement was, over time, to be punctuated by a series of significant and debilitating power plays between the two parties. Reynolds had been very open with Dick Spring and the latter had been intrigued by the fact that he had got a briefing from Reynolds that had, in effect, been deliberately withheld from Des O'Malley when he was a coalition partner of Fianna Fáil. This is hardly a surprise on reflection. The PDs were virulently antipathetic to the republican movement and the IRA. O'Malley had made his political reputation as a Minister for Justice who advocated a tough crackdown on the IRA's activities. It is symptomatic of Reynolds' lack of trust in O'Malley that he did not share with him the groundbreaking moves that were going on behind the scenes. Spring was clearly intrigued by the briefing he received from Reynolds on the North, so much so that he did not share any of its detail with any of his inner group of advisors, thus underlining its significance even more. Spring clearly felt positive about the assurance from Reynolds that he was telling him something he had not told O'Malley.

The Programme for Partnership agreed between Fianna Fáil and Labour ran to fifty-eight pages and was endorsed by both of their parliamentary parties:

> Reynolds was happy to adopt the bulk of the Labour agenda on issues like ethics in government, Dáil reform, the introduction of divorce, the decriminalisation of homosexuality and extra health and social welfare spending. In return he insisted that Labour accept the budgetary constraints necessitated by the Maastricht Treaty. This was a major modification of Labour's position in the election campaign but Labour bit the bullet of fiscal rectitude.[1]

In other respects, Labour drove a hard bargain and achieved six positions around the cabinet table with Dick Spring becoming Tánaiste and Minister for Foreign Affairs.

As the coalition was being set up, *The Irish Times* decided to focus on the extra cost of the arrangements to dedicate staff and budget to the new, more formal, Office of the Tánaiste. The cost was in excess of half a million pounds and it rapidly became a source of controversy for Labour. Unemployment was still stubbornly high in Ireland, despite the renewed growth in the economy and the future prospect of significant funding from Brussels. According to Fergus Finlay, 'What did the most damage were a number of staff who were, in fact, very badly paid – Niamh Bhreathnach's daughter, Dick Spring's sister, and Emmet Stagg's cousin'.[2] The net effect of these revelations was to add to a perception that the Labour Party was a group of individuals more interested in 'jobs for the boys' and nepotism. It appeared to many commentators that pretty much all of the key players in the party had been rewarded with ministries or posts advising ministers that had been deliberately invented to buy off the possibility of internal dissent against the coalition arrangement with Fianna Fáil. The media and the opposition had a field day, with the result that Labour felt on the back foot right from the outset of the new coalition.

In the midst of this, there had been precious little time afforded to Labour ministers to settle into their briefs, and the normal grace or honeymoon period given to new governments, in this case, never happened. There had, additionally, been a crisis over the European monetary system as soon as the government had formed in 1993, and the media onslaught never stopped. There was a sense in media circles that Labour had led them on a merry dance, campaigning against Fianna Fáil very heavily in the election, and then quickly changing their minds in the aftermath and re-installing Reynolds in power. In addition, Finlay freely admits, as some of the crucial people went into formal advisory roles in government, the much larger and newer ranks of their parliamentary party were left to fend for themselves. One of these, Jim Kemmy, a socialist TD from Limerick, became a regular feature, along with others, vocalising dissent on the front plinth of Leinster House. Despite the army of advisors, to outward appearances at least, the new coalition seemed to be a lightning conductor for leaks, dissent and sudden backbench rebellions over policy. Reynolds and many of his ministers harboured deep suspicions about Finlay, believing him to be the author and source of many of the damaging leaks about the government's work. This perception, and the fact that he enjoyed the unchallenged confidence of Spring, as well as a myriad of significant contacts in the media, made him something of a *bête noire* for the Fianna Fáil side of the coalition. His competence as a spin doctor of sorts only fed Fianna Fáil paranoia further. In my own dealings with Finlay as a journalist, I found him to be fair and truthful.

Seán Duignan, still government press secretary, caught the tensions in the new government well: 'Reynolds was manipulative and impatient of opposition to his wishes, Spring was moody and quick to take offence.' Duignan confesses a liking for Spring, despite his obvious 'touchiness', but adds that when Spring wasn't being touchy, 'Fergus is touchy for him.'[3] The moral disdain that Labour had maintained against Reynolds and Fianna Fáil while in opposition was coming back to bite them, and their careful cultivation of the media was rebounding on them. In one notable example, the media went to town on a story that Spring had stayed in the Waldorf

Astoria while attending meetings at the UN in New York. The use of the government jet by Spring also attracted headline media coverage.

By mid-summer, Spring was deployed to Brussels to fight the coalition's corner in a high-wire negotiation with the EU on the level of funding Ireland would get. This was in relation to the fabled £8 billion secured by Reynolds at Edinburgh. There now seemed to be renewed doubt over whether the country would, in fact, end up with this kind of money. There was an all-night negotiation in Brussels and Finlay was put in charge of totting the numbers. Spring eventually settled on a figure of £7.85 billion. Finlay was deputed to ring Reynolds and fill him in on what had been agreed. According to Finlay:

> He quizzed me backwards and forwards, asking me to recite the conversion formula that had been used, and apparently checking it against a formula he had developed himself, before pronouncing himself satisfied that at least the arithmetic was right. 'Good man,' he said, before going back to sleep the sleep of the just. You wouldn't think that this was a deal that might make or break his reputation.[4]

At various points in his book, *Snakes & Ladders*, Finlay expresses admiration for Reynolds' coolness under pressure. There is no doubt but that these expressions of admiration for Reynolds are sincere and well observed, but, despite this, there remain, to this day, deep suspicions about his own motives in relation to the coalition in Fianna Fáil. The negotiation of the structural funds from Brussels and, of course, the later negotiation of the Downing Street Declaration would appear to represent rare examples of unity between Reynolds and Spring in what was otherwise a bumpy and very fraught relationship.

In addition to the larger, more formal, Office of the Tánaiste formed for Spring in the Taoiseach's building in Merrion Street, a new system of programme managers was created with each cabinet minister now entitled to one of these, as well as a special advisor, to help smooth the business of coalition government. This new system was designed to act as a clearing house for decisions and to reduce tension before matters which needed resolving landed on the formal cabinet table. The system was widely praised by those involved and by ministers. In spite of this kind of arrangement, however, the coalition was shaky, and one fascinating insight into why things did not work out well comes from then cabinet minister Charlie McCreevy. Whilst he felt that the programme managers system, introduced by Labour, added greatly to the government's capability to process business and take decisions, he also made the following remark:

> As I observed it, the downside of the programme manager system, while mightily efficient, was that traditional interplay of ideas and debate was reduced, because items had been pre-cleared. It mitigated against building a relationship with ministers from the other party through robust debate. This often puts a strong camaraderie between ministers. It was too clinical. When it came to the row, the friendships weren't there.[5]

It might also be noted, though, that the coalition got through a huge workload and a great deal of Labour policy and programme commitments were actually delivered.

One of the foremost controversies, on a policy level, that confronted the coalition was the idea that a tax amnesty be given to those who had defaulted on their tax payments. This promised to bring in £200 million to the exchequer by way of much-needed revenue. Ministers with ambitious plans for public spending saw it in practical terms. However, it opened up a rift in cabinet and exposed the Labour party to accusations of abandoning their high moral tone on this type of issue in contrast to their stance during their time in opposition to Fianna Fáil. The media depicted the measure as a 'Cheat's charter' and it was advanced as yet another departure from the high standards Labour had set for itself in government.

In the early months of the new coalition, there were also policy clashes between the two parties that left their own scars. A proposed sale of 30 per cent of Greencore to a US multinational food group was shot down by the Labour side of the government. A similar intervention by Labour put a stop to the part sale of a 25 per cent stake in the state telephone company to telecommunications giant Cable & Wireless. Reynolds and the Fianna Fáil side of the government were clearly in favour of the disposal of or reduction in the state's shareholdings in public companies, but Labour dug in its heels and resisted. There were also tensions around the state's role as a shareholder in Aer Lingus, which was having difficulties with its Team Aer Lingus maintenance subsidiary. Labour largely won these battles, frustrating the Fianna Fáil side of the government. Tit-for-tat victories for either side seemed to dominate the life of the coalition with many of them being played out through the public media. Trust and energies seemed to be eroded by many of these controversies.

One significant controversy in March 1994 cascaded for the coalition partners. Newspapers started writing of a possible homosexual encounter in The Phoenix Park between a junior minister from Labour and a young man. Rumours abounded in media circles as to who it was and, before long, the media broke the identity of the minister involved. Fergus Finlay takes up the story: 'Although homosexual activity between consenting adults had been decriminalised within the previous few months, if money had changed hands in any of the transactions that were being spoken about, a crime had been committed.'[6] Eventually the Labour party handlers shepherded Emmet Stagg, the minister involved, to make a full public statement. At the time, there was a raging public debate about whether he should be allowed to stay in his position. Reynolds sent out instructions to his party's TDs and press officers that Fianna Fáil was to take no position on the matter or make any comment on the controversy. In the event, the scandal blew over and Stagg survived, but Reynolds and Fianna Fáil felt that they received very little gratitude from Labour for their decision not to become involved and for the support they gave to Labour as it went through this crisis.

Another source of tension between the two parties related to Labour's efforts to pass new ethics legislation which they had insisted was part of the programme for government. Given all that had happened under the previous Haughey regime, the time was well overdue for this type of legislation. However, Fianna Fáil TDs felt, perhaps inevitably, that the whole effort was directed against them and that Labour was introducing this legislation to draw an ethical line between themselves and Fianna Fáil.

There was little doubt in many media commentators' minds that Labour was holding the whip hand in relation to the coalition with perceptions growing that it was going all Labour's way. This sense on the Fianna Fáil side of the government was only exacerbated by the fact that Finlay and the Labour special advisors appeared to be much more effective than their Fianna Fáil opposite numbers when it came to handling the media and leaking generally. As a journalist covering the coalition, I often felt it was Labour which set the tone and was much more ready to brief the media on government events. This closeness between the media and Labour undoubtedly annoyed Fianna Fáil ministers.

However, the real tension was between Reynolds and Spring. The veteran political correspondent Stephen Collins sums up the situation well: 'Unfortunately for Reynolds, his relationship with Dick Spring was never remotely as good. The two men were like chalk and cheese and seemed always prepared to think the worst of each other. In contrast to Reynolds' bright and breezy style, Spring was thoughtful and reserved and quick to take offence.'[7] Spring was handling a lot both as Tánaiste and Minister for Foreign Affairs, as well as fulfilling his duties as the leader of a Labour Party that had dramatically swelled its parliamentary ranks. As Minister for Foreign Affairs, he was endlessly jetting off to meetings and this does not appear to have helped communication between him and Reynolds. In addition to this, it could also be argued that Reynolds spent too much time on visits and investment promotion trips abroad – certainly more than any previous Taoiseach. Many of the seminal controversies of the coalition were ongoing when the Taoiseach and Tánaiste were in different corners of the world fulfilling their busy diaries.

In June 1994, there was a defining controversy, in terms of the Fianna Fáil–Labour relationship, around a wealthy Arab called Masri who had invested £1 million in the Taoiseach's C&D Petfood company in return for a number of Irish passports. Reynolds insisted the transaction, under the state-sponsored scheme, had occurred at arm's length and without his knowledge. This assertion was backed up by the key officials at the Department of Justice who had handled the Masri application. Spring, as noted earlier, took on the task of investigating the matter directly before even discussing the issue with

Reynolds, a fact that Reynolds felt uncomfortable about. Tim Dalton, the Secretary of the Department of Justice, appears to have enjoyed the trust of Spring and, as it turned out, his assurances were enough to convince Spring that nothing untoward had happened. The compromise agreed with Labour was that there would be legislation to overhaul the well-nigh anonymous scheme and put it on a more transparent footing. However, Reynolds compounded Labour's embarrassment on the matter by stating, in a technical reply in the Dáil, that there was no formal commitment to bring forward this legislation. Although he was strictly observing the usual protocols on these matters, the effect was not pleasing from a Labour perspective.

As the tensions played out between the two parties, the summer of 1994 saw two by-elections and a European election. Labour did badly in the Europeans, but Fianna Fáil won a majority of European seats for the first time. However, Reynolds and Fianna Fáil lost both by-elections. Fine Gael and the Democratic Left won the seats, meaning, at a technical level at least, that there could now be an alternative to the Fianna Fáil–Labour coalition should Labour choose to leave their coalition arrangement with Fianna Fáil. Few, if anybody, seemed to realise the full importance of this at the time, but this change in numbers in Leinster was to prove catastrophic for Fianna Fáil, and Reynolds most of all, when his rows with Labour eventually reached boiling point.

Then, in late July 1994, the long-awaited report of the Beef Tribunal was given to the Taoiseach. Amid much secrecy, Reynolds gathered his key officials, advisors and state lawyers together in his office to examine its contents. He had been greatly goaded earlier in the summer by a prominent leak from Finlay that suggested that if the Tribunal made any adverse findings about Reynolds, then the Labour party would not be shy about pulling the plug on the government. Finlay was not just blamed for the leak but took full responsibility, arguing, when the article finally appeared, that a casual comment to a journalist had been inflated in importance. Reynolds saw the article as a direct threat to the government and himself. Finlay tried, in vain, to meet the Taoiseach to put the matter into context, but he was not invited to give an explanation. The whole episode was like a red rag to a bull for Reynolds.

The group gathered to read the Beef Tribunal Report included the Secretary to the Cabinet, speech writer Donal Cronin, communications advisor Tom Savage, various lawyers and, inevitably, Seán Duignan, the government press secretary. Having scanned the 900-page report, all of the officials present concluded that it did not do Reynolds any great harm. One of the political advisors confirmed to Reynolds, 'You're in the clear.'

It was Reynolds' reply, however, that worried a number of people present including the Secretary General of the Department of the Taoiseach, Paddy Teahon, and Duignan. 'I've taken this shit long enough. I'm not taking another minute of it,' Reynolds told them. 'They told the dogs in the street they would bring me down on this if they didn't like the judgement. Now I've been cleared and I don't need their permission to tell it as it is.'[8]

Reynolds instructed Duignan to get the story out to the media before anyone else had read the report, despite appeals for caution from both Duignan and Teahon, who felt that such an action would simply provoke Labour. The decision directly contradicted a previous agreement Reynolds had with Spring about how the government would respond to the report.

On the night that Reynolds had gathered his officials in his office, Labour had got wind that the report was out. Spring rang Mrs Reynolds to establish contact with the Taoiseach, only to be told by her that he was still in the office. When multiple efforts to contact Reynolds failed, Finlay was sent to the Taoiseach's office to see if he could find the Taoiseach and secure a copy of the report. However, Reynolds could not be found and Finlay suspected that he had been deliberately locked out of the Taoiseach's office while they planned Reynolds' response. Spring's reaction, as quoted by Finlay, was both telling and ominous from Reynolds' point of view: 'That's it. Collective responsibility, my eye! How can I stay in a Government where I'm told that I cannot speak to my Taoiseach about an absolutely crucial matter like this?'[9]

The paranoia felt by Reynolds about his treatment at the Beef Tribunal had now fed into his response and led him, in effect, to deliberately snub his coalition partner in a way that was bound to sour Spring utterly about remaining in government with him. The media smelled a rat and soon got wind of the fact that the relationship between the two was now in tatters.

Political correspondents were quickly informed that Duignan was speaking only for the Taoiseach and not the government as a whole. The entire episode set in motion a ticking time bomb inside Reynolds' government.

It is hard to imagine why Reynolds behaved in this way. His choices were barely defensible as good conduct when it comes to coalition colleagues. At best, it was sharp practice on his part; at worst, a spell-binding misjudgement with enormous consequences. The peace process had been progressing very well for Reynolds by this point and the last thing he needed was instability with his coalition colleagues. I, and other journalists at the time, knew the implications of what had happened and concluded it was only a matter of time before Labour would get their own back for this indignity inflicted by Reynolds.

CHAPTER NINETEEN

War

Many commentators expressed particular surprise when Albert Reynolds, on becoming Taoiseach in 1992, had declared the situation in Northern Ireland to be one of his top priorities. His rise to the top of Irish politics had occurred without him publicly enunciating his own beliefs on the issue. There are, of course, many reasons why this was the case. In the first instance, he was largely defined by his previous career as both entrepreneur and businessman. The ministries he had held were, for the most part, economic and investment-focused. His contacts were largely at the level of investment and business. His best friends, outside politics, were people he had encountered through business. Yet, around the time he took up the position of Taoiseach, Mick Quinn, a businessman based in Nigeria and lifelong friend of Reynolds, told Frank Dunlop something that has been little noted: 'Mick told me that solving the Northern Ireland problem was Albert's only remaining political ambition, though Albert himself never mentioned this.'[1] Quite separately Noel Dempsey, one of his key ministers, states, 'Albert Reynolds believed that unless you solved the problems of the North, you could not solve your economic problems in the South.'[2]

Another man, Benny Reid, a party supporter who played cards regularly with Reynolds, vividly remembers finishing a victory tour of the constituency when he was made Taoiseach. Reynolds made a speech in the village of Aughnacliffe in North Longford, pointing north to the border and stating that he would do his best to solve the situation in Northern Ireland. As Reid remembers it, Reynolds pledged, 'Be it long or short he would put an end to the slaughter up the road.' It was an off-the-cuff speech by Reynolds, but significant nonetheless. North Longford is close to the border, and reading

Reynolds' autobiography of his younger years in Roscommon, one is also reminded of the proximity of the border to the young man growing up. According to Reid, in Counties Longford, Roscommon and Leitrim there was a core republicanism, but also quite a few people, mainly Catholics, who had settled there because of the conflict in the North.

When Reynolds was starting C&D as a business, the cans for the petfood were purchased initially in the North of Ireland and he would have come to know a good number of unionists from his business dealings. Additionally, one significant contact he made in his dancehall days was Sammy Barr, the owner of a large club in the North. Barr was close to the Reverend Ian Paisley. Reynolds contacted his old friend within days of becoming Taoiseach with a request to speak with Ian Paisley. He was told by Barr that Paisley would only engage when he was the top person in the unionist political set up. As it turned out, that is exactly what Ian Paisley did, but it came about after Reynolds' departure as Taoiseach and under the leadership of Bertie Ahern.

Reynolds' happiest time, prior to his involvement in politics, was when he was running the dancehalls. It was in this period that he made his first real money and forged friendships that lasted a lifetime. The friendships made then are dotted across all aspects of his life subsequently. Many of the characters from his dancehall days pop up, again and again, as he climbed the ladder in politics – people like Mick Quinn, Eamon Monahan, Fr Brian Darcy and Oliver Barry to name just a few. The show-business sector also gave him unrivalled exposure to journalists at a young age. One particular incident linked to the music scene and the Troubles in the North may well go some way to explaining his determination to rid the region of violence rather than invoking political rhetoric.

In July 1975, five members of The Miami Showband, a popular cabaret band from the South, were travelling back to Dublin, having performed a concert in Banbridge in County Down. They were stopped at a bogus military checkpoint and asked to get out of the van. Two of the gunmen died when a time bomb exploded prematurely. The band members themselves were lined up on the roadside and three of them shot dead, while the others were left wounded on the road. It was a shocking massacre and acted as a vivid reminder of the sectarian conflict and its innocent victims. It rapidly brought the showband era to an end for bands from both political traditions; there was to be no more travelling back and forth across the border to entertain young people. It was like a macabre closing curtain on the industry itself. Two serving members of the Ulster Defence Regiment and a former UDR man were subsequently convicted of the murders – a reminder of the lethal crossover, or collusion, between soldiers and loyalist paramilitary groups.

One further incident was of particular significance when Reynolds began brokering peace. On 8 November 1987, the IRA planted a bomb which exploded during the Enniskillen Remembrance Day ceremony. It was an appalling atrocity and Gordon Wilson, a drapier, lost his daughter Marie in the blast, having shared a few last words with her as she lay dying in the rubble created by the bomb. In a televised interview, Wilson described his daughter's last moments: 'Daddy, I love you very much, those were her exact words to me and those were the last words I ever heard her say.' The emotional impact of the interview with Wilson spread around the world. Viewers and listeners heard Wilson say: 'But I bear no ill will. I bear no grudge. Dirty sort of talk is not going to bring her back to life. She was a great wee lassie. She loved her profession. She was a pet. She's dead. She's in heaven and we shall meet again.' Wilson said he would pray that night and every night for his daughter's killers.[3]

The public reaction to his words was immediate. Wilson went on to become a vigorous campaigner for peace. In 1993, Reynolds chose to make him his own personal appointment to the Irish Senate. It was an inspired recognition by Reynolds of the need to have the voice of the victims of the violence in Northern Ireland heard. 'I just want you to be a voice for reconciliation and forgiveness in the Senate, and on any occasion which might advance that process,' was the advice from Reynolds when he met with Wilson to discuss the appointment. In his first Senate speech, Gordon Wilson made reference to his attempts to make contact with the IRA: 'The IRA is composed of human beings like ourselves and they have suffered too, just as we have at their expense.'[4]

As a journalist covering Leinster House, I would often meet Wilson. Though he made very impactful speeches, he felt a little out of place in Dublin. Occasionally, I would meet him for a drink when business had finished in the Senate. Wilson was a plain-speaking Protestant with no particular politics. He thought a lot of Reynolds for appointing him and was very struck by the fact that the Taoiseach made no demands of him. When he spoke of Reynolds, he praised him as a family man. Wilson spoke to me about the possibility of meeting directly with the IRA. In his conversations with me, he wondered whether it would have any influence over them. I was unable to say. In any event, he went about making contact with them and requested a meeting. He was successful, but afterwards he described the exercise as 'pointless'. In private, he admitted to me that he had probably being expecting too much. He was quite disillusioned by it all and asked me if I thought they would pay any heed to his view. So, as a journalist, I made my own discreet enquiries and discovered from my contacts within the IRA that they had been quite affected by him – seeing him as an ordinary man, rather than just the latest expression of a peace movement about which they were cynical. Unknown to me and Wilson, the IRA was making moves at this time behind the scenes to see if there was some way of getting out of the conflict. Wilson may not have been fully aware of the role he played, but he did go on to serve on the peace forum set up by Reynolds in the wake of the Downing Street Declaration. His contributions were modest but very impactful. It cannot have been easy for him to share a forum like this with members of Sinn Féin, many of whom were also members of the IRA.

Despite Gordon Wilson's pessimism, after his meeting with the IRA, there were further rumblings in the undergrowth of the republican movement. Behind the scenes, meetings were still taking place. However, the sensitivity of such contact was so delicate that virtually nobody at a public level was aware of what was going on. Brendan O'Brien, the author of several books on the IRA, makes the telling point that, around this time, 'while the IRA leadership was preparing to enter political dialogue they were also gearing up for a bombing offensive in Britain and Northern Ireland. This time the essential difference with the past was that the IRA was thrusting to get into talks rather than trying to destroy them.'[5] By 1992, Adams and Sinn Féin had launched a document entitled 'Towards A Lasting Peace' at their Dublin conference in March of that year, which I attended. Intense speculation about a possible IRA ceasefire accompanied the launch of this document, but the rumours were quickly discounted by Martin McGuinness.

The IRA had ramped up its efforts to arm in the years previous to the launch of the Sinn Féin document, which was a source of serious concern on all sides. From 1985 through to 1987, there had been five huge shipments of weaponry and explosives from Libya thanks to the generosity of one Colonel Gaddafi, the then leader of the North African country. Four successful imports were landed in Ireland and secreted safely in secure storage. Among this deadly cargo were tons of semi-automatic assault rifles, Kalashnikovs, RPG rocket launchers, pistols, revolvers but, more importantly from an IRA perspective, a shipment of the deadly explosive Semtex. There were also Russian machine guns with armour-piercing bullets. The fifth and final import, aboard a ship called the *Eksund*, was intercepted in 1987; it contained more weaponry and material than the other four shipments put together.

From my own conversations with the Special Branch, during and after this event, it was clear that the shipments posed a distinct threat to the security of the southern state. Had the fifth and final shipment been landed, it would have meant that the IRA was better equipped and resourced than the official army of the state. It would have tipped the balance in favour of the IRA, which had already developed a sophisticated engineering department, supply line and an extensive financial operation that funded their efforts. Both Reynolds and my late father strongly believed that it was necessary to pursue a peace initiative, if only to prevent the inevitable repercussions for the stability of the Republic if the balance did tip in favour of what now appeared to be almost a 'state within the state'. Some propagandists during the peace process tried to suggest that the IRA had come to the negotiating table only because they were facing defeat. Neither the conventional security assessment of Special Branch nor indeed that of Reynolds supports this view. Reynolds, through his own contacts with Libya, and through conversations with Colonel Gaddafi, had a fairly accurate grasp of the level and sophistication of weaponry that the IRA had at its disposal.

The escalation of the IRA's bombing campaign in Britain in the period that followed these importations featured a direct rocket attack on Downing

Street that very nearly wiped out John Major and his entire cabinet. A month after the launch of the Sinn Féin 'peace document', the IRA struck at London, killing three and smashing the Baltic Exchange. As Brendan O'Brien points out, 'the compensation damage for this one bomb, estimated at more than £600 million, was more than the entire compensation pay-out in Northern Ireland to that point'.[6] Bombing incidents were a sharp source of division between people analysing the effect they had on the British government. Seán Duignan, Reynolds' press secretary, makes the following point in regards to the Baltic Exchange bombing:

> The incident produced the only division of opinion on the process that I observed between the Taoiseach and his chief adviser. Mansergh did not believe, then or subsequently, that the British Government was materially swayed by the London bombing. Reynolds however, suspected the British were deeply shaken – the IRA had hit the same district a year previously – and that the vulnerability of London to such attacks was a factor in terms of subsequent developments.[7]

What is clear is that this type of IRA attack against British economic and financial targets was very costly for the British Exchequer and also something of a reputational embarrassment.

In the same period, the Garda Síochána discovered a huge IRA bomb factory in Clonaslee in County Laois, the biggest they had ever found. Apart from the explosive capability, they also discovered forty or so electrical boxes that had been designed to be installed in London. These boxes would be packed with explosives and the clear intention of their manufacture was to take out the fibre optic telecommunications system in London. If this operation had been successful, it would have brought Britain's huge financial district to a standstill for several weeks and crippled its financial trading system.

Sean 'Spike' Murray, a leading Belfast republican who is believed to have served on the IRA's Army Council, makes the following point about this type of attack: 'If you know you are entering negotiations you have to use your muscle. Hitting Britain's financial sector was sending a message. You are not dealing with a defeated army.'[8] Apart from sending a message, operations like this boosted morale amongst the IRA back in Ireland and, at a certain level, they were a good deal less risky to their people than operations in the North. In effect, the IRA moved towards negotiations precisely because neither side, the British nor themselves, could ultimately win the war. Things had reached a standstill and there was a certain war weariness on both sides. By targeting London, the IRA was escalating the conflict and seeing if the British would bite at their feelers for peace. Albert Reynolds, more than anybody else, was aware of what was going on.

CHAPTER TWENTY

Hume–Adams

The real genesis of the Sinn Féin peace initiative lay with Fr Alec Reid and his willingness to become a go-between for Gerry Adams and the SDLP leader, John Hume. Fr Reid was adamant about the whole notion of bringing violence to an end. His role as mediator started in September 1988. 'There was a real change of tone. It was the first time the republican movement were dipping their toes in the real world of politics,' according to Irish diplomat Sean O'Huiginn, who headed up the Anglo-Irish division of the Department of Foreign Affairs between 1991 and 1996. Of Reid, he said:

> His main function was to act as a conduit from Gerry Adams. He also did some drafting on documents. He had the mindset of the republican movement. He was a sort of guarantor. He didn't tell lies or exaggerate things. Gerry Adams was toxic at the time. The way of communicating with Adams was via Alec. Everyone understood he wasn't pushing them on his own behalf. He was a real saint. Gerry Adams trusted him.[1]

Up until the IRA ceasefire of August 1994, there was no direct contact between the civil service and the republican movement. O'Huiginn and others were aware that there were lines of communication with the IRA, including that used by Reynolds himself at a personal level, but the general sense of it was that they, the permanent civil service, did not need to know of these communications and that they trusted Reynolds knew what he was doing. Reynolds had told Seán Duignan:

I'm breaking a few rules. First, instead of continuing to marginalise these people (IRA/Sinn Féin), I'm going to try pull them in. To do that, they must be shown the benefits of ending the 'Armed Struggle' and going the constitutional road. And that means they'll have to be talked to, by whatever means, but they'll have to be talked to.[2]

How much Reynolds was prepared to break rules is attested to by Noel Gallagher of Derry, who says that meetings between Martin McGuinness and Reynolds were held in his home well before any IRA ceasefire was forthcoming.[3] The fact of these meetings and their failure to come to light to date is testament to the extreme secrecy and personal risk that Reynolds was prepared to take to pursue his simple objective of bringing about peace. There is no doubt that if news of these meetings with the republican movement had become known, it might well have ended Reynolds' tenure as Taoiseach. According to former Irish diplomat Eamon Delaney:

The Peace Process starts with Albert. Or rather with Albert running with the ideas coming out of the Hume–Adams discussions. Albert's can-do, 'Let's sort this out' attitude to the economy and the liberal agenda was now applied to the North. Albert came relatively baggage-free. The fact that he wasn't even a rhetorical nationalist, like most Fianna Fáilers, was a big help. Nor was John Major a British nationalist.[4]

In the period between April and September 1993, news emerged publicly of what a handful of insiders already knew – that John Hume had been conducting a series of very engaged, behind-the-scenes discussions with Gerry Adams. Despite the obvious public backlash against this, the two men reiterated they would continue their discussions.

On the British side, John Major was privately sceptical of this initiative even though he was given insight into their contents, via his own officials, whom Hume had briefed on the content of the discussions. Fergus Finlay notes, 'The British government was forever seeking to get the all-party talks that had been abandoned in 1992 re-started. For our part we were now firmly embarked on a process aimed at getting everyone into those talks.'[5]

Reynolds, since the collapse of the previous all-party talks, had become fully intent on reversing what was, up to then, the way things usually worked in the world of Anglo-Irish relations. He, along with Hume, had effectively jettisoned the notion of trying to get time-consuming and difficult-to-agree all-party talks going, followed by applying pressure on the various paramilitaries to participate in new governmental-type structures. Reynolds' significant input was to focus, almost exclusively, on establishing peace first and then kick-starting talks. It proved to be very effective but was a highly risky choice in the circumstances in which he was operating. Throughout the prolonged negotiation between Dublin and London over a draft document for peace, there was intense suspicion on the Irish side that Major had a secret deal with the Unionists for their support at Westminster, which prevented progress being made and explained a lot of the stalling tactics being employed by the British in the negotiations.

Kevin Rafter tells us, 'In May 1993 Reid met with Mansergh in Government Buildings. He had reached the conclusion that Sinn Féin was agreed in principle to the latest draft document. "I think this thing is okay," he told the Fianna Fáil advisor who immediately brought him into see Reynolds in the Taoiseach's office.'[6] The priority now would be to work out how to bring the British on board for this document and to construct some kind of declaration on their part. Reynolds had the idea of having a secret meeting with Major in London to give him the document, at which he would attempt to bounce him into accepting it. But the idea of meeting in secret seemed to unsettle both Labour's Dick Spring and John Major himself, who told Albert it couldn't be done. Major was concerned about a meeting in secret spawning suspicion and conspiracy theories of all kinds. Reynolds, however, knew a permanent ceasefire was within his grasp and was desperate to underline the serious opportunity this represented. So, instead of a secret meeting, Chief Secretary to the British Cabinet Sir Robin Butler was dispatched, via military aircraft to Baldonnel, to meet directly with the Taoiseach, and the draft document was handed over. Reynolds briefed him on its contents.

There then followed a series of discussions during 1993 between British and Irish officials, mainly around drafting and re-writing documents. On the Irish side there was O'Huiginn and the Secretary to the Cabinet, Dermot Nally, while on the British side there was Sir Robin Butler, Sir John Chilcott of the Northern Ireland Office (NIO) and Sir Quentin Thomas, also of the NIO. A lot of the drafting around the language was done by Thomas and Mansergh, as advisor to Reynolds. O'Huiginn, after his retirement, applied for permission to look at the archives of the period and was surprised at the level and detail of Reynolds' personal involvement. 'Albert never got worried about people who were obstructing things. He would work around things. There was very little turf, or territorial, wars around the Irish side. Reynolds focused on getting us to concentrate on the goal.'[7]

There had been four months of effort by officials and others devoted to enhancing the work delivered to Reynolds by Adams and Hume. In the midst of these and later discussions, the British side became suspicious and irritated by the tough-minded approach of O'Huiginn in the negotiations, whom they viewed as a 'deep green' nationalist. Some British media sources habitually dubbed him the 'Prince of Darkness'. The British could barely conceal their irritation at his approach in the negotiations and, according to O'Huiginn, made efforts to disrupt or prevent his input in the usual manner, via judicious media leaks. He subsequently went on to be an ambassador to Washington and to Germany.

At one point, Roderic Lyne, Major's private secretary, was dispatched to Dublin to make known the British concerns about O'Huiginn. It was a strange mission but indicated that the British wanted him out of the way. Reynolds agreed to meet Lyne in his office. However, before sitting down to take the meeting, he rang O'Huiginn to tell him that Lyne was coming over with the single purpose of getting him off the negotiations. Reynolds asked O'Huiginn to come over and attend the meeting, to act as note-taker for what was being said. In O'Huiginn's mind, this underlined the seriousness of what was being contemplated, as the Taoiseach could have called on plenty of other people to take notes rather than bringing him over from the Department of Foreign Affairs. In the event, Lyne got the message and cannot have been in any doubt that O'Huiginn had the full support of the Taoiseach. The issue of O'Huiginn's removal at the request of the British was hardly going to be raised with O'Huiginn present, silently taking the notes for the meeting. O'Huiginn saw the attempt to remove him as a kind of standard operating procedure of British diplomacy, but he deeply appreciated the support that Reynolds had offered him.[8]

The Hume–Adams dialogue, previously conducted in secret, broke cover with a joint statement from both men in April 1993. There followed a wave of criticism, doubt and outright condemnation from a variety of quarters. To many of Hume's admirers, he was now in 'league with the Devil' in the shape of Gerry Adams. Even members of his own party privately complained of not being in the loop on these talks. Public criticism of Hume reached its crescendo in the pages of the Dublin-based *Sunday Independent*, one of the country's biggest-selling newspapers, where columnist Eoghan Harris stated, 'If we persist with the peace process it will end with sectarian slaughter in the North, with bombs in Dublin, Cork and Galway, and with the ruthless reign by provisional gangs over the ghettos of Dublin. The only way to end this abyss is to cut the cord to John Hume.'[9] Other big-gun columnists and writers, such as Eamon Dunphy and former minister Conor Cruise O'Brien, also took aim at John Hume.

The confused and un-coordinated response to the Hume–Adams conversations was made worse by a series of public statements from the two men, culminating in a statement from Hume that he had given a document to Dublin and London about the state of his dialogue. He made this statement and then disappeared for a week or so to the United States on an investment visit.

Despite the public criticism, in the run-up to the Fianna Fáil Ard Fheis that winter there was a growing groundswell of support for Hume and his endeavours, and also a clear annoyance that Reynolds and his government might be seeking to distance themselves from him. My father started hitting the phones and calling friends and colleagues in the party to shore up Hume's position. Despite the high-profile media campaign being run against Hume, the ordinary grassroots members of the party were anxious that Reynolds should endorse his efforts with Adams. The script of his keynote speech which was circulated to journalists attending the party's Ard Fheis was mild and contained little or no reference to the Hume–Adams initiative. However, the speech delivered live contained the vital line: 'History will not forgive us if we waste this opportunity.' Thunderous applause met Reynolds as he uttered this line and the perception grew that he was not just running with the Hume–Adams dialogue but fully endorsing it. The speech, sometimes described as the 'Peace First' speech, put Reynolds onside with his party and, more importantly, with Hume–Adams. Reynolds was now in the fast lane in a process that would evolve swiftly between the spring and the end of 1993.

Violence in the North continued at pace, even as these groundbreaking discussions were going on behind the scenes. On 23 October 1993, the IRA detonated a huge bomb in premises on the Shankill road that had previously been used by the Ulster Defence Association, a loyalist paramilitary group. The bomb exploded prematurely and ten people were killed, amongst them innocent men, women and children. One week later, a revenge attack at a Catholic bar in Greysteel left seven dead and raised significant public apprehension that efforts to pursue the Hume–Adams efforts were only leading to an escalation of sectarian tensions and violence. There were also whispered concerns about John Hume's health and well-being since he had broken down in tears at one of the funerals of the Greysteel victims. Much later, Hume revealed that the reason for his tears was because a daughter of one of the victim's told him 'that her family prayed for me around the coffin of her loved one the night before and they prayed that I would be successful in my work to get the violence ended so that no other family would suffer what they had suffered'.[10]

No matter what personal solace Hume took from these words, condemnation from both sides of the Irish sea, in the Westminster parliament and in Dáil Éireann, was heading his way for his efforts. The sense of revulsion in the aftermath of these attacks was only added to by photographic evidence of Gerry Adams carrying the coffin of the IRA bomber who had been killed in the premature explosion on the Shankill road. The photograph showed Adams in a provocative light – a peacemaker who was openly prepared to be associated with an IRA man who had committed a horrible atrocity. Strangely, both John Major and others, privately, took encouragement from the fact that Adams took the inevitable public flak associated with such an act.

At a European summit meeting in Brussels, the two leaders, Reynolds and Major, made it plain that the two governments that they led were now taking the issue of peace under their joint control. Reynolds, for his part, shared what really happened at the Brussels summit with Duignan, some weeks later: 'Hume–Adams was being declared dead, in order to keep it alive, in the same way as Adams carried the bomber's coffin because otherwise he couldn't deliver the IRA. He says Major agreed with this reasoning. Albert added, "So it had to be done – but I hated that Brussels joint statement."'[11]

Reynolds had not been idle in the wake of his successful party Ard Fheis. He had taken his 'Peace First' message to the airwaves and made several, single-purpose visits to London to record interviews with the British media on John Major's own turf. The idea was to ramp up the pressure on the British to run with the ball and do something. He was also signalling that the end of the year was a kind of deadline for this process to work. This kind of agenda setting and fixing of deadlines was not the kind of thing the British expected from Irish governments.

Hume, clearly annoyed that he had been sidelined, threw down a challenge to Major in the House of Commons, effectively stating that if his initiative had been accepted, there would have been peace within a week. Reynolds, too, was feeling a bit peeved, in his case at the extent to which his opposite number kept repeating the fact that he (Reynolds) supported the rejection of the Hume–Adams initiative. Clearly Reynolds calculated that his own party would start to turn on him if he threw Hume out on a limb. In my own conversations with Reynolds around this time, there was a sense that the British were consuming each concession he or others made with no real interest in reciprocating the gestures. Reynolds was also becoming more and more paranoid about what might be described as the baleful influence of various behind-the-scenes interests on Major's judgement. According to him, there were prominent right-wing figures in the Tory party, influential funders and operatives from the hard-core of the intelligence services, trying to stymie efforts in this period.

There was a fair bit of brinksmanship in the air. Reynolds told Major bluntly that if the British were going to play games and string things out then he would push ahead in his own right. This particular declaration on his part was masked as an impromptu interview he gave while attending a Whitney Houston concert with his daughter in Dublin. The two journalists concerned were convinced it was on the record, although it was later maintained by Reynolds that he believed it to be off the record. One way or the other, he was putting it out there and more importantly putting it up to John Major to deliver.

Reynolds had an ingenious way of turning up the temperature whenever he felt it necessary. This high-pressure technique was probably a trait he had inherited from his showbiz days – hyping up a shortage of available tickets was and remains the oldest stock-in-trade of a concert promoter. There was this distinct feeling that the Reynolds–Major relationship was being frayed to the limits of its natural elasticity. In the simplest terms, Reynolds, with his entrepreneurial flair, wanted to move fast on peace, whereas Major, with his innate managerial caution, wished to slow things down. There was also a suspicion on the Irish side that the British wished to be in control and run the process, rather than allowing the Irish to be in the driving seat.

CHAPTER TWENTY-ONE

Downing Street Declaration

The Shankill Road bombing had sent a shockwave of revulsion through the political systems on both sides of the Irish Sea. In his memoirs, John Major saw it as something of a turning point. However, at the time, according to Reynolds, he said, 'How do you expect me to continue with any process when I take up the papers and in every paper on the front page is Gerry Adams carrying a coffin?' Adams had responded to the incident by stating that while the bombing could not be excused, he could secure an end to IRA violence if the British responded to the Hume–Adams initiative. Major described Adams' statement as 'tantamount to blackmail'.

In a bid to retrieve the situation, Tánaiste and Labour leader Dick Spring made a Dáil speech on 27 October 1993 which set out six basic, well-understood principles that would underpin the government's approach to the process now unfolding. The speech, according to Reynolds, was well received by unionists and the British, but, inevitably, it was a source of annoyance to republicans. It set the scene for a certain distancing of the two governments from the Hume–Adams initiative and enabled the meeting in Brussels between Reynolds and Major to take the entire process under Dublin and London leadership.

With the Hume–Adams dimension now, symbolically at least, cast to one side, Reynolds was keener than ever to re-ignite enthusiasm for peace, saying, 'I was being heavily criticised by [Secretary of State] Patrick Mayhew for pushing the idea of peace before Christmas. He also insisted that talks and the peace process must run in parallel, but the move to seize the opportunity for peace was growing and I firmly believed it should be grasped by both governments.' Despite the despair over the Shankill Road bombing, Reynolds was undeterred and used the temporary crisis that it caused to double down on his pressure on the British government. Major, though wishing to slow things down, did acknowledge, in a keynote speech at the Lord Mayor of London's annual banquet, that this presented a better opportunity for peace in Northern Ireland than they'd seen for many years. This admission by him was an indication of his sincere intention to be loyal to Reynolds, despite the obvious apprehension everywhere and his ongoing dependence on Unionist MPs at Westminster.

I had, by this stage, been co-opted by Reynolds as a conduit in his efforts to mobilise and co-ordinate many of the intermediary networks that he had both spawned himself and responded to behind the scenes. Reynolds, to my mind, was hugely impressive in this task of steering a bewildering array of revolving and conflicting interests towards a single objective. I had come into this role while still carrying out duties as a political reporter at Leinster House. It started with me carrying messages from different players and grew out of my father's efforts. My own involvement became more pronounced due to my father's intermittent illnesses and hospitalisation as a result of complications related to a liver transplant. As a backbencher, for the first time in his career, he was free to meet with people in private with whom frontline ministers or the Taoiseach could not meet. In this role, he and my mother provided hospitality for the likes of the Reverend Roy Magee, a vital link to the loyalist paramilitaries, and Gusty Spence, something of an icon among loyalist paramilitaries. He was helped in some of this by a man called Tommy McCann, originally from Belfast, who lived locally in my father's constituency.

Up to this point, my father had often been somewhat dismissive of Reynolds' talents but, during this period, he was in constant contact with him, sometimes up to two to three times a day and often in Reynolds' home in Hazeldene, Ballsbridge. It is a testament to Reynolds' resilience and capability that my father became a huge fan of his. He often remarked that Reynolds was far more decisive than Haughey and more prepared to act quickly on things. At an intellectual level, he was impressed by Reynolds' capacity to absorb the microscopic details and different nuances of a situation.

I, for my part, was frankly amazed at the amount of time and effort Reynolds was putting in. He was like a human sponge when it came to processing information and insight. From time to time, he would call me into his office, impassive, but encouraging me to talk. He had this posture and concentration that downloaded information from you. I knew and suspected he had many more people like me who were volunteering help and information, but he rarely, if ever, breached a confidence. The more I became involved with him, at this time, the more I began to spot the telltale signs of the others he had co-opted into his network. He was a superb confidential operator and never seemed to drop his guard.

In Leinster House one day, he called me over and then quickly conveyed me to the Taoiseach's office. Once the door closed, a string of curses, directed at me, followed. He was now sitting behind his desk telling me that he had told me not to use my home telephone when communicating. Reynolds threw me over a telephone transcript of my conversation which meant, rather shamefacedly, I was in no position to deny any indiscretion on my part. The one thing I learned from this dressing down, though, was that, with Reynolds, it was never personal. We were chatting away amiably within a few minutes and he was already pressing me to make further inquiries and dig out information for him. John Major has made the same point about him. He could be robust in argument, but it was hard to fall out with him.

Reynolds was, like never before, upping the ante and renewing his pressure on the British to move in his direction. He was flying back and forth to London to do high-profile media interviews with British TV, American networks and international outlets. As ever, he was mobile, sometimes flying in for a few hours, then jumping back on the plane to Dublin. The effect of these interviews carried out in John Major's backyard was to raise the stakes. He was, in effect, daring the British to pull down the process. He was also creating fears about the consequences of failure.

One of his most relevant moves was to create an intermediary-led outreach to loyalist paramilitaries who, because of their internal factions, could often be paranoid. They were, as Reynolds discovered, feeling left out in the cold and a good bit resentful at all of the attention Adams and the republicans were getting from both governments. It was taken for granted by some in Dublin that London would have much greater influence with them and could attend to their concerns. Reynolds, however, discovered that they were not getting the attention that was their due from the British side and moved in to fill the vacuum. The paranoia amongst loyalist paramilitaries was fed by commentators referring constantly to a pan-nationalist front of Dublin, the SDLP and Sinn Féin.

The Reverend Roy Magee became the link man to the loyalists and Archbishop Eames, the Church of Ireland Primate of Ireland, was a vital connection and conduit to both the Official Unionist Leader Jim Molyneaux, as well as to Major. Confidential messages passed back and forth by both these clergymen built a significant amount of confidence amongst the key players in the process. In effect, they were fulfilling the role on the unionist–loyalist side filled by Fr Alec Reid with Sinn Féin and the SDLP. I found meeting all of these clergymen fascinating and their dedication to the mission they had been set quite impressive, not least because they were not seeking any great recognition for their role.

Yet, despite all this frenetic activity in the background, there remained a level of distrust about British intentions and significant tripwires lying in wait for Reynolds. One was a British media interview where Reynolds was to be asked about his official (Martin Mansergh) meeting with representatives of the IRA. A British official tipped off Reynolds that he would be asked about this. Reynolds believed that elements in the British intelligence services were deliberately trying to destabilise him – a theme he would constantly return to in both conversations with me and, as it turned out, also with John Major.

With documents and draft documents being passed back and forth between British and Irish civil servants, the plan was to bring the contents of a joint declaration by both governments to fruition with a summit in Dublin Castle at the end of November or early December. Doubts about whether this summit would even be held continued right up to the moment it began, in early December, and continued while it was being held. In the run-up to it, all the players were working on a shared document for discussion. However, just days before it began, Fergus Finlay, who had been privy to the shared document, noted:

There was astonishment at every level of the Irish government when on 25 November, the British handed in a new text that no-one had ever seen before. This was after months of slow and painful work towards an agreed text. What was worse, the British were coming to Dublin Castle, for a summit meeting on December 3rd, clearly believing that in this new text (which would have produced an unrecognisable Declaration) they had played a trump card.[1]

This new document caused significant surprise and anger on the Irish side. The normally mild-mannered Secretary to the Irish Government, Dermot Nally, went into a rage, saying to Reynolds, 'Who do these people think you are – the Prime Minister of Togo? They can't be allowed to ignore months of detailed negotiation, and tell us that we have to start all over again just because they click their fingers.' Reynolds calmed Nally down, but it was agreed that the British proposal had to be taken off the table. At the summit in Dublin Castle there was a storming row with Reynolds complaining, 'You're making a fool out of me, John', to Major. Reynolds quickly followed up by accusing Major of 'bad faith' which resulted in the British Prime Minister snapping in two the pencil he had been holding in his hands.[2] Finlay, despite the tensions with Reynolds in coalition, was filled with admiration for his approach.

A private meeting between Reynolds and Major ensued. Finlay asked Reynolds what had happened at the private meeting and received the following reply: 'It wasn't too bad. He chewed the bollix off me, but I took a few lumps out of him.'[3] Major returned to the meeting indicating work was to be intensified on the existing document, with the late and unexpected British document set to one side. From an atmosphere of utter distrust, a result had been won and it was, according to Finlay, down to Reynolds' preparedness to gamble all and not back down. Much of the private disagreement between Reynolds and Major had been behind the scenes, and was kept that way, though it was noticeable to the waiting journalists that something was not quite what it seemed given that Major left the summit without staying for dinner. Notwithstanding this, civil servants and diplomats on both sides were given strict orders to finish up and complete the necessary text for a declaration to be issued at a follow-up meeting or summit in Downing Street, London.

There is a plausible explanation as to why Reynolds was able to stand his ground so strongly at the Dublin summit and force Major to back down on his proposal to introduce a new text. Prior to the summit, the British government had been subject to enormous embarrassment in parliament as full details of their behind-the-scenes contacts with the IRA became public. The important thing to understand here is that these British contacts had been initiated surreptitiously and without reference to Dublin, whereas Dublin and Reynolds had shared updates of their own contacts with the IRA with the UK. In addition, in the wake of the Shankill bombing, Major openly had told parliament that it would turn his stomach to sit down and talk to the Provisional IRA. Yet evidence emerged, via a British Sunday newspaper, that he had specifically authorised such contact with the IRA. The British claimed that they had made contact to double-check on what John Hume was telling them about IRA intentions.

Meanwhile, prior to the Dublin summit and unbeknownst to Major, Reynolds had been fully briefed and had all the details on the scale of the British contacts with the IRA. Reynolds' old friend from Derry, Noel Gallagher, a member of the IRA who had been appointed by the organisation as a long-term link person to the British government, was responsible for this. 'I produced documents signed by Major and gave them to Reynolds,' says Gallagher.[4] All this caused further ill will at the Dublin summit, but the advance knowledge put Reynolds in a position of significant leverage over his British counterpart when he sat down for a private discussion with Major, without officials present, in Dublin Castle.

In addition to the information on British contacts with the IRA, Gallagher gave Reynolds a copy of the letter which Major had received on that grey February day many months before. It was from the IRA to the British Prime Minister, but there is some dispute about whether it reached Major in its original format or whether there had been some edits along the way. In his autobiography, Reynolds says that Gallagher was in the Hotel Excelsior, near Heathrow, when Fred, the British government's representative, compiled and sent the letter to John Major. The document was the source of huge controversy, when it became public, as it suggested that the IRA was, effectively, a beaten army now beseeching the British government's help to bring the conflict to an end. Martin McGuinness, along with the IRA, vigorously disputed the British spin on this letter's contents, which included the controversial phrase 'the conflict is over'.

The British description of the ongoing contact with the IRA as 'sporadic' over the years is vigorously contested by Gallagher. He says that from 1972 on, they met with the IRA pretty much every eighteen months and sometimes more frequently than that. In that time, Gallagher himself received a present of a painting from Mrs Thatcher, letters from Peter Brooke, and had meetings with Major, Tony Blair and many others. 'It was far from sporadic. It was a structured contact with key officials located for the purpose.' A new specific person to conduct the contact would be appointed for the purpose, with the connection renewed on a regular basis. Key officials appointed for this task included 'Mountain Climber' Michael Oatley (MI6), senior civil servant John Chilcott, and Robert McLennan, codenamed Fred.[5]

With the rows now over, the stage was set for a dramatic and exuberant meeting at No. 10 Downing Street, office and home to the British Prime Minister, in mid-December. Reynolds travelled to the UK with the Tánaiste, Dick Spring, and his Minister for Justice, Máire Geoghegan-Quinn. John Major had done his homework with the Official Unionist Jim Molyneaux, who committed not to reject the Joint Declaration on Peace (commonly known as the Downing Street Declaration). This rather minimalist, or grudging, acceptance of the *fait accompli* of the Declaration eased the way for Major and made for broad acceptance of its contents:

> The text which was finally agreed by the two governments was a masterpiece of diplomatic ambiguity. It reconciled the irreconcilable in one serpentine paragraph, which laid out: 'It is for the people of the island of Ireland alone, by agreement between the two parts respectively, to exercise their right of self-determination on the basis of consent, freely and concurrently given, North and South, to bring about a united Ireland, if that is their wish.'[6]

John Major poured champagne for his Irish guests in the British Cabinet Room at Downing Street, although Reynolds stuck to the orange juice, as befits a teetotaller.

There was to be one last twist in the tale, however. As the officials checked the Declaration prior to it being signed, Roderic Lyne, Major's private secretary, sidled up to Reynolds with what appeared to be an innocent request from Major – that the Prime Minister would appreciate it greatly if Reynolds could describe himself in the press conference as a 'unionist'. Reynolds told him this was not a good idea. That was the end of that, but Duignan notes in his diary that Major greatly resented this refusal.[7]

Not everyone was happy with the Declaration, but it was something of a personal triumph for both Major and Reynolds. There was euphoria amongst the assembled crowd outside Downing Street and strong supportive comments from all the European capitals, as well as from the United States. When Reynolds, Spring and Geoghegan-Quinn returned to the Dáil chamber later in the day, there was a spontaneous standing ovation from all sides of the house. However, although the Official Unionist leader, Jim Molyneaux, following his conversation with Major, had made it clear he was not going to stand in the way of peace, Sinn Féin, while not rejecting the Declaration, was insisting on clarification of its contents. This process would continue for quite some time, with Reynolds willing to engage, but the British and Major less keen to do so. 'I was convinced that nobody should be afraid of peace,' said Reynolds afterwards.

Reynolds had managed – with his steely determination, friendship with Major, and his ability to negotiate forcefully – to manufacture an agreement which, despite its many ambiguities, was set to become the template for peace on the island of Ireland. At vital points in the negotiation, Reynolds, in comparison to the British, proved himself better informed and better aligned to the conflicting interests involved. He had faced great resistance along the way, not least from British officialdom and a deliberate effort by the British to turn him onto another course – cornering the IRA and forcing them to compromise before being brought into a peace process – but subsequent events would prove that Reynolds had made the right call.

CHAPTER TWENTY-TWO

Peace

In the wake of the Downing Street Declaration, there was something of an impasse on the Sinn Féin side and on the part of the British government. Sinn Féin was asking both governments to give clarification on the document. Major initially refused to do so, seeing it as an attempt by republicans to renegotiate the agreed Declaration. On a pre-Christmas visit to Belfast, he brusquely brushed aside their request for clarification, declaring, 'There is a gauntlet down on the table. It is marked peace. It is there for Sinn Féin to pick it up.'[1] This declaration by Major, and his government's refusal to give clarification, held up progress for months.

Reynolds was not resting on his laurels, however, and told Duignan that he would 'hook' and 'reel in' a somewhat reluctant Sinn Féin in regard to their commitment to bring about a ceasefire. Reynolds was throwing out bait for republicans, suggesting that demilitarisation of the situation in the North could begin and that while the British would not become 'Persuaders' for Irish unity, they may be willing to consider a new agreement on the future of the island. Unlike Major, he was determined to meet all requests for clarification from Sinn Féin: 'I knew that the call for "clarification" was a delaying tactic by Sinn Féin. They needed time to study the complex document, as well as time to relay its meaning and content not just to the IRA's Army Council but to its many supporters around the world.' John Major, for his part, says, 'we always realised that Adams and McGuinness had their own problem with the IRA and it wasn't in our interest to make their problems more difficult.'[2]

In the background, my father had been busy. A friend and fine art dealer, Joe O'Meara, had been brought in to assist him with his contacts with republican and loyalist paramilitaries. He accompanied my father to two crucial meetings, the first of which was in the Conrad Hotel, opposite Dublin's National Concert Hotel, and involved IRA veterans and members of the IRA's Army Council. O'Meara says:

> We all knew the ceasefire was coming. It was the build-up. The meeting included people who had yet to be convinced about the Downing Street Declaration and the process itself. Brian came out of the meeting after a few hours muttering about the awkwardness of the questions. They wanted to pore over every sentence, comma and apostrophe in the document.[3]

The second meeting was attended by Reynolds himself, as well as Gusty Spence and David Ervine, who came to the Berkley Court Hotel and made their way from an underground car park up to the hotel's Suite 7 by private lift. This meeting was the first of its kind between loyalist paramilitaries and representatives of the IRA. Other significant meetings between loyalist paramilitaries and republicans were hosted at the Ballymascanlon Hotel, close to the border, in County Louth. Reynolds was, at all stages, ready to participate and meet with players and figures who could influence the process towards a resolute conclusion.

For my own part, I had a lot of work to do. Towards the end of 1993, I had been told by a close advisor to Michael D. Higgins, the then minister responsible for broadcasting policy, that the government was going to get rid of Section 31 of the Broadcasting Act. This was the law which prevented members of Sinn Féin, the IRA and/or their supporters from appearing on radio or television. Having covered the party's annual conferences and developments on my return from Britain to Ireland some years before, I now met with the Sinn Féin press officer, Rita O'Hare, and requested the first interview with Gerry Adams if the ban ended. She agreed. A decision was made to lift the ban from the end of January, with both Higgins and Reynolds pushing for its abolition as a carrot to Sinn Féin to push ahead with the plans for a ceasefire.

There were some nervous weeks in the run-up to the interview with Adams, as the mainstream media speculated about who would do the interview from amongst RTÉ's star-studded cast of celebrity presenters. But Rita O'Hare stayed true to her word and it came as a surprise to everyone that a journalist from a lesser-known, commercial station was the one chosen. The interview, once recorded and put out, led to a welter of publicity, with local and international media beating a path to the radio station. As time went by, O'Hare proved to be a great friend to me and a formidable operator in the peace process that was unfolding.

In conjunction with the dropping of Section 31, Reynolds went into battle to ensure that Adams got a four-day visa to visit the United States to attend a conference being organised about the conflict in Northern Ireland by Bill Flynn, of Mutual of America, a prominent businessman and leading light in the Irish-American community. Prior to the visit, over Christmas 1993 and into the new year, Senator Edward Kennedy had come to Ireland to stay with his sister, the US Ambassador to Ireland, Jean Kennedy-Smith. During his visit, he met and dined with Reynolds in his apartment in Ballsbridge, sounding him out on the Adams visa issue. Reynolds told him that Adams was serious and was trying to avoid all possibility that the IRA might split. He encouraged Kennedy to support the granting of a visa for Adams. Kennedy set great store by Reynolds' advice but was equally impressed that John Hume also endorsed this idea. In addition, Kennedy had sought out the opinion of Tim Pat Coogan, a former editor of *The Irish Press*, who had close contacts with Adams and the wider IRA circles in Belfast. For Nancy Soderberg, a key Clinton White House advisor, the letter of support from Kennedy was decisive in the visa issue: 'For Ted Kennedy to advocate anything for Gerry Adams or the IRA was a stunning shift.'[4]

The British government and its embassy in Washington went into overdrive, seeing the battle over the Adams visa issue as a vital test of their influence over the Americans. Major also believed it was not the time to make concessions to Sinn Féin, given that they still had not signed up to the Downing Street Declaration. Despite British objections, the visa was granted. This was something of a high-profile victory for Adams and did much to underpin US involvement in the unfolding peace process. As Reynolds had hoped, it also allowed Adams to convince those within the IRA who were wavering over peace that a lot more could be achieved through political action.

The visit to New York was an unqualified success from Adams' perspective. He was met at the airport by a phalanx of international and domestic US media. The excitement of interviewing and covering a person who had largely lived in the shadows, up to this point, was too much for the media to resist. The popular US talk show host Larry King introduced Adams as 'a man so controversial, his very voice is barred from British television, the political leader of the Irish Republican Army, Gerry Adams'.[5] Adams was mobbed everywhere he went. A friend of mine tried to attend one of his speaking engagements in New York only to be left outside with hundreds of others on the street with fistfuls of dollars being pushed into buckets being used to collect money for the cause.

Reynolds reckoned the hype and popularity surrounding Adams would mean that there would be no going back to the old ways. The fact that British anxieties about the visa had been brushed aside had sent its own message to the IRA. Perhaps the most significant element of the visit was that it formalised the involvement of the US administration in the process and ensured that President Clinton would act as a kind of guiding influence and guarantor that the process would succeed. Reynolds, in pushing the visa issue, had raised the stakes again, so that, from that moment on, few had an interest in seeing the enterprise fail. According to Reynolds, 'For the Americans, the visa was a very significant move and they expected it to deliver peace within a couple of weeks. I'm sure they thought the visa gave them the right to call the shots, but it doesn't work like that. Sinn Féin and the IRA are a law unto themselves; they deliberate, they discuss and they confer.' Adams, who did not want to disappoint his American audience, declared in one speech, 'It is our intention to see the gun removed permanently from Irish politics.' However, he clearly recognised that the IRA's Army Council would have to do a great deal more soul-searching and consultation with their rank-and-file units before getting the go-ahead for a ceasefire.

Maintaining confidence in the positive intentions of the IRA was difficult in this period, not least for Reynolds. There was a high degree of paranoia on both sides of the Irish sea as the IRA continued with their operations. Speaking to British diplomats at the time, I became aware of a kind of feedback loop between officials, security and intelligence people, which often influenced thinking in political terms. Adams and McGuinness, for their part, and largely for propaganda purposes, emphasised that there was a material difference in their 'political' opinion and that of the Army Council of the IRA. By deliberately playing up the difference between Sinn Féin and the IRA, McGuinness and Adams were able to effectively spook the British and leave them confused about their actual intentions until they could manage absolutely the obvious dissent and potentially lethal opposition from within the ranks of the IRA. It was a difficult high-wire act they were performing. British paranoia, one British diplomat informed me at a social event, was based on the idea that Adams–McGuinness would lure the British government into full negotiations and then blithely assert they had no formal control over the IRA when things were not going their way. This was a significant anxiety on the British government's part, given the fragility of Major's position within his own party and in parliament.

In March 1994, Reynolds was en route to the United States and the traditional St Patrick's Day celebrations with President Clinton in the White House when the IRA carried out a series of mortar bomb attacks on Heathrow Airport. These were daring attacks, carried out over three nights, with nobody killed and explosive charges that did not go off. However, the attacks caused chaos and cost the airport hundreds of millions of pounds as flights were diverted. In his autobiography, Reynolds made the following comment: 'Though none of them had gone off – they were all duds or not primed – once more the IRA were demonstrating their power and their determination not to surrender easily. It did not bode well for the peace initiative. The news was very black from Downing Street and very pessimistic on the streets of New York.'

I was rather intrigued by the audacity of the whole thing and asked an intermediary contact what the IRA was up to. The reply I got was a rather simple one – to the effect that the British had asked for some form of validation that the senior Sinn Féin leadership could, in fact, turn IRA attacks on and off. This was confirmed to me later by a military ordinance contact of mine, who said there had been no intention of creating any explosive effect from the mortars lodged in the runways at Heathrow. Additionally, I was later informed that there was a large bomb lodged under the archway of one of the main bridges over the Thames. When inspected, British ordinance professionals concluded that it had been put in place at short notice with the wires and priming devices placed in such a way that the device could never have been detonated, not even from a distance with a radio control mechanism.

Reynolds, over in the States, was in the dark about this and fielding questions from Clinton administration officials who had helped with the Adams visa issue. They were angry and perplexed by the Heathrow incident. In spite of the difficult context, the social side of the visit was a success, however. Reynolds had brought his entire family to the White House to meet with Bill and Hilary Clinton. A whole floor of the White House had been opened up for the party with the administration's key officials who were dealing with the peace process, along with celebrities and the big connections in Irish America. The evening at the White House finished, somewhat incorrigibly, with Reynolds, Clinton and Hume on stage singing 'When Irish Eyes are Smiling'. In the aftermath of this event, Adams wrote to John Major requesting a face-to-face meeting in his search for clarification. Major batted off the request, stating that it would not happen without a cessation of violence.

Reynolds came home from Washington to a fresh wave of sectarian killing. The IRA then offered a three-day Easter ceasefire, which was viewed as a huge disappointment in the context of expectations of a fuller or permanent cessation of violence. In the wake of all this escalating tension, Sir Patrick Mayhew, Major's Northern Ireland Secretary, conveyed to Reynolds that the British government might be prepared to relent on its refusal to supply Sinn Féin with clarification, in Reynolds' words, 'as long as it was clearly understood there would be no renegotiating whatsoever'. The significance of what was being conceded was not lost on Reynolds and he immediately set about securing the clarification requested by the republican movement and ensuring that whatever questions were asked did not create further misunderstanding or distrust on either side. He states in his autobiography:

I went through their questions myself, vetting each issue raised. Those that I knew were answerable and acceptable to the British I passed on, but there were some I refused to transmit. I insisted my stamp was on all the questions that were sent, because only in that way could I ensure there would be no excuses for the British to react negatively.

There is a sense here that Reynolds' intervention was guided by a frustration at the approach being taken both by Sinn Féin and the British government. In any case, he was leaving nothing to chance. He was at his most assertive in this run-up to the permanent IRA ceasefire.

Not long afterwards, he was back in the USA, facing into a follow-up meeting with Clinton to reassure him that the clarification obstacle was now out of the way. Martin McGuinness, always closer to IRA thinking than Adams, confirmed in his interview for the Reynolds autobiography: 'That decision was only ever going to be taken by the seven members of the IRA Army Council. They were the people who had to decide.' There was a hope that a ceasefire would be announced at a Sinn Féin all-island gathering in Letterkenny over the summer. A leak to the British newspapers that this would happen, however, led to an IRA leak investigation and the ceasefire was called off.

In my capacity as a journalist, I attended the Letterkenny conference. I arrived a day or two early in the hope of meeting some of my contacts inside the IRA who might, for security reasons, also arrive early. Letterkenny is situated right beside the border with the North. There was a strange atmosphere in the town with a distinct absence of gardaí, either of the uniformed or undercover kind. In fact, the whole security of the town had, in practical terms, been handed over to the IRA itself. Armed IRA people were discreetly patrolling the streets with many of the retail outlets closed down for the occasion. The normal complement of media that followed the peace process was there, in addition to many others. The latter, while not aware of the fine detail of the process, were clearly present on the presumption that this gathering would signal the arrival of a ceasefire. This expectation dwindled to disappointment when the Sinn Féin conference passed motions that were unsympathetic to the Downing Street Declaration.

The night before the gathering, I met a senior commander of the IRA. I had not met him before this and he introduced himself while both of us were waiting for a drink in Gallagher's Hotel in Letterkenny. He was a modest man and spoke, for self-protection reasons, in a conversational riddle, something I was used to, having dealt with IRA people in the past. This man was a member of the Army Council. He was a senior commander and had a security detail scattered around the bar keeping a vigilant eye on him and the people he was talking to. Nobody interrupted us as we spoke. We went through the reasons for a ceasefire and his own motivations. In short order, albeit through riddles, he informed me that the decision to call a ceasefire had been taken by the Army Council and that the gathering in the morning was to settle down the troops and consult at a wider, more informal level. He, for his own part, had been active for thirty years, perhaps staying in his own home only once or twice a month. His grown-up children were going to university and, for him, this would provide an opportunity to catch up on his relationship with them. He indicated that he and the other operational commanders were confident in the assurances they had been given by 'the top table' – namely McGuinness and Adams. It was a fascinating insight into the IRA's thinking. Their only worry was that the British might double back on their promises.

The uncertainty about the Letterkenny event was magnified by media that were not used to the nuances of the republican movement's statements. A negative message of rejection was fed out over domestic and international channels. Sinn Féin was genuinely upset at the coverage, so much so that, the next day, still in Letterkenny, Rita O'Hare and her press office team hurriedly assembled a team of journalists whom she felt could be trusted. She specifically urged us to get the message out that the event was much more positive than was being portrayed. The event the previous day had been attended by all the significant people in the IRA from almost every level, but few of my media colleagues would have noticed this. Key people wore delegate badges that did not approximate to their real names. It was a qualitatively different Sinn Féin Ard Fheis than the others I had attended over the years. There were people there with delegate passes who had never been members of Sinn Féin. When I got back to Dublin, I filled in Reynolds, assuring him that things had not been as negative as the media reaction had indicated.

Reynolds, due to go on a family holiday in mid-July 1994, was becoming more and more impatient with Sinn Féin's stalling. On the eve of his holiday, he spoke to McGuinness and Adams: 'I could not live with the uncertainty any more. I demanded a ceasefire by the end of August or I was closing everything down. I'd put my life and career on the line to support them: now they had to call it, or I was walking away and the chance for peace would be lost for another twenty-five years.' Reynolds was, again, taking a deliberate risk, pushing the IRA to come to a decision. It was the kind of high-stakes gambling he was used to, but behind it lay a real frustration at the tortoise-paced way the IRA was going about its decision-making. While he understood their reluctance, he was becoming understandably impatient.

As it happened, at around this time, the IRA and Sinn Féin were busy preparing the orchestration of an IRA ceasefire announcement in the wake of a visit from a high-profile delegation of Irish-Americans that included former Congressman Bruce Morrison, philanthropist Chuck Feeney and Bill Flynn, the CEO of Mutual of America. This group, gathered together by the editor of the *Irish Voice*, Niall O'Dowd, were Irish-American heavy hitters, close to Bill Clinton and hugely connected with Adams and his Belfast-based operation. A previous visit had led to an unannounced ceasefire. On 25 August 1994, they met with Reynolds and Dick Spring in the Taoiseach's office. Their understanding was that the IRA would announce a ceasefire of limited duration. Reynolds basically exploded, stating, 'There's no way. If you come back from Belfast with your six months I'll not be taking it. You can tell Gerry Adams that if six months is on the table, he can take it off again. It's permanent or nothing! You may accept it from them but I won't.' His American listeners were a little astounded. Reynolds believed he had, at this stage, turned himself upside down to facilitate the IRA, citing the lifting of the broadcast ban, commitments to release prisoners, and the opening of border roads. He wanted a permanent ceasefire and he was now using the visiting Irish-Americans as a high-pressure tool to deliver it. People of the calibre of Feeney, Flynn and Morrison knew they could not head back to the States with anything less than a permanent ceasefire.

A week before the Taoiseach's end of August deadline for a permanent ceasefire, Fr Alec Reid called to his office with what can only be described as a last-minute request. The IRA wanted to send Joe Cahill, as a prelude to the ceasefire, to the United States to brief their key people there on what was about to occur. Cahill was a veteran republican; he had more than simply 'totemic' importance within the movement. Apart from a murder conviction back in the 1940s, he had held a number of important posts in the IRA, North and South. He was in charge of the IRA's fundraising operations for many years and this, more than anything else, made his connection with the organisation's Irish-American helpers very important.

The request could not have come at a worse time. Most of Washington, like Dublin, takes its summer break in the month of August. Reynolds was like a man possessed trying to track down the key officials with whom he'd had dealings in the White House and the wider US administration. He had been told by Fr Reid that this visa issue would trigger the ceasefire. The IRA, it seems, was very keen not to lose control over its US operation, which probably involved a lot more hardliners than had to be dealt with at home. If they, the American supporters, felt they were being bounced into something, it might derail the Adams–McGuinness wing at the first hurdle. Bill Clinton was on his summer break, but Reynolds worked into the early morning, hitting the phones to talk directly to his advisors.

Clinton rang him back from his Martha's Vineyard summer retreat at 3 a.m. in the morning. He began by asking Reynolds if he had seen Cahill's CV. Clinton was still a bit annoyed that he had conceded the visa for Adams back in January and there was still no sign of a ceasefire. Reynolds took another risk over the telephone, telling Clinton he had a copy of an IRA statement with an assurance of a ceasefire and could read it to him once he got permission from them to do so. Reynolds was back to Clinton some six to seven hours later with approval to share the wording of the IRA ceasefire statement with him. He had worked all through the night on this last outstanding visa matter. He read the key part of the IRA statement to Clinton, who responded: 'We'll go for it. But this is the last chance. And if this one doesn't run, I never want to hear from you again! Goodbye.'[6]

Back in my newsroom, a colleague who had worked with me, giving behind-the-scenes guidance from his own knowledge, looked at me and said, 'Joe Cahill is travelling to the United States. This means it really is on!'

Reynolds had taken huge personal, political and practical risks, often against all sorts of advice, but the risks were about to pay off. Peace, in words he had frequently used in speeches over the past year, 'comes dropping slow' – a pointed paraphrasing of the poet W.B. Yeats. Reynolds, since he had become Taoiseach, had immersed himself totally in the language, history and culture of the IRA and the republican movement. He had earned huge respect behind the scenes and his vindication would now come in a very public way.

CHAPTER TWENTY-THREE

Loyalists

The formal announcement of the IRA's 'complete cessation of military operations' was accompanied by a clandestine operation of its own involving selected journalists north and south of the border. The statement announcing the ceasefire was signed 'P. O'Neill', a familiar code word used, down the years, for announcements of a more sinister, violent kind. Selected journalists were brought to undisclosed locations and given both the statement and a rudimentary micro-cassette of a woman reading the statement, clearly designed for broadcast use. The voice on the tape was deliberately distorted to prevent identification. Shane Harrison, the BBC's Dublin correspondent, met with 'An IRA contact who was given the statement written on paper remarkably similar to [that] which the IRA used for smuggling messages in and out of the prisons.'[1]

Experienced observers of the conflict, Eamonn Mallie and David McKittrick, make the point that 'although Reynolds, Hume and some others knew it was on the way, all the intelligence resources of the British government did not. The people whose mission was to work out what the IRA was up to – the RUC Special Branch, military intelligence, MI5–MI6 – did not see it coming.'[2] Reynolds did, and put a call in to his friend John Major, who sounded hopeful but was still sceptical. On the fifth floor of Leinster House, Reynolds was attending a routine, weekly meeting, with his party's TDs when the news came through. The mood is captured well by Máire Geoghegan-Quinn, one of the Taoiseach's closest advisors: 'Everyone jumped to their feet, everybody clapped and screamed and roared, shouted, whistled and everything. I mean it was like a crucial goal in a nail-biting game, and there were tears in people's eyes.'[3] In the traditional republican enclave of West Belfast, people hit the streets, waving Irish tricolours and hooting car horns. In the days and weeks that followed, there was continued euphoria, but also a distinct and lingering apprehension about how the loyalist paramilitaries would respond, and speculation as to whether they would see the obvious nationalist jubilation as some kind of provocation.

Within a week of the IRA announcement, Reynolds hosted a meeting at Government Buildings with John Hume and Gerry Adams. It was designed to give momentum to what the IRA had announced. After their meeting, the three came down to the steps of the Taoiseach's office and gave a public, if somewhat pedestrian and matter of fact, report of their meeting. I was in attendance. The press briefing was about to come to an end, with reporters and camera people turning away, when one of the photographers shouted out to the three men to ask whether there was a possibility of a handshake. All three looked sheepish. Of the three, Reynolds was the most keen to respond to the photographer's request and he sealed a handshake between Hume and Adams with his own hands. This triple handshake became an iconic moment in the whole process, confirming, if it were not already obvious, that nationalist Ireland was united in its desire for peace. It was also a public acknowledgement of what had been, albeit behind the scenes, a long road of surreptitious dialogue conducted in secret by all three men present. However, to others more sceptical and/or hostile, it seemed to confirm the existence of a threatening 'pan-nationalist front' that had been at work for a long time.

Despite the high-profile handshake with Hume and Adams, Reynolds had been working away quietly in the background with the loyalist paramilitaries who had most to fear from such a photograph. Billy Hutchinson, a leading loyalist paramilitary, takes up the story: 'Although there was no direct contact with the British government, the Irish government was slightly more accommodating and Albert Reynolds met representatives of the Ulster Volunteer Force (UVF) to lay out, from his perspective, what the Irish position was. Things were slowly falling into place in a manner conducive to a loyalist ceasefire.'[4] The truly novel aspect here is the frank admission that there was very little if any cultivation of the loyalist paramilitaries up to the ceasefires by the British government. It was Reynolds, in anticipation of a potential violent backlash, who had made contact with the loyalists to avoid the creation of a vacuum.

In the wake of the IRA ceasefire, I went for a celebratory lunch with a contact, in the Unicorn restaurant, just around the corner from Reynolds' office. On the street after lunch, I ran into an old college friend, Eamon Delaney, whom I had not seen for a while and who now worked in the Department of Foreign Affairs' Anglo-Irish Division. He asked me directly if there would be a loyalist ceasefire. I was slightly surprised at his apparent lack of knowledge and, in an unguarded moment, gave him the precise date of the forthcoming announcement by the Combined Loyalist Military Command (CLMC). In Delaney's memoir on his time in the department, he reveals his colleagues' astonishment at this news; it seems that none of them had any expectations that this was even a possibility. What surprised many, and was widely remarked upon at the time, was the tone of contrition expressed in the formal statement issued by the loyalists on 13 October 1994. This was in stark contrast to the IRA statement. The loyalist ceasefire announcement used the phrase 'abject and sincere remorse' for the violent actions they had carried out. This addition to their statement had been at the prompting of Archbishop Robin Eames, the Church of Ireland Primate of All Ireland. Eames had played a crucial role as intermediary between Major, Reynolds and the loyalist paramilitaries. His role in the peace process was beyond reproach; throughout, he conducted himself with huge sensitivity and confidentiality.

Reynolds had worked very hard to read himself into the mindset of loyalist paramilitaries, hosting meetings with David Ervine, Billy Hutchinson and, of course, Gusty Spence, something of an icon within the movement. In Reynolds' own words: 'The trouble was, the Loyalists were somewhat out on their own. Traditional Unionism did not really appeal to them; most of them were poor, working-class Protestants outcast by discrimination, poor housing, poor education and no jobs.' Clearly, they were deeply suspicious that they were being sold out to Irish nationalism, and a degree of republican triumphalism would only feed into this anxiety. Spence had, with the assistance of intermediaries working with Reynolds, informally arranged meetings directly with Army Council-level members of the IRA to assuage the loyalist anxieties and fears. My own experience from contact with the loyalist paramilitaries was that they were deeply suspicious of the British government's intentions throughout the process. Factions within the loyalist paramilitary organisations were far more fragmented and prone to violent feuds than their republican counterparts. Moreover, the danger of being part of one of these organisations was added to by the fairly open awareness within these structures that they were deeply penetrated by people who were working for the British security services. Reynolds worked carefully to cultivate the loyalists in spite of this and, at times, at great danger to himself in a security sense.

Details of one meeting he held were given to me as part of the research for this book. Prior to the loyalist ceasefire announcement, Noel Gallagher received a call from Reynolds to come over from his native Derry and meet him in a hotel in Belfast. Reynolds duly arrived in the hotel with his driver and no security escort, where he met Gallagher and asked him to accompany him to a meeting. They left the hotel by a rear kitchen and jumped into a waiting and relatively anonymous car. 'We suddenly realised the risk we were both taking: me the Taoiseach, in a car with Gusty Spence, former commander of the UVF and a leading Loyalist. If we'd been caught, he could have been arrested for kidnapping me!' said Reynolds. Following a circuitous route to east Belfast, Reynolds and Gallagher were shown into a room, where they held a meeting with individuals drawn from the ranks of the diverse loyalist paramilitary groupings. Gallagher, a resolute republican and no stranger to clandestine work, was a little frightened by being there, but Reynolds, for his part, was totally relaxed. It may well be true to say that nobody else as taoiseach has taken such extraordinary personal risks.

This aspect of Reynolds' personality was vividly captured by the veteran *Irish Times* columnist Mary Holland, when she noted that the very characteristics that had brought the peace process along were the same characteristics that had attracted unfavourable commentary from his critics:

It has been precisely the skills of a Huckster, well, successful entrepreneur – his readiness to take a risk, cut corners, drive a hard deal and, crucially, to back an instinctive hunch with the necessary action

– which not only wrested the much longed-for 'complete cessation' of violence from the IRA, but since provided, almost single-handed, the momentum to keep the peace process on course ...[5]

Holland concluded her article by stating, 'Looking back over the past 25 years it is impossible to imagine any other Taoiseach capable of pulling off this outrageous coup de theatre.' This was quite a compliment from someone who had diligently witnessed, written and reported on some of the key events in the bloody history of Northern Ireland. Like many others, including my late father, she was more than ready to acknowledge Reynolds' talents, notwithstanding the fact that she, like pretty much everybody else, had started out with few expectations that he would apply these talents in relation to Northern Ireland. In his compelling diaries of his time working with Reynolds, Seán Duignan is also frank in his acknowledgement that it was these characteristics that propelled the peace process forward.

In the weeks immediately after the loyalist ceasefire, Reynolds moved swiftly to consolidate the opportunity for peace. He set up 'The Forum for Peace and Reconciliation with all Southern parties, and many Northern parties, except the Unionist ones. Assembled in Dublin Castle under the chairmanship of Judge Catherine McGuinness, [it] heard a wide range of evidence and drew up a report. Increased international aid was made available from the EU, the US and Australia.'[6] Reynolds' speed in setting this up was to give constitutional politicians, as well as members of Sinn Féin, an immediate opportunity to contribute ideas for the ultimate resolution of the process through all-party negotiation. It also offered a new platform to allow smaller, loyalist political groupings to participate, and played a role in allowing disparate community and business groups to have their voices heard. It commissioned valuable reports and allowed for various rival political groups to come into contact with Sinn Féin.

At this time, Reynolds was also keeping up a relentless personal schedule, with regular visits abroad where he was praised for his achievements. Prior to the announcement of the loyalist ceasefire, he had travelled to Australia. On this, he writes:

We were feted in Sydney. There is a big Irish population in Australia and many IRA supporters. Peace in the North had been headline news throughout the continent and the crowds were out on the streets to celebrate. After the tensions of the last few days it was a relief to be part of these emotional and joyful demonstrations. It made the quarrels over a judicial appointment seem very insignificant indeed.

Reynolds was basking in the international credit he was receiving for delivering peace. However, the seemingly small matter of the appointment to the High Court of his pick for Attorney General, Harry Whelehan, was about to engulf him in a way that he, like many others to this day, find hard to believe.

Prior to departing for Australia, Reynolds had pushed for Mr Justice Liam Hamilton to be appointed as the new Chief Justice in charge of the Supreme Court. The Labour leader, Dick Spring, was out of the country in Hong Kong, and Hamilton, although a Labour man in political affiliation terms, was not Labour's first-choice nominee. Given that their first choice was ineligible for appointment, the Labour ministers agreed to the appointment of Hamilton but, in exchange, had asked for a delay in filling the position of President of the High Court, a role for which Harry Whelehan had put himself forward. Two Labour ministers consulted on the issue with Spring by telephone. Reynolds' impatience on the matter was uncomfortable for Spring, as he had previously indicated his belief that Whelehan was not the man for the job. The row under the surface in relation to Whelehan's appointment quickly became a matter for national media speculation. On 26 September, *The Irish Times* made the following comment, in an editorial:

> There is a game of brinkmanship in play here. The Taoiseach is on a winning roll. He has a breakthrough in the North, he has survived the worst of the Hamilton report, the passports affair, the tax amnesty and sundry irritations. Mr Spring is seen by many in the rank and file of his own party as out-manoeuvred and humiliated.[7]

Irish journalists travelling with Reynolds in Australia were told that Spring would leave the government if Whelehan was appointed. Another piece in *The Sunday Business Post* had Labour figures telling the media that Reynolds was 'power-drunk following the IRA ceasefire'. These media briefings by Labour confirmed the party's resistance to Whelehan and also a view expressed by the Taoiseach's key advisor, Martin Mansergh, that the Taoiseach was politically soaring and could do with being pulled down to earth.

Prejudicial media briefings by Labour had become a huge annoyance to Reynolds. The Labour party figure most blamed for a number of negative leaks was Spring's closest advisor, Fergus Finlay. As has been discussed already, Finlay was a sophisticated spin doctor and well respected by the media. The problem for Finlay, as I saw it as a practising journalist, was that he rarely seemed to cover his tracks. Even though he had relinquished his role as press secretary, he continued to consult, have coffee and mix socially with the Leinster House correspondents. Rumour thrived on rumour and it was very difficult for him to deny that he was the source behind the many hostile leaks and briefings that seemed to target Fianna Fáil. Seán Duignan and John Foley, the Labour-appointed head of the Government Information Service (GIS), kept a much lower profile, avoiding mixing with journalists around Leinster House. Through his very open contact with journalists, rumours were spawned that Finlay was behind every leak, whereas Foley and Duignan preferred to get their message out over the phone.

Once again, Reynolds' and Spring's constant overseas trips were adding to the difficulty of resolving this latest difference of opinion between such uneasy coalition partners. Finally, both were able to air their grievances over the Whelehan appointment in person, albeit at a midnight meeting at Baldonnel military aerodrome, after the two had flown in from separate destinations. Labour ministers and TDs exerted their own pressure on Tánaiste Spring, urging him to resolve his row with Reynolds over what was considered a minor matter of a judicial appointment. The so-called Baldonnel Agreement between the two was further prompted by Labour TDs taking to the airwaves and urging their leader not to break up the government over the matter. Clearly Labour TDs and ministers were in no mood for a general election over a simple legal appointment. There had also been mutterings of disquiet amongst Reynolds' senior cabinet colleagues and friends.

Spring extracted a promise from Reynolds that the system of judicial appointments would be overhauled and a new piece of legislation drafted for this purpose. The implicit trade-off between Reynolds and Spring was that the latter would sanction the Whelehan appointment in exchange for this judicial reform. The veteran commentator Stephen Collins observed: 'As far as Reynolds was concerned, he had won, but he was prepared to give Spring time to eat humble pie. It was one of the biggest mistakes of his political career.'[8] Reynolds was of the view that the objections by Labour to Whelehan were spurious and without foundation. He felt that in pressing ahead with Whelehan's claim to the appointment, he was steering an honourable course. Prevailing cabinet custom and practice was that a serving Attorney General was entitled to a forthcoming judicial appointment once he expressed a wish to be considered. Whelehan, for his part, felt he was ideal for the job of President of the High Court, given that it was a largely administrative role, rather than one requiring the appointee to sit actively as a judge on cases. He felt that his experience as Attorney General meant he was well suited to the position.

Reynolds, for his part, felt he owed Whelehan the appointment. Whelehan had been appointed by Haughey and then continued in the role once Reynolds took over. Reynolds believed Whelehan to be an honest person, as he had gone to bat for him on the matter of cabinet confidentiality in relation to the Beef Tribunal. Whelehan had presented the case on the cabinet confidentiality issue in person to the Supreme Court, thus amplifying the importance that the government attached to the matter in the eyes of the sitting judges. It meant that Reynolds did not have to face the prospect of former ministerial colleagues, such as Ray Burke whom he had sacked, giving testimony before the Tribunal about the precise nature of the discussions and opinions around the cabinet table in relation to his very generous export credit allocations to Goodman's and others' companies. There was a sense that a quid pro quo was being observed in relation to the Whelehan appointment.

Labour, of course, felt no such loyalty to Whelehan and persistently muttered that they believed him to be too conservative to be appointed a judge, citing, *sotto voce*, his actions in relation to the X Case on abortion rights as an example of this. At one point during the crisis that unfolded, rumours were flying around that Whelehan was, in fact, a member of Opus Dei, a secretive Catholic organisation not unlike the Protestant Masons. Although Whelehan, for his part, vehemently denied any such membership, suffice it to say that even Reynolds was sufficiently concerned about the rumours in circulation to ask Whelehan's successor as Attorney General whether Whelehan was a member.

Despite the mutterings, in the aftermath of the Baldonnel Agreement, Reynolds, in typical business style, believed 'Dick and I have a deal', and he was ready to press ahead with Whelehan's appointment. This assumption on Reynolds' part, that he had a firm agreement, was to prove disastrous in light of new information that would emerge in the weeks that followed. A controversy arose over how the Attorney General's office had dealt with a controversial paedophile priest case and the ensuing crisis was set to cost Reynolds his job. The bewildering series of legal and media scandals which were raked out were as simultaneously sinister and baffling to all bystanders as they were to Reynolds himself.

CHAPTER TWENTY-FOUR

Headless Chickens

In October 1994, Fr Brendan Smyth – a Norbertine priest and known paedophile and child sex abuser who had remained at large for the best part of thirty years – became a household name. The controversy around this priest was to play a decisive part in the departure of Albert Reynolds as taoiseach. A programme entitled *Suffer Little Children*, broadcast on UTV in Northern Ireland, told a horrible story about how the Catholic Church, though it knew of his offences, had simply moved him from parish to parish. Fr Smyth's catalogue of sexual abuse could be traced both north and south of the border, and even across to the United States. From 1961 onwards, a priest called Fr Bruno Mulvihill had tried to warn the Abbot of the Order of his concerns about Fr Smyth, but these warnings went unheeded. Fr Smyth had been involved in a minimum of forty-three sexual assaults and, by his own admission, his sex abuse could have involved up to 200 children from the 1960s onwards.

After the investigative *Suffer Little Children* programme, it began to emerge that there had been a seven-month delay in processing an extradition request from the Northern Ireland authorities while Fr Smyth was being sheltered in Killnacrott Abbey in County Cavan. In November, the revelations about this delay were to unleash a political crisis in the Dáil which played out live on television over ten days. Nature, as the saying goes, abhors a vacuum. As the controversy played out in public, few, if anybody, in authority, could explain what the cause for the delay had been. As a journalist covering the unfolding events, it was easy to succumb to the wild rumours that were travelling the corridors of Leinster House. The rumour mill was working at full tilt and I remember being told that a further 'bombshell' revelation was to come in the form of a direct intervention by the Catholic Primate of All Ireland, Cardinal Daly, in a letter to the then Attorney General, Harry Whelehan. As I sipped coffee in the Dáil's visitors' lounge, this rumour was everywhere and I noticed Pat Rabbitte, an outspoken deputy with the Democratic Left, in a corner in animated discussion. Literally minutes later, he was in the chamber of the Dáil stating that a document existed in the Attorney General's office 'that will rock the foundations of this society to its very roots'. His party colleague and leader Proinsias de Rossa went further in support of Rabbitte, asking, 'Is it true that a memorandum has been found in the Attorney General's office which indicates that there was outside interference in the decision by the Attorney General not to proceed with the extradition for seven months?'[1]

What had, up to that point, been treated as wild speculation and unsubstantiated fact was now on the parliamentary record. I and many other journalists raced to our offices and hit the phones to see if something else was about to emerge. It is testimony to the hysteria around the Fr Smyth allegations that this, apparently baseless, rumour was allowed to be aired in public. Cardinal Daly issued a firm denial and was subsequently interviewed on a broadcast denying any involvement in the extradition delay. Despite a thorough investigation, including an extensive trawl of documents in the Attorney General's office, no such letter or interference has ever been substantiated. Whoever set these fevered rumours in motion was determined to link Church and State with the scandal.

A series of conflicting explanations of the case badly destabilised Reynolds' coalition partnership with Dick Spring. In *The Power Game*, Stephen Collins points out that with the disclosure of the delay in the Fr Brendan Smyth case, 'Spring suddenly had a weapon in his hands to renew his resistance to the appointment of Whelehan to the presidency of the High Court'.[2] The weaponisation of the Fr Brendan Smyth case was to the benefit of everybody except Reynolds. The opposition and the media had a field day over the case and the apparent contradictions from government about how the delay had occurred, and Reynolds was very slow to realise the full impact Fr Smyth was having on his relationship with Spring and the Labour Party. John Foley, Spring's spokesman, was quick to tip off Duignan, in blunt terms, on the implications of the Smyth case: 'The priest changes everything.'[3] Despite this timely warning from the Labour side, it did not immediately register as a threat in Reynolds' mind. He was still clearly of the view that the deal he had secured in his midnight meeting with Spring in Baldonnel would remain in place.

Reynolds continued to push for the appointment of Whelehan as President of the High Court and a decision was scheduled to be made by the cabinet. Whelehan reported to colleagues on the reason why there had been a delay of seven months in the Smyth extradition case, the crux of which explanation was that there was no suggestion this was an urgent case and it was dealt with in accordance with policy. But on the basis of body language alone, it was clear that the Labour side was not satisfied with the Attorney General's explanation. When it came to a vote on the appointment, the Fianna Fáil part of the cabinet voted to appoint Whelehan, while the Labour side, led by Spring, left the room. This led to confusion amongst Reynolds' ministers about what precisely had transpired. Some believed that Labour was merely abstaining from the actual vote, while others felt the situation was more serious and this a signal that Labour was, in fact, leaving the government. Reynolds himself tells us, 'I was not particularly perturbed. At the time we all thought that the walk-out was a means of having their dissent recorded in the cabinet minutes – in other words, facilitating the recording of a non-vote as a tactical move.'

Then, in a way that significantly compounded matters, the swearing in of Harry Whelehan as President of the High Court by President Mary Robinson was scheduled for that very evening, with Reynolds and some of his key ministers dashing to Áras an Uachtaráin for the event. The appointment, from a Labour perspective at least, seemed to be happening with indecent haste. The official explanation was that Robinson was going away on the Friday evening and, from a scheduling point of view, the appointment needed to be made official that very evening.

Given the lack of clarity over Labour's intentions, it seems like a foolish decision on Reynolds' part to press ahead with the swearing in and, unsurprisingly, Spring was none too pleased about it when Reynolds told him. Following this Friday stand-off between Reynolds and Spring, the whole weekend was dominated by media speculation about whether the coalition would survive. In a significant escalation of the rhetoric involved, Spring told his TDs, 'We have allowed a child abuser to remain at large in our community, when we had it in our power to ensure that he was given up to justice. Is no one to explain why? Is no one to take responsibility? Is no one to account to the people of this country for so grievous a lapse?'[4]

The problem with Spring's speech to his party's backbenchers was that it seemed to depict Reynolds and Fianna Fáil as complicit in covering up information about why it took so long to process Smyth's extradition. In reality, the facts were quite different. Over the weekend, Fianna Fáil and Labour ministers moved into action with discussions to try to prevent the collapse of the government. The next few nights were to be exhausting for Reynolds, his ministers and his closest advisors.

At the heart of Reynolds' difficulties had been the premature appointment of Harry Whelehan and the perception, in the public realm and in Labour's mind, that there had been some kind of shielding of the paedophile priest or, at the very least, an incompetent delay in handling the extradition case. The events, as they played out before Reynolds' resignation, represent something of a playbook of 'what not to do' in terms of crisis management. Ministers were struggling with complicated legal arguments, different and often contradictory documents and scripts, while simultaneously trying to de-escalate rising tension with their coalition colleagues in Labour.

The official responsible for the extradition warrant for Fr Brendan Smyth was Matt Russell, someone with huge experience and direct, day-to-day responsibility for dealing with extradition requests. His title, as Senior Legal Assistant to the Attorney General, meant that it was him rather than the Attorney General who did the bulk of the legal work on cases like this. As it has transpired, Whelehan was only marginally involved in any of the considerations around the Smyth case. Though the seven-month delay in the case was the major issue causing public controversy surrounding the Fr Smyth case in the media, in the minds of Labour TDs, members of the opposition at Leinster House and lawyers representing victim groups, it was not an issue in substance. Neither the British Attorney General, nor indeed the authorities in Northern Ireland, were pressurising Matt Russell for a quicker decision on the case. The standard of proof required for extradition cases can be legally complicated and in the Smyth case, even more so, in that some of the offences he was sought for reached back over twenty-nine years. Russell was taking into account significant consideration of the principles and the individual circumstances of the Smyth case, making sure that the issue of the amount of time that had elapsed since an offence had been considered, as well as the delay between the actual offences and the eventual request for extradition. There were many other higher priority demands on his time and he had no indication from the British legal authorities, with whom he would have had numerous contacts on a week-to-week basis, that they wanted him to move more quickly on this case.

On the day of his appointment as the new Attorney General, filling the post left empty by Whelehan's new appointment, Eoin Fitzsimons was immediately plunged into the public and governmental crisis over the Smyth case. In a matter of days, he and Russell were having a serious difference of opinion over another, earlier extradition case, the Duggan case, which, it was being suggested, had a material comparison to the Smyth case and meant that the argument that the Smyth case needed lengthy consideration due to there being no precedent for it was incorrect. Fitzsimons had been summoned to a meeting with the Minister for Justice, Máire Geoghegan-Quinn, and Russell was pleading with him not to attend until he had read the file in relation to the Duggan case. The failure to address the Duggan case and, frankly, its irrelevance played into the wider political crisis in a way that led many to believe that there was some form of cover-up going on with regard to the facts. Senior Legal Assistant Russell believed that the Duggan case had no bearing on the Smyth case, but Fitzsimons, new to the office, appears to have inflated its relevance in front of ministers and in his own mind.

Reynolds became the political casualty of a disagreement of opinion amongst lawyers which was, in fact, never fully clarified as the issue of the 'seven-month' delay was played out as a public controversy with full twenty-four-hour media 'crisis' coverage. Journalist Vincent Brown has written that the Duggan case was not just 'irrelevant', but also 'a storm in a teacup in which Reynolds, Whelehan and Matt Russell were drowned'.[5] Part of the problem was that Reynolds had, quite rightly, not made any reference to the Duggan case when addressing the Dáil earlier in the week on the issue of the Smyth case. The chairman of the parliamentary inquiry into the circumstances of the government's collapse, Dan Wallace, concluded that 'Reynolds was absolutely correct not to have mentioned the Duggan case in his Tuesday speech in the House because the implications were too great for its introduction without absolute written confirmation by the new Attorney General.'[6]

However, the failure by Reynolds to mention the Duggan case was presented as evidence that he had been less than truthful in his pronouncements. In this instance, Reynolds' due caution about the Duggan case became a kind of rope to hang him with in the eyes of his opponents, as well as for the Labour side of his government. In the crisis that ensued, late night meetings, complex legal issues and even confusion about the concept of 'delay', not just Duggan, threw chaos into the mix. There were two forms of delay that were the subject of heated debate – the alleged delay in dealing with the extradition warrant and the actual issue of 'delay' as a legal concept in terms of the amount of time which had passed between an offence and trial, and whether there was an appropriate limit to extradition. It was quite obvious to me, as I covered the unfolding crisis, that there was confusion, amongst both ministers at critical meetings and observers, about which of the 'delay' issues people were speaking about.

As the full enormity of Labour's position became more apparent to Reynolds, he began to turn away from his own initial misgivings about the Duggan case. He asked his new Attorney General to visit Whelehan in his home and see if he could prevail upon him to resign. Whelehan, now the duly appointed President of the High Court, told Fitzsimons that he viewed any effort by the government to get him to resign as constitutionally incorrect and improper. Another later visit also led to a refusal to resign, even though Whelehan was reminded that the peace process was perched on a knife-edge and the last thing that was needed was a collapse in the coalition government.

In the midst of all this, Leo Enright, a BBC journalist with significant experience in both London and Dublin, was contacted by Reynolds to meet with someone he believed was a member of the IRA's Army Council:

I met this member of the Army Council in the precincts of Leinster House. The meeting was organised by Albert. This man was not connected to Sinn Féin in any way. His concern was that Spring was going to collapse the government and he specifically threatened Dick Spring. He said if Spring went ahead with this, they would shoot him.[7]

Enright had become very close to Reynolds during the peace process and was often used by him to get messages directly across to the British through pieces he put together for the BBC news. Enright reported directly to BBC London rather than through BBC Belfast. He took the threat to Spring sufficiently seriously to alert the British to what was being said. His first instinct was to tip off President Mary Robinson, as he had a contact who worked with her and could pass the message on. Ultimately, Enright was told that Spring's people were aware of such threats and the possibility that they were under some form of surveillance by the IRA.[8]

The behind-the-scenes appeals to Whelehan to resign had fallen on deaf ears and Whelehan had dug in. Reynolds spoke darkly to his press secretary, Duignan, about the prospect of Whelehan becoming the first ever High Court Judge to be 'impeached'. Effectively, because of Reynolds' failure to mention the Duggan case in his first main speech on the Smyth affair, Labour was now requiring him to do an about face, denounce Whelehan and assert that if he knew then what he knew now he would never have appointed him in the first place. The words and speech that Reynolds' was being forced to make would not just be a humiliating climbdown, in terms of what he had said a mere matter of days before, but he would also have to publicly apologise to Spring. Duignan, indicative of the paranoia at play at every level, confided in the Head of the Taoiseach's Department, saying, 'Spring is on for the treble. He gets rid of Harry; he gets rid of Albert, and gets into bed with Bertie without an election.'[9]

Such was the paranoia in the minds of Fianna Fáil ministers about Labour's intentions that they insisted that this last-minute agreement be formally signed on paper by Dick Spring. Spring duly signed a document at 10.22 a.m. on 16 November stating that he and his cabinet colleagues would stay on in government with Reynolds. Reynolds illustrates his own degree of paranoia in his autobiography with the words: 'I'm being led to my execution, somebody is doing this, somebody is orchestrating this.' He also confesses to being apprehensive about the constitutional propriety of publicly casting aspersions on a sitting judge while his own Attorney General still appeared legally uncertain about the Duggan case, but he admits to having 'little or no choice' but to go down the road he was now choosing. Even Fergus Finlay, on the Labour side, was anxious about the denunciation of a current or serving judge.

In any event, the last-minute deal signed off on by Spring hardly lasted an hour beyond its actual signature. Preparing for the Dáil debate in the chamber, Spring was approached by one of his experienced backbenchers, Michael Bell, who informed him that a contact and friend of his in his local newspaper had further details on the Duggan case that were important for him to know. Spring left the chamber to speak on the telephone to Bell's informant. The person on the end of the line provided Spring with proof that Reynolds had known fully of the Duggan case on the Monday night prior to his Dáil speech on the Smyth matter. This information had the effect of spooking Spring. The informant had the information directly from journalist and society columnist Angela Phelan, a close family friend of Kathleen Reynolds. Phelan had, in fact, been in the Reynolds' home on the Monday night when Albert had come home complaining volubly to his wife that there was now another case in the whole Smyth affair. This piece of information, inadvertently given by Phelan to a friend, had the effect of pushing Spring towards the view that Reynolds had, in fact, lied to the Dáil in his earlier statement.

Spring then checked with Fitzsimons about when he believed the Taoiseach had known of the Duggan case and Fitzsimons confirmed that Reynolds had learned of it on Monday. There then followed an emergency meeting between Spring, two of his ministers and Reynolds, who was accompanied by Ministers Dempsey, McCreevy and Geoghegan-Quinn. In these discussions, Reynolds tried to explain the sheer confusion on the Monday night over the status of the Duggan case and why he refrained from mentioning it. The suggestion that Reynolds should call for the resignation or impeachment of Whelehan was not something he felt he could do.

Labour's Ruairi Quinn, underlining the seriousness of the situation, then memorably concluded, 'We have come for a head, Harry's or yours. It doesn't look like we are getting yours.'[10] This quote subsequently entered the annals of political legend, and as a cryptic summation of events it was to prove both prescient and prophetic. Spring told the Dáil that day that he no longer had confidence in the government and all the Labour ministers resigned. Reynolds had finally run out of road. The next day, 17 November 1994, he stood up in Leinster House and formally announced his resignation as Taoiseach.

Mary O'Rourke, then serving as a Minister of State under Reynolds, said that the crisis leading to his premature departure had serving and senior ministers running about from office to office akin to 'headless chickens'. It is hardly a remark for which her colleague ministers would have thanked her, but it seemed to sum up the confusion that characterised this affair. Even with the benefit of twenty-six years' hindsight, the whole debacle appears incredible. Ultimately, however, it was Reynolds' mishandling of Spring that left him with little or no chance of blaming anybody but himself for how things turned out.

CHAPTER TWENTY-FIVE

Resignation

In his resignation speech to the Dáil, Albert Reynolds was valedictory, gracious and anxious to vindicate his public life. There were two memorable quotes. The first was: 'Above all in politics and in business I was delighted to have been a risktaker because I believe that if you are not a risktaker you'll achieve nothing.' Seán Duignan asserts that, in conversation, Reynolds confessed he would like the word risktaker on his tomb and, in a way, he glorified this aspect of his own character.[1] The second quote, an aside to the press gallery, was given as he trudged up the steps to leave the Dáil chamber. He had spent the previous few minutes taking congratulations and commiserations from colleagues and opponents alike. Turning his gaze to the reporters and media who had shadowed him as Taoiseach, he said, 'It's amazing. You cross the big hurdles, and when you get to the small ones, you get tripped up.' He had paid a big price for his support for Harry Whelehan. In the event, under huge duress from his judicial colleagues, Whelehan himself, belatedly, resigned as President of the High Court, but not in time to save Reynolds.

Reynolds' private passions, quite apart from his business and political life, were around the card table playing poker, or more frequently at the racecourse, having a gamble on a horse that might win. When you met him in the betting ring at the Galway races, he looked the epitome of a happy man. He would quietly whisper a tip for a race that was on that day. He appeared to like the sociability of it all and the prospect of making money on a winning horse. For all his wealth, he was not a huge gambler, but he always had a few hundred in his right-hand jacket pocket, just in case someone gave him some insight on a horse. While Duignan was privately sceptical about Reynolds' ability to win at the racecourse, believing that many of his exploits were exaggerated, he did believe that, in politics, as in other things, 'It was the nature of the man – he wasn't going to be a loser.'[2]

In building his personal business career and in public life, Reynolds had not had the same good fortune to begin with as his erstwhile coalition colleagues, Des O'Malley and Dick Spring. Both of these men were, by profession, lawyers, and solidly middle class in their upbringing. They were also both scions of significant political dynasties. O'Malley was the nephew of a political legend in Limerick, Donogh O'Malley, who had died young but made a great impact through his introduction of free secondary education in Ireland in the 1960s. Dick Spring had gone to a rugby-playing school, togged out for Ireland, and become a Labour TD off the back of his father's popularity as a Tralee-based deputy. In comparison to them, Reynolds would have regarded himself as having come up the hard way. These social and occupational differences between Reynolds and his coalition colleagues explains a lot, without even going into the political and personality rivalries that set them apart. By instinct, lawyers are analytical and cautious. Reynolds, for his part, was impulsive and quick to seize an opportunity when it presented itself. A lawyer, by training, likes to peruse a lengthy document, whereas Reynolds, in a phrase that was to bedevil him, was a one-page man. He saw the written page as a prelude to action rather than lengthy further discussion. He had once admitted that he liked to get briefings from his civil servants digested down to a tight note or on one page. The media and his opponents delighted in calling him the 'one-page man.' The phrase was exploited mercilessly to taunt him.

His relationship with O'Malley was, in a sense, bound to be bad. Reynolds had been elected leader of his party on a specific promise to control or downsize the influence of O'Malley's smaller party over Fianna Fáil in power. Neither O'Malley nor Spring would have seen a great deal of difference between Fianna Fáil under Haughey and under the leadership of Reynolds. Reynolds, in their eyes, may have been guilty by association given his long years of loyal service to Haughey. In Spring's case, he had achieved his huge electoral success in the 1992 election because of Haughey and what he would have decried as corruption and low ethics in Fianna Fáil. The manner in which the Fr Brendan Smyth affair was escalated to the point where Reynolds lost his job as Taoiseach probably came about because the Labour Party believed, without proof, that there was something going on in the background that they were not aware of. There was a strong perception in Labour's ranks that some form of insidious or furtive clerical influence was at play in the drama. This whole fear on Labour's part seems only to have been added to by rumours that a secretive Catholic Church organisation, Opus Dei, was at work exerting its influence. Such was the paranoia on this point that the new Attorney General, Eoin Fitzsimons, asked his staff to declare if they were members of Opus Dei or any other such clandestine Catholic organisations. Willie O'Dea, a supporter of Reynolds and minister in the then government, feels: 'Labour probably thought that there were more skeletons in the cupboard and it wouldn't do their own popularity any good if these came out. Albert was dealt with very harshly. He wasn't holding anything back.'[3]

Former Taoiseach Bertie Ahern believes: 'Albert Reynolds was not protecting anybody with regard to abuse. The political controversy that led to his resignation was one of those things that took off. There was no suggestion of a cover-up. None of us thought it would collapse the government. It escalated from the Whelehan appointment and Labour simply didn't want him appointed.'[4] The frenzy around the Smyth case led to a profusion of conspiracy theories about clerical influence, Labour party orchestration and even suggestions that the British intelligence services were trying to stop Reynolds in his tracks. Years and years later, precious little has emerged to justify the conspiracies. Nevertheless:

On Friday 11 November, Labour withdrew from cabinet, when Albert Reynolds persisted in forcing through the appointment, regardless of its effect in undermining the spirit of partnership government. That same day the government lost two by-elections in Cork, having lost another two the previous summer. It was assumed that Labour would not want an election. But unnoticed by most, the arithmetic of the Dáil had been altered, and now made viable Labour's original preference for a Rainbow Coalition consisting of Fine Gael, Labour and Democratic Left, to which Fine Gael had now dropped its objections.[5]

The effect of this change in the Dáil numbers was to strengthen Labour's hand in their dealings with Fianna Fáil and Reynolds. If the worst came to the worst, they had options. Reynolds, as it turned out, had none. The numbers had changed irrevocably. A change of government could now happen without recourse to an election. It was testament to Fianna Fáil and Reynolds' innate self-belief that nobody had foreseen the prospect of this actually happening.

Seán Duignan believes Labour was conscious that the party could, in effect, avoid an election but insist on Reynolds' departure as Taoiseach. While this demand was never made explicit, it became obvious, the longer the stand-off continued, that Labour would be able to do business with Bertie Ahern and continue with the coalition. Reynolds' faithful advisor, Martin Mansergh, made the comment, 'the Taoiseach was engaged in a power play that went hideously wrong – what he wanted, he had to have, and that was the end of the matter'.[6]

The power play and the legal confusion clearly exhausted a great many of the players in the drama, which probably exacerbated things on both sides. Reynolds, at one point, confessed to Duignan that he felt he was 'being led to his execution'. A number of Fianna Fáil ministers interviewed for this book formed the view that Labour wanted out of the government anyhow. A sort of fatalism began to form that this was a pre-ordained outcome, despite ministerial efforts to patch up late night or early morning compromise deals. On top of this, Donal Cronin, Reynolds' former speech writer, makes the point: 'Towards the end of the crisis I myself was sleeping on a sofa. Sloppiness and carelessness crept in. You cannot underestimate this.'[7]

Bertie Ahern suggests that the whole thing and the reaction to the crisis was made worse by the fact that it was being dealt with by a big committee of ministers and officials; had only two or three people been involved, the management of the crisis could have been tightened up. Johnny Fallon, a lifelong friend of Reynolds, believes the Taoiseach succumbed to a degree of fatalism about his position, stating, 'if people become detached, at that level, in a crisis, it becomes difficult to get them to focus on the issue at hand'.[8] Prior to the crisis Reynolds had been abroad on an investment visit and had taken the plaudits for his immense efforts on the peace process. When he was out of the country there had been a calculated Labour party leak designed to bring him down a rung or two. An anonymous Labour source described him as 'punch-drunk' in the wake of the IRA ceasefire and behaving like 'the High King of Ireland on a roll'. Willie O'Dea believes 'hearing things at a distance, briefings in the media like that – I got the distinct impression that he was extremely angry about this kind of coverage when he came back.'[9] Labour's Fergus Finlay is fairly open about the fact that he was often suspected to be the perpetrator of such leaks: 'In the weeks leading up to the fall of that government, I came to realise that Albert Reynolds saw me as a malevolent influence, determined to wreck his government.'[10] Finlay believes Reynolds was driven by a need to be vindicated or given respect, and that he was unable to accept responsibility for the events that resulted in his undoing. In any event, Reynolds was bounced out of office, Ahern was denied the opportunity of replacing him, and Fianna Fáil was now out of power and in opposition. A parliamentary committee was set up to investigate how the government had fallen, but it went on to be hamstrung by rows over its remit.

Back in 1992, Frank Dunlop, a former government press secretary, had been drafted in to take control of the Fianna Fáil election campaign. The campaign had got off to a bad start:

> Albert's weakness was that he had a stubborn streak and once he got an idea into his head it was very difficult to shift him. He was not very good in a crisis – and Fianna Fáil was in a deep electoral crisis in November 1992. In such circumstances he tended to get strident, his style became domineering, and he alienated experienced figures in the party who, although they might not have been supporters of his, could have helped him with the difficulties in which the party found itself.[11]

Precisely two years later, in November 1994, Albert Reynolds was the subject of yet another crisis. As in 1992, his management of that crisis was suspect and lacked coherence. Bertie Ahern offers the view that the fact that he operated a kind of 'kitchen cabinet' of ministerial colleagues did not help him when it came to concerted action and support from colleagues when it was perhaps needed most.

Noel Whelan, the late commentator and party strategist, observed of Reynolds:

> Like many people in the country, the majority of his party colleagues and the party grass roots had a mixed attitude towards Reynolds. They respected him most of the time and had some affection for him, but they were always wary of where his words and deeds might lead. He seemed to be uninterested in party management, he was frustratingly bad at day-to-day political tactics, he was often gauche in his communications and he appeared blind to the need for either party unity or subtle coalition management. But he could do the big things well.[12]

A more prosaic explanation of Reynolds' deficiency, in terms of party management, was the fact that he had come to power following a debilitating power struggle to replace Haughey. Reynolds had taken over the party leadership and the position of taoiseach after Haughey had been in power for five years. The fate of leaders who take over mid-stream, or on the cusp of an election, can often be chequered, not least because they lack a direct electoral mandate from the people. Reynolds was in a desperate hurry to prove himself and did not have the time to assert himself over the party's election machinery. He had also alienated a significant faction in the party – the old Haugheyite rump. When it came to his own survival in 1994, the pro-Haughey faction was ruthless in ensuring he, Reynolds, was moved on. They had a willing, as well as a capable, replacement ready in the shape of Bertie Ahern. The speed with which Ahern replaced Reynolds is testament to the party's forlorn need to retain power and provide Labour with a more consensual figure with whom they could be comfortable.

Reynolds himself tells us:

> I was no longer Taoiseach, no longer worth guarding, and my privileges would slowly be stripped away. I was so utterly exhausted by the long hours of the last few days, the sleepless nights, the mental agonies, the devastating situation, the emotion of the day that I was now like

a zombie on automatic pilot completing the final ritual of my office, my resignation. I went home to Kathleen and closed the door on the world.

Tiredness and late nights do not make for a great performance in a crisis. The fabled 'night owl' status that Reynolds had enjoyed since his dancehall-promoting days had finally left him.

Freed from the burdens of high office, Reynolds was not going to allow himself rest for too long. He soon turned his gaze to the prize of becoming his party's nominee for the presidential election. It was a tantalising prospect for him and perhaps represented an opportunity for a modicum of validation of his life's work in politics. His departure as Taoiseach had damaged him and clearly the role of President would offer a certain redemption.

CHAPTER TWENTY-SIX

Presidential Nomination

Albert Reynolds may have been bounced out of his job as Taoiseach, but he soon dusted himself off. Within a month of leaving office, he was signed up by the New York-based Harry Walker Agency – a specialist company that offered elite opportunities for people who wanted to make some money on the international speaking circuit. This move saw Reynolds featured in the pages of *The Irish Times* in December.

The prospect of Reynolds committing to speaking engagements on the peace process, so soon after leaving office, appeared to fill senior British officials with a degree of apprehension. Roderic Lyne, a senior diplomat with Russian experience and private secretary to John Major, expressed his 'deep gloom' about the potential of a Reynolds speaking tour to the US. Lyne, according to the British state papers released subsequently, wrote to his opposite number in Sir Patrick Mayhew's office in the NIO, to outline countermeasures to any such tour noting, 'I think we should keep a careful eye on Reynolds' movements.'[1] Amongst the measures suggested were a direct appeal to Reynolds to mitigate his remarks and the activation of Irish intermediaries to influence him. Lyne also suggested 'some steps to shadow the Reynolds tour and try to counteract its influence on gullible American opinion.'[2] This note, written in the wake of Reynolds signing up for the Harry Walker Agency, shows the extent of British fear, as well as regard, for Reynolds. Notwithstanding the strong friendship between Reynolds and John Major, the British would be keeping tabs on him.

As it turned out, Albert Reynolds was to prove both telling and prophetic in his pronouncements on the peace process. With Fianna Fáil in opposition and John Bruton of Fine Gael in power, Reynolds held strong personal concerns about the direction of policy. 'I was not so sure about John Bruton. He was seen to favour the Unionist side more than the Nationalists, and I feared that progress in the peace process would now slow down,' he confides in his autobiography. Taoiseach Bruton was more hostile towards Sinn Féin, but had asked Reynolds' key advisor, Mansergh, to stay on in his role. However, Mansergh refused to remain, believing he could not work in the same way with Fine Gael.

Reluctant to stand back from the process he had done so much to advance, Reynolds contacted many of the main players to express the view that he was available if they needed help. Sinn Féin responded and Martin McGuinness was swiftly appointed to liaise with him. Reynolds had a better relationship with McGuinness than Adams and was never too shy about expressing this opinion. In the wake of the IRA ceasefire, the British government and unionists continued to drag their feet over the issue of the ceasefire itself – they held it suspicious that the word 'permanent', in relation to the end of the IRA's campaign, was absent from the formal statement. This kind of nit-picking was not to Reynolds' liking.

Reynolds insists, 'Bruton was not part of that continuity, as was evident when he joined with the British in making decommissioning a precondition for talks, in breach of my agreement with Sinn Féin.' He believed that the British understood, while he was Taoiseach, that decommissioning could not be framed as a demand as a precursor to Sinn Féin's inclusion in formal talks. Reynolds said he had a 'gentleman's agreement with John Major that Sinn Féin would be included in talks after six months of non-violence'. Major confessed, when interviewed for Reynolds' autobiography: 'I wasn't being obstructive or inflexible. I was just boxed in.' He still needed the unionist votes at Westminster and realpolitik meant he could not move on admitting Sinn Féin to talks. In fact, Major finished his premiership without once coming into contact with anyone from either Sinn Féin or the IRA, despite having authorised a flurry of back-channel contact throughout.

In early 1995, Bill Clinton appointed his friend George Mitchell as a formal US envoy to Ireland and the latter sat down with Reynolds to map out outstanding issues. Reynolds subsequently warned that 'if they [the IRA] went back to the armed conflict people won't blame them because they have shown good faith'. With this rather stark warning, Reynolds was attempting to warn the British directly of the prospect of the IRA ceasefire breaking down. He followed up his warning with a personal message to Downing Street on the issue. His appeal fell on deaf ears. Within months, on 9 February 1996, the IRA broke their ceasefire with a massive bomb in London's Canary Wharf. In the weeks prior, Reynolds had warned Major about the possibility of a collapse of the fragile peace.

Major believes that the IRA had carefully calculated this event. In Reynolds' autobiography, he is quoted as saying: 'They thought they might get a different and better deal from an incoming Labour government and so they were holding back [from engaging with the British government]. If we had been ahead in the opinion polls instead of behind I think we would have made much faster progress because they would have continued to deal with us'. Years later, as a member of the British–Irish parliamentary body, I discovered from a veteran Labour MP, Roger Stott, that there had been behind the scenes contact between the IRA and the British Labour Party, prior to the British general election, where certain assurances had been given.[3] The Stott admission to me has an uncanny resonance with Major's assessment.

Within a short time frame, both the Major and Bruton governments would be voted out, with Labour stepping into power in the UK and Fianna Fáil in Ireland. Reynolds, despite his lucrative earnings on the international speaking circuit, would again be a candidate for his party in the Longford–Roscommon constituency in the 1997 general election. Given how busy he was with business and speaking engagements, it was somewhat surprising that he opted to stand. Johnny Fallon believes that the party had nobody ready to replace him and that Ahern, facing his first full election as leader, was anxious to optimise the number of seats the party could win. Fallon also believes that Reynolds put himself forward so that he could be in a position to win the party's nomination to run for president later that year, from a position as a member of the parliamentary party.

The prospect of becoming president was, as Reynolds admitted, 'very tempting' and according to him, Ahern met with him and 'pointed out that my son Phillip could hold the seat in a by-election if I succeeded in winning the presidency, which he was sure I would, or so he said'. The meeting between

Reynolds and Ahern occurred in McGrattan's restaurant, near Government Buildings, a location frequently used by Ahern for confidential discussions. In the event, Reynolds was easily elected, with his colleague Seán Doherty winning a further Dáil seat for the party from the Roscommon side of the two-county constituency. Reynolds did not, however, top the poll on this occasion.

As soon as he was elected, Reynolds threw himself into the challenge of securing the party's nomination to run for the presidential election, which would happen towards the end of the year. I had been elected for the first time to the Dáil in the same election and sat for the constituency of Dublin South West. Reynolds and I had coffee, one day, at his request. He asked me for my support and advice on how he should win the nomination to run. I said he should put himself about in the Fianna Fáil deputies' constituencies by attending local functions. I suggested that he accept invitations to social events and launches of one kind and another, and parallel this with his contact with local members and representatives of the party. I gave Reynolds my assurance of support; later it emerged that my aunt, Mary O'Rourke, and brother, Brian Lenihan junior, had separately given their support to the other runners, Mary McAleese and Michael O'Kennedy respectively. My brother was friends with O'Kennedy as a fellow barrister, while O'Rourke supported McAleese on the basis that she was a woman and not Albert Reynolds. I had pledged to Reynolds due to my friendship with him as a journalist and as an intermediary of kinds in the peace process. The cynics around Leinster House tried to suggest that, as a family, we had a foot in every camp, but our decisions were arrived at entirely separately and without consultation with each other.

Reynolds went everywhere around the country and, in some cases, he was reported in the media to be at two geographically separate venues in different parts of the country on the same evening. Some of those who tried to piece this together felt he had hired a professional PR person to drop his name into every social diary event. This was not the case. Reynolds had appointed wealthy millionaire Eddie Haughey to the Senate and, at the time, he owned one of the few private helicopters in the country that could fly safely at night. Haughey, later created Lord Ballyedmond and appointed to the House of Lords, was a good friend to the ex-Taoiseach, as well as keeping him posted on business opinion in the North, where he owned a huge pharmaceutical company, and the helicopter had been made available to Reynolds.

Between the election and the formal nomination meeting of Reynolds' parliamentary party colleagues, a strong candidate was to emerge in the form of Mary McAleese, originally from the North. TDs, including myself, were sent letters from different parts of the country apparently from disinterested individuals, pushing for the party to nominate her as our candidate. It had the feel of an organised campaign. Mansergh, now Ahern's advisor, was sounded out on the prospect of McAleese as a candidate by none other than Fr Alec Reid. She had been an unsuccessful candidate for Fianna Fáil in the 1980s but had then moved back up to the North, where she was a prominent law lecturer in Queen's University Belfast. The idea for her to run had first been mooted before the general election and, in September, over a month before the contest, Mansergh was present when McAleese pitched Ahern on her bid in Government Buildings. 'Her quarter-of-an hour monologue on her vision of the presidency was a tour de force. Very persuasive, flowing and articulate,' recalled Mansergh.[4] Over the summer, McAleese had made private and personal contact with those deputies who would have been hostile to Reynolds, in some cases in their own homes, including Mary O'Rourke. Dermot Ahern, a previous chief whip, also became a vigorous supporter of McAleese, having lost his ministerial job in the big Reynolds' clear-out of Haughey loyalists. Quite a few Fianna Fáil TDs were taken by the potential of McAleese. Reynolds was not aware of these contacts at the time and was pressing ahead with his own campaign on the presumption, perhaps mistakenly, that he had Ahern's fulsome support.

David Harvey, a TV presenter who owns his own media production company, would have advised Fianna Fáil under different leaders on its annual Ard Fheis events. Harvey became an informal advisor to Reynolds in his bid to become the party's nominee for the presidency. The night before the formal nomination vote, he, Peter Finnegan who owned a PR firm, and Brian Crowley MEP met with Reynolds to discuss the communications strategy. When the discussions had finished, Harvey brought Crowley by car back to the Burlington Hotel. On the way, they passed Fianna Fáil headquarters on Mount Street. 'As we drove down Mount Street it was like a Mercedes Showroom. There were ministerial cars lining the street. We concluded that Albert was bunched,' says Harvey.[5] Inside party HQ, P.J. Mara, a key strategist, was co-ordinating with ministers and other party luminaries on how they would mobilise a vote for McAleese.

Bertie Ahern, in his own autobiography, sets out his position as follows:

> Once she [McAleese] declared, a lot of people were saying inside and outside of the party that it was time to put the controversies of the past behind us and move forward. That was how the balance started to swing. I recall the day before the election talking to Charlie McCreevy, who had been a big supporter of Albert, and to Tony Kett in St Luke's. 'It's slipping away from Albert,' Tony told me. 'What do you want us to do?' I told them to tell people the truth: that I was voting for Albert, because I had promised it to him, but that this was my personal vote. It was up to the parliamentary party to make its choice. I did not see it as part of my role to influence the vote.[6]

Johnny Fallon believes some of the key people around Ahern chose to give their backing to McAleese because they wanted a candidate with no baggage or link to the party's past. He says of Ahern: 'He didn't do anything to help. He didn't influence people to vote one way or another. From a cold strategist's point of view, the McAleese option was more desirable.'[7]

Prior to the actual vote in the parliamentary party, I warned Reynolds that they might spring on him the opportunity to speak at the meeting. He was of the view that there would be no speeches on the day and that members would simply nominate the three candidates standing. He assured me that he had been told this by party headquarters, which was organising the meeting. On the day, due to the fact that McAleese was not a member of the parliamentary party, she was ushered in to make an address. She then promptly left the room and Reynolds and Michael O'Kennedy were given their chance, in turn, to speak to the gathered TDs. Both of them seemed unprepared for this opportunity. They clutched notes and essentially made appeals to their colleagues on the basis of having known them for a long while. McAleese, as she had previously done in her presentation to Ahern at Government Buildings, had made a forceful impression and, on this occasion, it was to have a telling effect on wavering members of the parliamentary party.

There was palpable tension in the fifth-floor room where the parliamentary party met. Those like me, who were voting for Reynolds, sat near each other. It was hard to gauge how others, in particular the new intake of TDs, would vote. When the first vote was read out there was shock in the room. Reynolds had the most votes, but McAleese was within striking distance of him. The dozen or so votes which had gone to Michael O'Kennedy, who came third, would now come into play in a second ballot. It was something of a foregone conclusion that most of these would be harvested by McAleese. When the final result was announced, McAleese was the victor and Reynolds sat ashen-faced, wondering what had happened. Ahern, true to his word, had voted for Reynolds. Sitting close to Reynolds, he had gone so far as to show him his ballot. Seeing this gesture, Brian Crowley apparently turned to Reynolds and stated, 'You're fucked now, Albert.' As happens on such occasions, this vignette from Crowley became the most quoted story from the party meeting in the weekend media. The incident seemed to confirm Haughey's description of Ahern as 'the most skilful, the most devious and the most cunning of them all'. Ahern, in his own autobiography, concedes 'some of his supporters seemed to blame me for his defeat. They should have been asking why they hadn't run a better campaign for him.'[8]

David Harvey had gone into Leinster House that day to be with Reynolds in his hour of need: 'They just shafted him. There were a lot of old scores being settled. McAleese won it. People didn't want the potential controversy in an election around Albert.'[9] Quite a few of those sacked by Reynolds when he took over as Taoiseach back in 1992 were still members of the parliamentary party. Revenge was a definite motive, with people whispering in the corridors the old cliché: 'Those who live by the sword, die by it'. Reynolds had, once again, become the victim in the cruel business that is politics.

Mary McAleese went on to win the presidential contest and secure two terms, the second uncontested. Reynolds never quite forgave Ahern for what had happened. It was a bruising defeat and humiliation at the hands of someone who was a complete outsider. Reynolds' days of hanging around Leinster House were over. He did not stand as a candidate for the general election of 2002. Instead, he turned his attention back to his business interests. In addition, he pursued a hugely costly defamation action against the London-based *Sunday Times* over articles which had appeared in the paper. The action had begun shortly after he ceased being Taoiseach, but did not come to full trial until October–November 1996. Reynolds had gone to law in a London court this time and was on the hook for massive legal bills if the gamble didn't pay off.

CHAPTER TWENTY-SEVEN

Reputation

On 19 November 1996, after a five-week defamation trial before the British High Court in London, Albert Reynolds achieved something of a hollow victory. The jury, which took three days to deliberate over its verdict, decided, in answer to four questions put to them by the judge, that Reynolds had, in fact, been libelled by *The Sunday Times*. On hearing that the jury agreed he had been libelled, 'Mr Reynolds then smiled and winked at the press box.'[1] Reynolds' obvious joy was somewhat premature, however. In response to the further three questions put to the jury, the foreman of the jury indicated that the *Sunday Times* journalists who had written the article had not acted maliciously. The foreman simply said that Reynolds should get 'zero costs' with regard to damages or compensation. The trial judge later substituted 'one penny' in damages. It was a derisory award for a very inconclusive result. Reynolds was now facing legal bills of £1 million as a result of his search for vindication of his integrity in the British court. Some days later, he described the decision as unjust and immoral, and stated that he and his lawyers would be appealing the decision to the Court of Appeal – a decision that would then mean he faced £2 million in legal costs if he lost. Reynolds was raising the stakes.

The second trial was a strange affair, all the more so because an eleven-person British jury was being asked to adjudicate on the intricacies of Irish politics in relation to an issue that even Irish jurors would have found it hard to understand. The substance of the issue was two articles written by *The Sunday Times*, one in its Irish edition and the other in its UK edition. The UK edition had, in effect, stated that Reynolds had lied to his cabinet colleagues and the Dáil in relation to the issues that led to his resignation as

Taoiseach. Reynolds had no issue with what was printed in the Irish edition but highlighted the contrast between the two different articles as part of his evidence. The *Sunday Times* article, published in the aftermath of Reynolds' demise, carried the headline: 'Goodbye gombeen man – why a fib too far proved fatal for the political career of Ireland's peacemaker and Mr Fixit.'[2]

Reynolds' lawyer, Lord Gareth Williams QC, got to the nub of the issue quickly:

> If you call someone a fibber – let's not mess about it – what he is being called is a liar. *The Sunday Times* called Mr Reynolds a liar. They said he lied to the Dáil on November 15th, 1994, and misled his cabinet colleagues. If you call someone a liar, you have to prove it. And that is what this case is going to turn on.[3]

The jury in the original case had decided that, while the newspaper had not proven Reynolds was a liar, the gravity of the libel had not resulted in any great loss of reputation to the former Taoiseach.

Lord Williams then read one extract from the article itself to the jury:

> In another age, Albert Reynolds could have been the classic gombeen man of Irish lore; the local fixer with a finger in every pie. The fact that he rose from backwoods dance-hall manager to Taoiseach was a tribute both to his own brilliant cunning and the nature of Irish society. His slow fall last week, his fingernails screeching down the political cliff-face, has been welcomed with a whoop of delight by many Irish people who want to drag their country out of the past.

The article had only come to the attention of Reynolds thanks to his daughter Miriam, who was living in Edinburgh. Reynolds normally devoured the weekly as well as the Sunday newspapers, but on the Sunday after his resignation, he tells us, 'Yes, the papers were delivered as usual, but nobody, least of all me, had the stomach to read them. The entire family were completely exhausted, traumatised and shattered, both emotionally and physically.'

His eldest daughter agonised for hours over whether or not she should draw her father's attention to the article. According to Reynolds, she only finally made the call because 'she knew that she had been reared in a home where lies were not tolerated under any circumstances. The truth, the truth, the truth, she recalls that in our home, the truth was all that mattered.' Reynolds decided to take the matter further but ruefully conceded he never imagined that 'my issue with *The Sunday Times* on that day would play a major part of my life and my family's life for the next six years'.

The final round of the legal dispute would be a hearing before the British House of Lords – at the time, the final point of appeal in the British legal system. *The Sunday Times* finally settled their dispute with Reynolds with a frank admission that he had not lied to the Dáil or his government colleagues. The case and much of the coverage given to Reynolds during his active political career throw into relief the ambiguity of media attitudes towards him. Indeed, the *Sunday Times* article itself deployed adjectives and descriptions that many in Ireland would find hard to swallow if published in an Irish newspaper, let alone a British one.

Extra spice was added to the original trial by the presence of Fergus Finlay in the courtroom. While he was present in court, he was never actually brought into the proceedings to give evidence. Finlay had agreed to give evidence, when invited to by *The Sunday Times*, because the article written was 'based primarily on briefing given by me'. A lawyer for Reynolds had referred to him 'as a snake in the grass, a creature who skulked in the darkness and fashioned the dagger that Dick Spring had plunged into Albert's back'.[4] Finlay felt there was a tone to the *Sunday Times* article he did not like but, nonetheless, overall, he did not feel that the content justified a libel action. In the event, neither set of lawyers decided to call him as a witness. The Labour Party, which Finlay worked for, had put an element of pressure on him not to appear. Even Spring informed him that people were ringing him telling him that it was seen as wrong for Finlay to give evidence against Reynolds on behalf of *The Sunday Times*.

In his own book, *Snakes & Ladders*, Finlay struggles greatly with the personality or phenomenon that was Albert Reynolds. There is undisguised admiration for Reynolds' achievements in the peace process and Finlay expresses enormous gratitude to Reynolds for involving him so heavily in the discussions on the run up to the announcement of the Downing Street Declaration. He also perceptively talks about the importance Reynolds placed on reputation – the very concern which had driven him to take legal action against *The Sunday Times*. Finlay tells us:

> In the end I believe that Albert Reynolds suffered from an inferiority complex. He led us to a great achievement, in the form of an IRA ceasefire, and he presided over the greatest economic recovery in Ireland's history. His government, in a short space of time, introduced more far-reaching legislative reform than any other government. But it wasn't enough. His bottom line was respect, and he never felt he got enough. His endless quest for vindication about the events of that period, and his inability to accept some responsibility for the events that brought down his government, are proof enough for me that Albert Reynolds needed not just to be right, but to be seen to be right.[5]

Finlay attempts to attribute the fall of the Labour–Fianna Fáil government to Reynolds and his 'stubborn refusal to accept that he couldn't win every argument'.[6] This opinion, so eloquently expressed, has some merit, but it does not take into account any of the mistakes made by the Labour Party and its leader, Dick Spring, in the collapse of Reynolds' government. In the context of the peace process, it was a bad time to have a change of government in Dublin. In fact, subsequent events proved, beyond doubt, that the change of government in Dublin was to lead to a collapse in the IRA's ceasefire. At the time, however, the fragility of the peace process was deemed to be secondary to Labour apprehensions about further potential skeletons in the Fianna Fáil cupboard.

In taking on *The Sunday Times*, Reynolds had gambled again, at great personal cost, to vindicate his reputation in the British courts. His fierce protection of his personal reputation and rights was a consistent feature of both his business and public life. In his early business career, he was swift to resort to the law to carve out his own interests. Most notably, as referred to in an earlier chapter, he sued his brother Jim over what he felt was his due from their early dancehall business. This action led to a settlement but left a rift between Reynolds and his brother that took many years to heal. Formal contact between the two brothers was only finally restored in the period just before he became Taoiseach. One of Reynolds' earliest and most enduring personal friendships was with Dessie Hynes, a well-known Dublin publican and Longford man. Hynes expresses the opinion that 'if him and Jim hadn't disagreed, Albert would never have gone into politics'.[7]

Reynolds had also taken Matty Lyons – his co-founder at C&D Petfood – to court. This legal action, which saw Reynolds copper-fasten control over the company, also resulted in a legacy of bitterness and ill-will. Seán Duignan underlines the unease he felt at his boss's proclivity for vindication through the courts: 'Irrespective of the cost, he was not prepared to abide by Haughey's acceptance of the conventional wisdom that it would be counterproductive for him [Haughey] to take legal proceedings against those who smeared and vilified him.' Duignan, ever mindful of the impact suing the media would have on his own role, attempted to challenge Reynolds on this approach but was rebuffed: 'I don't care, Diggy. I'm not going to take that kind of thing lying down. Charlie felt he could do nothing about it, but if they tell lies about me, I will sue them, and to hell with the consequences.'[8]

Dessie Hynes believes that Reynolds was, first and foremost, a businessman in his attitude: 'He had a wonderful brain but it wasn't a political brain'.[9] The decision by Reynolds to confront the media directly on untruths that appeared in the coverage of him was principally directed at making the point that he was not prepared to endure the kind of coverage that his predecessor Haughey had endured. Reynolds, in my conversations with him, was hugely proud of the fact that he was a legitimate businessman who had achieved financial success through his own means. His open book approach to his own wealth and how it was earned is in stark contrast to that of Haughey. Haughey was, for his entire period in public life, surrounded by rumours and speculation about the source of his wealth and a belief that the money he had received was from dubious origins. It turned out later, after Haughey left public life, that he had been almost entirely supported by business friends or acquaintances. In this regard, Reynolds was quite different to Haughey. All of the wealth that Reynolds had acquired was due to his own efforts rather than the kindness of others. Effectively, Haughey was a kept man in financial terms, whereas Reynolds was the archetype of the self-made man – earning his own keep through his entrepreneurial skill. In personal, as well as financial, terms another lifelong friend of Reynolds from his show-business days, Eamon Monahan suggests that his success lay in the fact that he was straight in the transactions he entertained: 'I always found Albert to be right down the middle. There were no corners to Albert.'[10]

Reynolds once expressed to me his view that Haughey's personal finances meant he was utterly compromised in terms of his public duties. He also believed that Haughey's secretive banking and other arrangements meant that it was probably the case that he could be the subject of leverage due to the fact that his money was lodged in off-shore accounts in the British overseas territory of the Cayman Islands. It is implausible to assume that the British authorities, at the security level, were unaware of these off-shore arrangements, no matter how covert and secretive they were. There is, therefore, no mystery, given the revelations at public tribunals, about why Haughey was reluctant to become involved in legal actions against the media or indeed anybody else.

In his six years after leaving office, Reynolds kept himself busy. He was still a member of the Dáil, but not ready to run again. He had acquired a myriad of business involvements that took up much of his time. And, similarly, his failed bid to become his party's presidential nominee had taken up a great deal of his time too. In addition to this, the strain of the lengthy, six-year case against *The Sunday Times* had taken its toll. He was now going to have a quieter few years in retirement. Events arranged by the Harry Walker speaking agency would net him between $20,000 and $30,000 for a single engagement. According to the *Sunday Tribune*:

[H]e is said to be worth a cool £10 million on paper. His emergence as a fully fledged member of the seriously rich people's club is confirmed by the regularity with which rumours of his deals fly about business circles. The latest is that he reputedly made a million pounds profit in the last six months on a property transaction in Dublin.[11]

The same article indicated that Reynolds and his wife, Kathleen, had year-round tans and would be adding to them through their purchase of a ground-floor apartment in the Futura del Mar complex in Marbella, southern Spain. Justine McCarthy, the writer of the article, continued: 'Their seven children, who bought him a Jaguar when he resigned as Taoiseach, are well educated and embarked on good careers. One of them runs the Louis Vuitton shop in Brown Thomas. Like her daughters Kathleen Reynolds has a fondness for Prada suits with stitched in thousand-pound price tags.'[12] Psychologically and financially, Reynolds was kicking off the remaining dust of his public life with a full return to what he knew best – business. The disappointments of his Irish political life were behind him once and for all.

CHAPTER TWENTY-EIGHT

Business Again

Over the years, Albert Reynolds had built up an influential network of international contacts. Amongst these was the President of Pakistan, Pervez Musharraf, whom Reynolds knew from Musharraf's previous role as Prime Minister and Chief of Staff of Pakistan's army. In 1999, Musharraf effected a *coup d'état* and, in the wake of this, was concerned about his relations with the West. Pakistan was, according to Reynolds, 'seen as a haven for terrorists and most western countries had in place a policy of sanctions against it'. Musharraf rang Reynolds seeking his advice. His worry was that if he could not build a strong economy, Muslim extremists in his country would grow in power. Reynolds put in a call to Bill Clinton and warned him about the difficulties in Pakistan. As a result of Reynolds' intervention, Clinton amended his travel schedule for a visit to India and Bangladesh so that it also included Pakistan. Musharraf also wanted to do some bridge-building in the country's fractured relationship with India. Senator Ted Kennedy, another friend of Reynolds, was appointed as a mediator between the two countries and that led to meetings between the two heads of state. Reynolds also fulfilled advisory roles in Vietnam and Zimbabwe.

Life was proving to be busy for him in retirement from politics. 'I might be in my twilight years, but I am not finished,' he joked to a journalist from the *Irish Independent* in an interview in 2002.[1] Reynolds was invited to join a UN trust fund based in New York that was raising $10 billion in the fight against AIDS in Africa. That invitation came from his friend Bill Clinton. Additionally, it was reported that:

Since he left the Dáil, Albert Reynolds, who will be 61 this year, has, according to his daughter Emer, been far busier that when he was in office. He is a director of six companies, having joined the board of the Smurfit Group just last week-end, but the most time consuming of the lot appears to be China Strategic holdings (CSH), a Far Eastern investment group which holds a majority interest in 140 companies.[2]

His role with CSH was to broker European capital for investment in China for companies based there. The appointment to the Jefferson Smurfit Group's board was hardly a surprise given his strong friendship with its owner Michael Smurfit. Reynolds was the first former Taoiseach to be appointed to this board since Jack Lynch had become a director after stepping down as Taoiseach.

It was not all plain sailing for Reynolds, however, when he took on the non-executive chairmanship of Bula Resources, a public-quoted oil and gas exploration company. He was pushed out as chairman after three years, with shareholders expressing disappointment at his stewardship of the company. Reynolds told the *Irish Independent* he would not miss being chairman of Bula: 'Some shareholders that bought into Bula expected to be joining a get-rich club. When you buy shares you should expect to lose. Some people waited too long before selling their shares.'[3] The shareholders' annual general meeting had been a disaster, with much recrimination over failed deals in the Middle East, conflicts of interest and reference to another company Reynolds was involved in called the Life Energy Corporation – a US NASDAQ listed company. There were also stories about visits to Libya when an investment company owned by Colonel Gaddafi's son was due to invest in Bula. Reynolds cited a 'potential conflict of interest' as his reason for not putting himself forward again to be chairman.

Reynolds had paid a number of visits to Libya down the years, meeting with Gaddafi on a trade visit back in the 1980s. He also met him again while travelling there on behalf of Bula Resources. In the summer of 1997, he made a further trip at the behest of Purcell Meats, a Waterford-based company that had multiple contracts for exporting live cattle both from Ireland and other parts of the world. Due to a BSE outbreak, Irish cattle could no longer be exported to Libya. Seamus Purcell and his son, Gerry, accompanied Reynolds on a private plane to see if they could get Gaddafi to re-open the live cattle trade from Ireland, which would have benefitted the Purcell export operation and protected Irish farmers from falling prices. Purcell Meats had paid for educational exchanges for Libyan students studying in Ireland and had arranged previous visits to the country involving Irish ministers and also Charles Haughey, when the latter was in opposition in the 1980s.

The three men landed in Tripoli, accompanied by an agricultural vet, and the business delegation was summoned to a meeting in the desert with the Libyan leader. Gerry Purcell believes they simply would not have got the meeting were it not for the 'gravitas' and connections Reynolds had: 'Albert was brilliant and very commercial as well. There was a presentation from the vet on the BSE situation. Reynolds and Gaddafi discussed the state of play in Northern Ireland. Gaddafi was very well briefed and had a huge file in Arabic in front of him about Ireland.'[4] In the event, it proved impossible to lift the ban on Irish beef, but Purcell Meats managed to get the contract to supply the Libyans from Australia.

Also on their flight on a military transport jet to meet with Gaddafi in the desert was a Scottish politician, who was trying to intervene with the Libyan leader over the idea of compensation for the victims of the Lockerbie bombing. Two hundred and seventy civilian passengers had lost their lives in 1988 in an operation which Gaddafi had apparently authorised. According to Reynolds, 'During my talks with Quadhafi [Gaddafi] I had discussed the subject of compensation for the victims, and an idea had emerged.' It was the first time that families of victims of a terrorist attack had been offered compensation by a state that had sponsored this kind of terrorism. Reynolds rang Ted Kennedy and indicated the Libyan interest in offering compensation. He later recorded, 'I was not involved with the actual negotiations, only the principle – which was actually more of a business deal than an acceptance of responsibility by Libya; but it resolved an impasse and helped move things forward.'

The success of Reynolds' business ventures was now such that he decided, with Kathleen, to sell the apartment in Ballsbridge that had initially been his base in Dublin but eventually became the family home. This very up-market apartment was where most of his discreet political meetings had been held. It had also been a home for his children when they attended university and the family's primary residence was still in Longford. Now, Reynolds moved into the plushest of addresses on Dublin's Ailesbury Road, reputedly paying £600,000 for the property in 1995. He had struck it lucky again. This large house, perhaps too large for his and Kathleen's needs, was to be sold in late 2007 for a sum of £14 million. The sale of the house occurred at the top of the run-away property boom in Ireland during the Celtic Tiger years, after Reynolds and his wife decided to downsize to an exclusive condominium that was on the top floor of the five-star Four Seasons Hotel in Ballsbridge. The family was now all grown up and all the children had moved away from home.

During his retirement from politics, Reynolds was scheduled to appear before the Mahon Tribunal – a public tribunal of inquiry into alleged corruption in the granting of planning re-zonings in north Dublin, which soon expanded its remit to look at wider issues of financial donations to politicians. His appearance before it was widely anticipated. At the centre of his appearance was the issue of a donation of £80,000 that he solicited for the Fianna Fáil party from the Cork developer Eoin O'Callaghan. There was no suggestion that Reynolds had personally received the donation, but in its concluding report, Judge Alan Mahon deemed the soliciting of the donation in the first place to be an 'abuse of political powers and government authority'.[5] The Mahon Tribunal had come to this conclusion on the basis that Reynolds was Taoiseach at the time and O'Callaghan was lobbying government for a stadium project he was promoting in the western suburbs of Dublin. It may have seemed a harsh judgement to Reynolds, all the more so because he was eventually unable to give evidence before the Tribunal to defend himself due to ill health. A further adverse finding was that he had been told of a £50,000 donation to his ministerial ally Pádraig Flynn back in 1992 and had never pursued the matter further.

Lawyers on behalf of Reynolds had written to the Tribunal indicating he was unable to give evidence for health reasons. The tribunal was sent medical reports from his GP and two medical consultants stating that he was not in a fit state to testify. The Tribunal did not take this report for granted and appointed its own medical consultants to assess him. Chairman Alan Mahon concluded that Reynolds had a 'significant cognitive impairment which renders him unfit to give evidence'.[6] It was a sad state of affairs and all the more so for the pressure this must have placed on his wife and family. According to his eldest son, Phillip, some five years later, the family felt hurt by suggestions that it was somehow an illness of convenience, stating, 'He has been ill for a long time. He is in the very late stages of Alzheimer's. He has been suffering slowly with it for five years now.'[7] Phillip went on to describe how his father's illness began to become obvious: 'As a family we started to recognise it at various times and those of us who would see less of him rather than more of him would have remarked on it.'[8]

Prior to the onset of this terrible illness, Albert Reynolds had been a very active man. He and Kathleen had been frequent contributors to and attendees at prominent charity events. Reynolds had received awards for the generosity of his work for public charities of one sort or another. To the outside world, at least, he seemed active and well. However, to those who knew him and who met with him often, there were telltale signs even then that he was losing his memory. I remember on one occasion him whispering in my ear, 'Who is this fella we're talking to – remind me of his name.' It was often someone whom he would previously have recognised instantly and known well. It was a great testimony to Reynolds, his family and friends, that few spoke about his gradual disappearance from the social scene during this time.

Reynolds' autobiography, published in 2009, has the appearance of something put together quite swiftly. A gifted TV screenwriter, Jill Arlon from the UK, was drafted in to do the interviews with him, and some key friends and former ministers who were close to him. It is a mine of information about Reynolds' life but comes up short on detail. Like most autobiographies, it errs on the side of caution. The autobiography was published, but Reynolds himself was not available for media interviews about the book, though extracts appeared in the national media.

During his retirement, prior to the onset of his illness, Reynolds had impressed a great many people, in particular because few if any of his public appearances, interviews and utterances displayed any modicum of bitterness about his political demise. He had that quality of simply picking himself right back up after experiencing personal adversity or a set-back. Unfortunately, with the onset of his debilitating illness from 2008, he was not able to do this again.

CHAPTER TWENTY-NINE

Farewell

Shortly before Albert Reynolds died, I rang Kathleen and asked if I could come up and see him. They were still living in the penthouse apartment they shared in Dublin's Four Seasons Hotel. Kathleen poured me tea and offered me a bun. Outside, the noise of the Dublin Horse Show was getting underway. She seemed sheepish about Albert. His Alzheimer's was at an advanced stage. He was under round-the-clock care. She warned me that he might not recognise me. There was a television at the end of his bed, its big screen radiating out a folksy entertainment show. There was not a glimmer of recognition, but he was smiling, unaware of what was going on. The entertainment show was played and watched constantly. It was an awkward moment. Kathleen and I left him, and there was a trace of sadness on her countenance when she told me that this was all he watched.

Reynolds had lived a bustling life and it seemed sad that things should end this way. Kathleen and I chatted in her kitchen, over another cup of tea. She spoke about her children, grandchildren, and what they were all doing. In that small, social exchange, I got to understand how lucky Reynolds was. The two had met while very young and with nothing to show for themselves. But in choosing Kathleen, Reynolds had not gambled at all. Nor had she. Reynolds had provided well for his family and Kathleen had always been there for him. Neither of them could have imagined back in Ballymote, County Sligo, that life would give them so much.

Reynolds had conducted his business career and public life with a ruthless ambition, always to better himself and, at the same time, to ensure that his wife and family wanted for little. His life's journey had criss-crossed the worlds of media, showbusiness, bacon production, petfood, politics and the high altar of power. He had made big money and dealt with an enormous number of people along the way. He was a restless gambler, always with an eye to the main chance. Along the way, both in politics and business, he had rubbed up against and co-opted a strange collection of eclectic friends. It was all in the way of business – he was always moving on. He knew he had to make something of himself and, like someone accustomed to playing cards for money, always had to be involved in the next game. The extent and variety of his involvements after his premature retirement from politics spoke volumes about his ability to try virtually anything. It was as if he was endlessly trying to prove he could make a difference. This, despite the fact that by championing the ordinary notion of peace and bringing together the motley crew of moving parts that made up the dizzy, helter-skelter, bumpy ride to the Downing Street Declaration with its consequent IRA ceasefire, he already had. Peace, he was wont to say, came dropping slowly.

On 21 August 2014, Albert Reynolds died. His daughter Miriam told a hushed funeral mass that, in his life, he had often been reviled, isolated and set apart, alone. It came as a surprise to many, in that church in Donnybrook, that he had, in that sense, been a victim of his own success. His business life had been one of hard work, networking and trusting his own, often impeccable, judgement. There were very few enemies made from his involvement in the 'cut-throat' business of music promotion and entertainment. In fact, some of the nicest things said about him came from the people who inhabit that world. The reputation he took away from this business was one of honesty and plain dealing. His straightforward business attribute of acknowledging 'it is what it is' followed him into politics. Reynolds could listen to a lot and process things quickly. He never showed his impatience, so, to outward appearances at least, he seemed open to all. Behind that impassive expression, though, was a man who knew his own mind. He preferred to make quick decisions, moving on swiftly to whatever action was required.

His prickly concern about his own reputation came as a surprise to most of those he met in the world of politics. The journalists and politicos he had indulged imbibed the hail-fellow-well-met image that he conveyed.

Many of the people who praised this quality in him failed to understand that in the world of business, shaking hands is not how you earn your way. Reynolds frequently had to seek recourse to the law to get what he was, in fact, owed. There were High Court actions against friends and family in the dancehall business and at the very outset of the C&D Petfood venture. As we have seen, one of the lawsuits was against his old friend Matty Lyons, another against his brother Jim. In the context of the 1960s, Reynolds was wealthy by the age of 30, when he settled down to marry and secure himself with his family and a future. He only became involved in the public realm, Chamber of Commerce, County Council and Dáil when he had enough time and money to do so. His purchase of the *Longford News* was an inspired decision. In becoming a newspaper owner, Reynolds put himself on the map. He was no longer just another businessman from Longford; he had stepped unobtrusively onto the national stage. In the small-town setting of Longford, if you are not the doctor, the lawyer or the bank manager, then being the local newspaper owner makes you a figure in the town, someone to be reckoned with. By delegating the task of actually running the paper to someone else, the *Longford News* became a profitable venture as well.

Many newspaper ventures in Ireland stumble from profit to loss because they are family-owned, quixotic and involve a little bit of vanity on the owner's behalf. Not so the *Longford News*, which also gave Reynolds a certain standing and credibility with the journalism profession in Ireland. His many connections in business, media and show business hastened his progression up the political career ladder. Picked out as a supporter of Charles J. Haughey at the Arms Trial, he took the fast-track route to public office. He spent less than three years as a backbencher before becoming a cabinet minister. Coincidentally, he also spent less than three years as holder of the office of Taoiseach. There was a hurried and driven aspect to his character. His first ministerial appointment as Minister for Posts and Telegraphs was not the kind of role that would set most people alight, but Reynolds had a desire to deliver and was soon given the additional responsibility of Transport, something he must have considered ironic given that his first settled job was as a lowly administrator working for the rail company. As a minister, he was high impact, and the manner in which he took over and transformed the telephone system in Ireland was, at any level, impressive. His predecessor in the role, Conor Cruise O'Brien, was a public intellectual of some repute who had not fully grasped the challenge of transforming a ramshackle department of state. While Cruise O'Brien spent most of his cabinet energies pursuing and sounding the alarm about the IRA, Reynolds spent all of his time pushing for service delivery improvement. Reynolds never lost his Dáil seat and constantly focused on the job in hand. Of course, these two ministers operated in different times and under different styles of leadership but, while Cruise O'Brien spent most of his public life and commentary excoriating the IRA and seeking to marginalise them further, in a few short years as Taoiseach, Albert Reynolds pulled the IRA away from violence and into a process of compromise focused on basic aims.

Reynolds' decision to embark on a peace process was replete with danger. The early reaction of the country's largest selling newspaper, the *Sunday Independent*, to his efforts was negative and vitriolic in the extreme. Columnist Eoghan Harris said if the government persisted with the peace process, 'it will end with sectarian slaughter in the North, with bombs in Dublin, Cork and with the ruthless reign by provisional gangs over the ghettos of Dublin'.[1] The columnist went on to advise that if this abyss was to be avoided, 'the cord to John Hume' must be cut. In the same newspaper, Conor Cruise O'Brien was weekly warning of a doomsday scenario and civil war encompassing the whole island of Ireland.

The Hume–Adams dialogue, which lies at the very origins of the peace process, was gratefully embraced by Reynolds. Combined with his own efforts in the background, the initiative was integrated into an Irish government drive by Reynolds to prompt and cajole an often unwilling British government into steadfast action. Reynolds was no passive participant in what was to unfold. The demands made by him of John Major and Bill Clinton were both measured and awkward at the same time. He pushed them to the limits of patience and friendship, yet he was proven right. He had not, when it came to peace, gambled too far.

If the peace process itself was a source of extreme comment about Reynolds, there were plenty of other examples. As he made his way up the greasy pole of Fianna Fáil politics, there was ample opportunity for others to pull him down. His emotional commitment to Haughey was to become, for Reynolds, as in the case of others, a sort of metaphorical crown of thorns. He had willingly helped Haughey put down his internal critics – Colley, O'Malley and, of course, his old friend Charlie McCreevy. This was done on the basis of loyalty and the need for internal party discipline. When it became clear in the mid-1980s that Reynolds' previously dependable loyalty could no longer be relied upon, a strange but damaging narrative about him was built upon. He was increasingly defined as outside the Haughey 'Golden Circle', with all that this involved. There were subtle smears launched against him. He was, in the telling of these, a provincial 'grasping' businessman with no cultural insight to offer. It was ironic that the urban liberals and the Haughey toughs found common cause in sneering at Reynolds as an 'unlettered culchie' from Longford. Reynolds was more wounded than he ever cared to admit by the sneers, but he pressed on regardless, confident that the majority of Fianna Fáil TDs would back him. However, the sneering did colour his generally benign attitude towards the media and he issued writs against *The Irish Times* on a number of occasions.[2]

The question is – was Albert Reynolds hard done by? The answer is a definitive no. He had the humility to recognise that one took the rough with the smooth. He was the subject of social snobbery and, at times, very negative commentary. He took most of this on the chin and, like most politicians, was an over-eager consumer of what newspapers wrote. As a former journalist, who turned to politics, I was always amazed at the length of time my ministerial colleagues would spend analysing the tiniest detail of comment by the media. Having been in both professions, the paranoia that newspaper commentary induces in practising politicians was quite surprising to me. By and large, politicians over-read media, seeing quite a lot of significance where there is none at all. On the other hand, journalists quite often attribute conspiracy theories to randomly existing or unconnected facts.

Reynolds was very close to journalists over the years and did not mind openly mixing in their company; in this respect, he was part of a new breed of politicians who came into office in the mid- to late 1970s. This generation was very quick to realise the oxygen that publicity gave. The older generation, in political terms, was a little bit more wary and elitist in its approach. Reynolds, more than most, given his previous experience as a business promoter in the music scene, knew that the media was a key way to get your message across. When he transferred to politics, he continued to use this approach, perhaps sometimes forgetting that overfamiliarity with the media can, in some minds at least, breed a certain contempt.

Notwithstanding the money and power he accumulated, Reynolds was never a snob. He could and would talk to anyone. He processed a myriad of requests and conversations while staying alert. Some years previous to his death, he fetched up at a funeral in Roscommon for an uncle of mine. Uncle Paddy had been on the council but had split from the party to join Independent Fianna Fáil. Reynolds was a welcome presence on a cold day. His conversational skills, honed by years of practice, could always keep you in thrall. He was sociable but never afraid of being on his own. After the burial, he stood in the freezing cold in a graveyard that was elevated to the wind. He, my brother Brian and I fell into conversation about the uncle, politics and Roscommon. Reynolds offered great advice, in particular to my brother about the officials in the Department of Finance, where Brian was then minister. It was only as the conversation petered out that we realised all the other family and mourners had gone. We were on our own in the graveyard and quickly made our way to the cars. There was no entourage – just his driver and a car. It was my last time to see him in full health.

CHAPTER THIRTY

Legacy

Anthony Cronin, the distinguished poet, writer and literary critic, once assessed the life of Charles Stewart Parnell by stating: 'Alone amongst parliamentarians he never fell in love with parliament.' It was a fitting tribute to the Anglo-Irish, nineteenth-century, Protestant leader of nationalist Ireland, who had spent a lifetime fighting for Irish tenant rights and Home Rule. Parnell's life work ended in failure, his reputation in tatters, in what his once loyal colleague Tim Healy MP referred to as the 'stench of the divorce court'. Parnell, a single man, had defied conventional nineteenth-century morality by daring to have an affair with Kitty O'Shea, a married woman estranged from her husband, Captain O'Shea. When news of this emerged in divorce proceedings, he was harried by popular sentiment, but most of all by the British Liberal Party establishment and its supporters, who were then in the grip of what can only be termed Victorian morality. Parnell's sin was an affront to Gladstone's deeply religious, non-conformist political base. The political hounding of Parnell, both in Ireland and Britain, carries with it from today's perspective, the smell of rich hypocrisy. Like Parnell, Albert Reynolds realised that real power did not just reside within parliament, but in the great hordes of wisdom outside of its purview.

Reynolds, in his career trajectory, was the only leader of nationalist Ireland, since Parnell, to create a similar alliance, or new departure, that involved bringing together the forces of insurrection, or armed opposition to British rule, the parliamentary or constitutional impulse and the necessary heft of Irish America, with its incalculable influence, to the aid of the Irish cause at home in Ireland. In his iconic three-way handshake with John Hume and Gerry Adams on the footsteps of Dublin's Government

Buildings, he confirmed the overwhelming desire of Irish nationalism to come to a reasonable peace with its Protestant or unionist co-brethren. It was a powerful moment, symbolising a common purpose to take the gun out of Irish politics. Reynolds followed this up with an equally symbolic greeting and meeting with David Trimble, the then leader of Ulster unionism. The heady idealism of that period was followed by an intense and long drawn-out peace process. Reynolds, using his entrepreneurial instincts, risked all his political capital and his reputation in the cause of achieving peace. However, due to the long delay after his efforts, in a substantial sense he has not been given full and due credit for what he achieved.

Reynolds' simple pursuit of the idea of peace won him many plaudits and stands the test of time as his finest legacy for the years he spent in power. This was no simple matter and involved high stakes negotiation as well as great sophistication. In this respect, all of his skill sets and flaws as a personality became a distinct advantage in the high-pressure period between the emergence of the Hume–Adams dialogue, the signing of the Downing Street Declaration and the formal announcement of the IRA ceasefire in the late summer of 1994. There was so much suspicion of motives, on all sides of the conflict, that it was something of a political miracle that he managed to pull it off. He had nerves of steel and great *sang froid* at key moments in this rollercoaster period, perched between escalating acts of violence and the tantalising prospect of peace. Of course, he did not accomplish this on his own. Other notable public figures like John Hume, Gerry Adams, John Major and Bill Clinton were also taking big risks, as were loyalist paramilitaries, members of the clergy, key intermediaries, diplomats, and a whole cast of invisible people lending their weight. The key point is that Reynolds was at the centre of it and was one of the few players in the process, if not the only one, who managed to create the networks of influence and contact with those that could, materially, move things forward.

The crucial characteristic that Reynolds had in all this was an abiding refusal to discriminate against people. He had this intrinsic ability to listen and give time to people irrespective of what background, social origin or place they were coming from. It was this patient ear and mind that made him so amenable to the contradictory and toxic differences that existed in the Irish conflict. Anyone who, he felt, could have an influence was mobilised to his particular cause in this case. As a personal witness to his efforts, I concluded that there was none amongst his predecessors as Taoiseach, or those who followed after him, who could have operated with such calm in such difficult circumstances. It was his business instinct of striking a deal and, in a transactional sense, leaving enough in the deal for the other side that made him different.

Reynolds, like Parnell, lost public office and authority in a maelstrom of controversy. Parnell lost his British Liberal alliance partners and, in a slow, drawn-out conflict, Catholic Ireland, too. Reynolds, for his part, lost the confidence of his coalition partners in a bewildering series of provocations and pedestrian power struggles, defined by mutual suspicion. When distrust begins to fester in the corridors of power, tragedy is almost always the result. So dangerous and non-consensual was his approach to his dealings with Dick Spring that when one reads of them in retrospect it becomes an object lesson in how not to run a coalition government. Similar errors were made with his previous coalition partner Des O'Malley. It has become conventional wisdom to state that these failures were inevitable, but, in all honesty, the burden of responsibility for what happened lies squarely with Reynolds himself. When he spoke about failure in business, Reynolds was often speaking about the failures of management. In his own case, his failure to maintain stable coalition governments was mainly his own fault – the buck stops with the boss.

Not unlike Parnell, Reynolds was seemingly oblivious to the risks he was taking. He had that hauteur of a person who knows his own mind. He had a significant business and political career behind him before he mounted the podium of political leadership as Taoiseach. There was a steely obstinacy and determination to his character that spoke to the fabled notion of the 'self-made man'. This obduracy and obstinacy can work well in business, but it pays little dividend in the shifting sands of politics.

The words 'ruthless' and 'ambitious' were often used about Reynolds, and even more so when he began to climb the greasy pole of public life. These adjectives can be a compliment or a criticism, depending on whether you are in business or politics. Reynolds operated successfully in both fields. His entrepreneurial nature, impatience, practical directness and willingness or appetite for taking risks meant that he achieved extraordinary things in politics. These characteristics also, ultimately, led to his downfall. It may, of course, be the case that Reynolds in this, as in many other aspects to his life, saw himself as a congenital outsider in the very hostile world of politics, a man of action rather than words, and a risktaker against a very risk-averse establishment. He certainly seems to have taken this attitude into government and played foolishly high stakes with his own career and that of his party.

Historians, rightly, beg to differ over any historical comparison between Reynolds and Parnell. They operated in distinct and different eras of Irish life. The alliance Parnell put together was precarious and involved parliament, the 'Hillside men' and the large agrarian agitation for change of land ownership; from a funding perspective and influence perspective, he cultivated Irish America and was greatly assisted in this path by the Fenian Brotherhood; he was unique also in his dependence on support from the Catholic Church and its priestly power on the ground.

Reynolds lived in a very different era – an era of diminishing and diminished clerical power. While a devout Catholic, clean-living and a family man, he was not afraid to confront the Catholic bishops and hierarchy when they started to make discomforting noises about abortion. At one point, it appeared that the Church was prepared to oppose his support of the Maastricht referendum on the grounds that it did not safeguard Ireland from the introduction of abortion at a domestic level. Reynolds did not cede to them the right to dictate on this most important treaty for both Europe and Ireland. In fact, his open rift with the Church, most public in its expression, was a daring power play on his part and, substantially, he won. The eminent bishops retreated in front of him. Reynolds was, of course, helped by the coincidence of the revelations about Archbishop Eamonn Casey and his relationship with an American woman with whom he had a child. The fact that this relationship had not just been covered up for years, but also that it involved the use of Church funds, came as a real shock to Irish people. It marked a symbolic and formal end to ecclesiastical influence over matters of state in Ireland.

Reynolds' effort to respond to the public scandal of the X Case was considered, even though it did not resolve what was politely termed the 'substantial issue' – whether or not a woman had a right to have an abortion in Ireland. His preferred response was to constrain the right to have an abortion to very limited circumstances. However, the referendum he staged on the issue was to have far-reaching consequences. His proposal, on the substantive issue, was voted down by the public but, though it took many more years, it opened up a path for the removal of the Constitution's outright ban on a woman's right to choose. Reynolds was a conservative on this issue and was, in conscience, probably opposed to abortion. He was a most unlikely candidate to put the idea of introducing abortion in Ireland and calculated that he would be defeated if it went to a vote. Even if he had not been conservative, the political system was not ready, until many years later, to grapple with the issue in a liberalising direction. However, the two other liberalising changes put to the people on the same day were both passed – the right to travel abroad for an abortion and the right to information about abortion services outside the state. These were liberal measures in the context of the time and the issues thrown up by the X Case. They also made common sense, although they had the unfortunate consequence of opening the state and the constitution to the accusation of hypocrisy, in that an Irish citizen was now fully entitled to have an abortion provided they chose to have that abortion overseas.

Many of the characteristics Reynolds had learned as a youth, honed in business and then carried into political life, were a distinct advantage as he pursued his career in politics. His sense of political organisation learned at the feet of a great master of electoral politics, Neil T. Blaney, was one such skill. Such was his success in his own Longford constituency that one observer concluded that Longford, at times, resembled a one-party state. It was an amusing observation, but it indicated his determination to achieve stability on home turf while he scaled the dizzy heights of national politics. As the famous Speaker of the House in the US, Tipp O'Neill, once observed, 'all politics are local'. Reynolds was never going to allow local constituency vulnerability to threaten his determination to succeed. He also largely safeguarded his own fortune before dipping his toe into the shark pool of Irish politics. His family and marriage were a great source of stability and refuge in the context of his very busy climb to the top.

What marked him out most as a minister was his ability to both implement and execute the policy goals he set out to achieve. He deserves enormous credit for his transformation of the Irish telephone service. In the case of the Cork to Dublin gas pipeline, a big public piece of infrastructure which might have been very pricey and involved costly budget over-runs, he made a simple demand: that contractors, civil servants and everybody involved committed to bringing it in at cost and on time. Public life in Ireland is littered with examples of projects that over-run on cost and are mismanaged from start to finish. Reynolds' ability to become involved, hands on, was commented upon by civil servants who worked under him. This is in stark contrast to many ministers who came after him, in particular during the years of wealth creation with the Celtic Tiger.

This ability to get things done was a feature of his entire adult life. Many who knew him found it hard to believe the energy he had, even when he grew older and retired from politics. He retained a grace and alertness though he never shunted people off. If you put something to him that was not going to work, he would candidly tell you 'that's not on', but he was never rude in the way he said it. Politicians are often expected to shuffle people around and people-pleasing comes as second nature to them. Reynolds had the people-pleasing skills on an interpersonal basis, but he would also look you in the face when he said, 'No.'

Reynolds suffered very much at the hands and in the shadow of his first real political boss – Charles J. Haughey. For a period in his early career, there was nobody like Haughey for Reynolds. Haughey gave him all of his important promotions. Such was the emotional respect Reynolds had for Haughey that he was close to tears when he spoke of him in a film documentary recorded for RTÉ. He was far more sentimental and emotional than Haughey but, like any public person, sought to hide that fact. Yet some of those who witnessed his speech before his party colleagues on the occasion that he supported a formal challenge to Haughey's leadership depict it as almost the political equivalent of an emotional breakdown. He claimed he had been put under surveillance by Haughey and his cronies. Some who were present felt that Reynolds was acting; however, when it came to Haughey, there was a fifty–fifty chance that it could actually have been true.

While Reynolds got all his promotions from Haughey, Haughey also made his life a misery. As soon as he discerned that there was a potential wavering in Reynolds' loyalty to him, he moved ruthlessly to discredit him. The Haughey coterie of cronies was lethal when it came to low-level smears against rivals. The most famous rumour put about relating to Reynolds was that he had intentionally set fire to some of his business premises in order to make inordinate insurance claims. The derisive nickname 'Ronson Reynolds' was often used in the context of these stories.[1] To date, nobody has provided a shred of documentary or witness proof to substantiate such rumours. Still the 'Ronson Reynolds' tale is told and retold even to this day.

The most potent smear launched against Reynolds, again by Haughey acolytes, was the notion that he was some kind of country bumpkin. This particular smear spawned the description of Reynolds and those who supported him as being the 'Country & Western Alliance'. It was a blatant attempt by Haughey to depict his internal opponents as a hick, country mob, who were morally, culturally and intellectually his inferiors. The smear was very hard to shake off as Reynolds had, at one point, appeared on a TV light-entertainment programme dressed in a Stetson and cowboy regalia.

The default position for many of those spreading these kinds of stories was a kind of intellectual snobbery and depiction of Reynolds as some kind of brash businessman – in a phrase, *nouveau riche*. Despite demonstrable success in the business arena, Reynolds was often depicted in this way behind the scenes.

It is hard to imagine that these slights and cuts were not keenly felt by him and his supporters, and all of these put-downs and smears only made Reynolds more determined to dislodge Haughey. On one occasion, after Reynolds' failed heave against Haughey, supporters of Reynolds, waiting outside the Leinster House gates, were reprimanded by the Party's Chairman Jim Tunney with the words: 'You are not at a County Final.'[2] Reynolds' supporters, not surprisingly, resented the condescending chastisement directed at them by a leading Haughey supporter. Reynolds' people, like Reynolds himself, decided not to get angry but to get even instead.

Haughey's long period of time in politics and in power, ultimately, deeply divided the party he led, almost down the middle. In his final years, he had become disdainful and arrogant about the merits of those who opposed him. Reynolds had formed the view, well before Haughey retired, that he was deeply corrupt and in danger of ruining the party's reputation in the long term. Part of Reynolds' political legacy, thus, is that it was he alone who decided to bring the Haughey era to an end. This was no mean achievement on his part. From his close observation of Haughey in his position as cabinet minister and finally in his role as Minister for Finance, Reynolds grew to understand fully and to his horror how corrupt Haughey had become. It was something he was very open about to political confidantes after he had left public life.

The two great ironies of Reynolds' career were that it was left to him to ruthlessly remove the leader, in many ways the one man he had most admired, and also to finesse the process of solving the problem of Northern Ireland, a problem with which Haughey had grappled for so long, but had signally failed to solve. Haughey spoke endlessly of his nationalism and his thoughts on Northern Ireland. Reynolds, by contrast, said little or nothing before climbing the final step to power. The North had defined Haughey's career but, somehow, he couldn't bring his knowledge of the place to the table with regard to solving the problems and thus, he achieved very little. Reynolds, on the other hand, took action in relation to his knowledge and hunches, and achieved what nobody else could. Haughey owed his early promotion to Seán Lemass, but seemed to learn little from his great early mentor and father-in-law. Reynolds, far less blessed in terms of early political mentors, held Lemass as his hero, taking on board his approach when it came to both the economy and the North. Lemass was humble and led a modest lifestyle but was very direct. Reynolds may have made a lot of money but he was also humble in his approach and very, very direct when he spoke. In terms of hard achievement, leaving aside Fianna Fáil's first founder, Lemass and Reynolds stand out as two of the most effective leaders the country has ever had.

If there is a last word to be included about the legacy of Albert Reynolds, the summary written by Kathy Sheridan, someone who observed him over a lifetime, seems fitting: 'Albert Reynolds was many things – ruthless, tricky, cunning, scheming, stubborn, clever, a generous boss, affectionate, loving and beloved – but he never pretended to be something he was not.'[3]

CHAPTER THIRTY-ONE

Demise

The big ballroom of the Four Seasons Hotel in Ballsbridge, Dublin was packed to the brim that August day in 2014. People from the world of entertainment, business and politics were present. There were laughter and smiles as people told their own stories about Albert Reynolds. It resembled a huge reunion rather than a formal funeral. Reynolds had been ill for six years and had totally withdrawn from public life. Such was his state towards the end that he had been moved from his apartment in the Four Seasons to an adjacent room where medical nurses and care assistants tended to him around the clock. Those who came back to the Four Seasons were, for the most part, friends. Reynolds' seven children mixed freely with the guests, hugging, embracing and smiling at people they might not have seen for years. It was a most enjoyable occasion and a fitting way to see out the man he was.

The funeral mass had been held earlier that day. Everyone who attended was asked to come back to the hotel afterwards for a meal. Between the mass and the function, there had been a formal state funeral with full military honours and a formal volley at the graveside. The religious ceremony at the grave was conducted in the teeming rain with the flurry of umbrellas.

Earlier, in Donnybrook church, the funeral ceremony had been conducted by Fr Brian D'Arcy, an old friend of Reynolds and the priest who looked after the music industry in the ballroom days. D'Arcy was very close to Reynolds, presiding at family events down the years. He was something of a spiritual and personal confidant to Reynolds. 'In showbands there was no religious difference. Long before he entered politics, we also spoke passionately about how violence was destroying our beloved country,' D'Arcy told mourners at Reynolds' funeral.[1] He also explained to the congregation how the monastery where he lived, in County Fermanagh, became a kind of post box for anonymous communication between Reynolds and key figures in the North. Reynolds would come up to the monastery to read the letters that were left for collection, then, in return, leave letters for his correspondents. According to D'Arcy, Reynolds had 'a wider field of contacts in the North than anybody ever knew. This was all the more valuable because it wasn't noticed.' D'Arcy believes Reynolds was trusted, in particular, by the 'militarists' on both sides of the equation in the North, because he was straight about things.[2]

Phillip Reynolds described his father as a 'simple, innately good and brilliant man'. He also suggested that he was a 'dealer', but was at pains to point out that he was not a 'wheeler-dealer', in his professional life. Phillip said the real tragedy of his long illness from Alzheimer's was that the real man was gone years earlier and that his grandchildren had not been given the opportunity to see 'the real Dad, the family man'.

In the Donnybrook church, there was spontaneous applause when the congregation was told of the presence of Sir John Major, the former Prime Minister of the UK. Major, when thanked by Fr D'Arcy for his attendance, responded, 'Where else would I be on this day?' There is little doubt about the genuine nature of the friendship between Reynolds and Major. It remains an example of what can be achieved between Ireland and Britain if there is a sincere sense of equality in the relationship. Both men had an inner toughness but seemed to delight in sparring with one another.

Louis Turley, a parishioner of Donnybrook church and neighbour of Reynolds, was present at the funeral. He had sat beside Reynolds on many occasions as they both attended Sunday Mass. 'He went every Sunday to mass. He had a deep faith but never pushed it. He was a person of innate humility and connected very easily with people he met.'[3] There was little that was pretentious about Reynolds.

The funeral service, state funeral and glowing media coverage accorded to Reynolds on his death were a belated recognition of all that he achieved. His death came twenty years after he lost power in 1994. His retirement had been dignified and, for the most part, during his last five years, Reynolds was gone to the world. Between his departure from office and his death, politics had become rather more managerial, duller and more risk averse. In the coverage accorded to his death, there was a tinge of regret that the kind of leadership he offered was now largely absent. At one level, Reynolds was a casualty of the transition from an era of 'conviction politics' to an era of the politics of 'spin'. The arrival of the twenty-four-hour news cycle began under him and, to a certain extent, his inability, in the words of John Major, to pass a microphone made him vulnerable to media attack. Reynolds' effort to operate a more open system of weekly briefings for political correspondents proved to be a mistake and got him into trouble, as these sessions were often used by the media as an opportunity for ambush. His career also exposed the natural limits of entrepreneurial values when set against the values of public service and the incorrigible inertia in the civil service system. As we have seen, he had arrived late to power and had been determined to move fast.

Reynolds' rise to power was largely achieved through his undoubted skill in economic portfolios. While this gave him great credibility, it meant he neglected the wider issues affecting society. A newer Ireland, ushered in with the election of Mary Robinson in 1990, was anxious to see a more intense expression of secularism from the state. Reynolds was a quiet and low-profile Catholic with little appetite for the social issues. He preferred to deal with social issues as matters of practicality rather than messianic belief.

Reynolds had also clawed his way up the political ladder under the influence and shadow of Charles Haughey. When Haughey's period as Taoiseach ended, it was after a full year of scandal and controversy. Some of the public suspicion that attached to Haughey had also attached to Reynolds and, at a wider level, Fianna Fáil. Reynolds found it hard to totally detach himself from the reputational damage that Haughey had caused, all the more so since it was clear to onlookers that he had solidly backed Haughey through all the internal party heaves with the party's dissidents. The final drive to power by Reynolds was at a terrible time for him with his wife being treated for cancer. This may well have inhibited him from developing a significant narrative about himself. To many in the outside world, away from Leinster House, Reynolds' ascent to power looked more like the result of an internal feud rather than a radical changing of the guard.

The simple fact of his personal achievement in office is this – few, if any, of his predecessors, or indeed his successors, could have produced the compelling case for peace that he did. What made Reynolds' intervention for peace so impressive was his networking skills. To maintain a listening ear from John Major, Bill Clinton, the IRA and loyalist paramilitaries was a difficult act to carry off. But carry it off he did, working very effectively with Major to ensure that the official unionists did not march away from the process too.

Perhaps most impressive of all, however, were the personal risks Reynolds was prepared to take for peace. Few politicians today, or in the past, would have travelled in a private capacity, without formal security, to meet with the high command of the IRA and with loyalist paramilitaries. This type of contact was not just inherently dangerous but could have ruined Reynolds' political reputation forever. However, he was not the sort of person to let advisors and intermediaries carry the can – he was prepared to put his own neck on the line. This type of personal courage is often absent as a quality in the political species. Reynolds was that rare individual in politics, cautious to some extent, but never risk averse.

Endnotes

PREFACE

1. Tim Ryan, *Albert Reynolds: The Longford Leader: The Unauthorised Biography* (Dublin: Blackwater Press, 1994).
2. Albert Reynolds, *Albert Reynolds: My Autobiography* (London: Transworld Ireland, 2009). All quotes copyright © Albert Reynolds 2009. Reprinted by permission of The Random House Group Limited.
3. Seán Duignan, *One Spin on the Merry-go-round* (Dublin: Blackwater Press, 1996).

CHAPTER ONE

1. *Hibernian Historical Trust* (n.d.), 'The Players – Michael Whelehan', available at: http://www.hibshistoricaltrust.org.uk/players/michael-whelahan?highlight=WyJ3 aGVsYWhhbiIsIndoZWxhaGFuJ3MiXQ== (accessed 12/03/2021).
2. The village where Reynolds grew up is commonly spelt both Rooskey and Roosky. Rooskey is used throughout this book except where the alternative spelling is used in a quotation.
3. Ryan, *The Longford Leader* (1994), p. 9.
4. Ibid., p. 10.

CHAPTER TWO

1. Ryan, *The Longford Leader* (1994), p. 13.
2. Ibid., p. 15.
3. Sam Smyth, interview with the author, 2020.

CHAPTER THREE

1. Peter Vacher, 'Kenny Ball Obituary', *The Guardian*, 7 March 2013.
2. Sam Smyth, interview with the author, 2020.
3. Vincent Power, *Send 'Em Home Sweatin': Irish Showband Story* (Cork: Mercier Press, 2000), p. 250.
4. Sam Smyth, interview with the author, 2020.

CHAPTER FOUR

1. The late Joe Sheridan quoted in Ryan, *The Longford Leader* (1994), p. 97.
2. Ryan, *The Longford Leader* (1994), p. 42.
3. Sam Smyth, *Thanks a Million Big Fella* (Dublin: Blackwater Press, 1997), p. 41.
4. Reynolds quoted in *New Spotlight*, August 1968.

5.   Derek Cobbe, interview with the author, 2020.
6.   Liam Collins, interview with the author, 2020.
7.   Ryan, *The Longford Leader* (1994), p. 104.

CHAPTER FIVE

1.   This and following quotes from Cumbers, interview with the author, 2020.
2.   The business achieved significant success up to 1990 and beyond until Reynolds' son Phillip, who was then leading it, sold it, having grown it into a much larger entity.
3.   Duignan, *One Spin on the Merry-go-round* (1996), p. 93.
4.   Ibid., p. 94.

CHAPTER SIX

1.   Derek Cobbe, interview with the author, 2020.
2.   Ryan, *The Longford Leader* (1994), p. 101.
3.   *Sunday Tribune*, 1 January 1989.
4.   Liam Collins, journalist, interview with the author, 2020.
5.   Ibid.
6.   Kathy Sheridan, 'The Longford man who brought the razzmatazz to midlands Ireland', *The Irish Times*, 22 August 2014.
7.   Derek Cobbe, interview with the author, 2020.
8.   Sheridan, *The Irish Times*, 22 August 2014.
9.   The decision by Albert's brother Jim to stick with Joe Sheridan and not canvass for his brother was known and something of an embarrassment to Reynolds. It would be a good few years before the two men patched up their row over their dancehall business.

CHAPTER SEVEN

1.   Dáil Debates, 30 November 1977, Industrial Development Bill, 2nd Stage.
2.   John Donlon, journalist with the *Longford Leader* and the *Star*, interview with the author, 2020.
3.   Stephen Collins, *The Power Game: Fianna Fáil Since Lemass* (Dublin: The O'Brien Press, 2000), p. 107.
4.   Vincent Brown, 'The Making of a Taoiseach', *Magill* magazine, January 1980.
5.   Finn McCool, former Finance official and hotelier, interview with the author, 2020.
6.   Brown, 'The Making of a Taoiseach', *Magill*, January 1980.
7.   Ibid.
8.   John Donlon, interview with the author, 2020.

CHAPTER EIGHT

1.   'Cash on the Line – the cost of the telephones', *Magill* magazine, 31 October 1984.
2.   Patrick Banks, interview with the author, 2020.
3.   Finn McCool, former Finance official and hotelier, interview with the author, 2020.

4. Sheridan, *The Irish Times*, 22 August 2014.
5. Article quoted in Ryan, *The Longford Leader* (1994), p. 128.

CHAPTER NINE

1. *Sunday Tribune*, 27 November 1988.
2. *The Sunday Business Post*, 21 January 1990.
3. *Sunday Tribune*, 27 November 1988.
4. Davy's Stockbrokers Budget 1990 report, 31 January 1990.
5. Don Bergin, former Department of Finance official, interview with the author, 2020.
6. Ray McSharry, former Minister for Finance, interview with the author, 2020.
7. Ryan, *The Longford Leader* (1994), p. 152.

CHAPTER TEN

1. Bertie Ahern, *The Autobiography* (London: Hutchinson, 2009), p. 108.
2. Liam Collins, interview with the author, 2020.
3. *Sunday Independent*, 25 February 1990.
4. Smyth, *Thanks a Million Big Fella* (1997), p. 86.
5. Collins, *The Power Game* (2000), p. 213.

CHAPTER ELEVEN

1. Ahern, *The Autobiography* (2009), p. 129.
2. Ibid., p. 136.

CHAPTER TWELVE

1. Duignan, *One Spin on the Merry-go-round* (1996), p. 7.
2. Ibid., p. 8.
3. Dáil Debates, 11 February 1992.
4. Ibid.
5. Duignan, *One Spin on the Merry-go-round* (1996), p. 9.
6. Ibid., p. 20.
7. Ibid., p. 21.
8. *The Irish Times*, 18 February 1992.
9. Duignan, *One Spin on the Merry-go-round* (1996), p. 28.

CHAPTER THIRTEEN

1. John Major, *John Major: The Autobiography* (London: Harper Collins, 1999), p. 203.
2. Ryan, *The Longford Leader* (1994), p. 174.
3. Major, *The Autobiography* (1999), p. 440.
4. Brendan O'Brien, *A Short History of the IRA* (Dublin: The O'Brien Press, 2019), p. 128.
5. Jonathon Powell, *Talking to Terrorists: How to End Armed Conflicts* (London: The Bodley Head, 2014), p. 112.

ENDNOTES

6. Ibid.
7. Duignan, *One Spin on the Merry-go-round* (1996), p. 97.
8. https://api.parliament.uk/historic-hansard/commons/1993/nov/29/northern-ireland-1.
9. Former Taoiseach John Bruton, interview with the author, 2020.
10. Noel Gallagher, interview with the author, 2020.

CHAPTER FOURTEEN

1. Conor O'Clery, formerly of *The Irish Times*, interview with the author, 2020.
2. Ibid.
3. Ibid.
4. Dermot Gallagher, quoted in Reynolds, *My Autobiography* (2009), p. 224.
5. Conor O'Clery, formerly of *The Irish Times*, interview with the author, 2020.
6. Ibid.
7. Tim Pat Coogan, interview with the author, 2020.
8. Frank Kilfeather, 'Kennedy-Smith criticises Seitz and says peace process can speak for itself', *The Irish Times*, 20 January 1998.
9. Niall O'Dowd quoted in Eamonn Mallie and David McKittrick, *Endgame in Ireland* (London: Coronet Books, 2002), p. 175.
10. Malie and McKittrick, *Endgame in Ireland* (2002), p. 176.
11. Former Ambassador Dermot Gallagher as quoted in Reynolds, *My Autobiography* (2009), p. 239.
12. Bill Clinton quoted in Reynolds, *My Autobiography* (2009), p. 241.

CHAPTER FIFTEEN

1. Ahern, *The Autobiography* (2010), p. 145.
2. Charlie McCreevy, interview with the author, 2020.
3. Collins, *The Power Game* (2000), p. 238.
4. Duignan, *One Spin on the Merry-go-round* (1996), pp. 23–4.
5. Collins, *The Power Game* (2000), p. 239.
6. John Bruton, former taoiseach, interview with the author, 2020.
7. Benny Reid, former schoolteacher, interview with the author, 2020.
8. Collins, *The Power Game* (2000), p. 237.
9. Ibid., p. 229.

CHAPTER SIXTEEN

1. Dáil Debate on the Beef Tribunal, 1 September 1994.
2. John Bruton, former Taoiseach, interview with the author, 2020.
3. Duignan, *One Spin on the Merry-go-round* (1996), p. 49.
4. Ibid., p. 50.
5. Fergus Finlay, *Snakes & Ladders* (Dublin: New Island Books, 1998), p. 121.
6. Noel Dempsey, former minister, interview with the author, 2020.

7. Duignan, *One Spin on the Merry-go-round* (1996), p. 61.
8. Ibid.

CHAPTER SEVENTEEN

1. Finlay, *Snakes & Ladders* (1998), p. 136.
2. Duignan, *One Spin on the Merry-go-round* (1996), p. 73.
3. Major, *The Autobiography* (1999), p. 370.
4. Duignan, *One Spin on the Merry-go-round* (1996), p. 29.
5. Noel Gallagher, interview with the author, 2020.
6. John Major quoted in Reynolds, *My Autobiography* (2009), p. 207.
7. Tommy Gorman, *RTÉ* European Correspondent, interview with the author, 2020.
8. Alan Murdoch, 'EC Summit: Luck of the Irish Lifts Reynolds', *Independent Newspaper*, 14 December 1992.
9. Finlay, *Snakes & Ladders* (1998), p. 138.
10. Ibid., p. 142.

CHAPTER EIGHTEEN

1. Collins, *The Power Game* (2000), p. 251.
2. Finlay, *Snakes & Ladders* (1998), p. 168.
3. Duignan, *One Spin on the Merry-go-round* (1996), p. 86.
4. Finlay, *Snakes & Ladders* (1998), p. 177.
5. Charlie McCreevy, interview with the author, 2020.
6. Finlay, *Snakes & Ladders* (1998), p. 210.
7. Collins, *The Power Game* (2000), p. 257.
8. Ibid., p. 264.
9. Finlay, *Snakes & Ladders* (1998), p. 234.

CHAPTER NINETEEN

1. Frank Dunlop, *Yes Taoiseach: Irish Politics from Behind Closed Doors* (Dublin: Penguin Ireland, 2004), p. 319.
2. Noel Dempsey, former minister, interview with the author, 2020.
3. Alf McCreary, *Gordon Wilson: An Ordinary Hero* (London: Marshall Pickering, 1997), p. 51.
4. Ibid., p. 107.
5. O'Brien, *A Short History of the IRA* (2019), p. 135.
6. Ibid., p. 138.
7. Duignan, *One Spin on the Merry-go-round* (1996), p. 102.
8. Sean 'Spike' Murray, interview with the author, 2020.

CHAPTER TWENTY

1. Sean O'Huiginn, interview with the author, 2020.
2. Duignan, *One Spin on the Merry-go-round* (1996), p. 99.
3. Noel Gallagher, interview with the author, 2020.

4. Eamon Delaney, *An Accidental Diplomat: My Years in the Irish Foreign Service, 1987–1995* (Dublin: New Island Books, 2001).
5. Finlay, *Snakes & Ladders* (1998), p. 190.
6. Rafter, *Martin Mansergh* (2002), p. 207.
7. Sean O'Huiginn, interview with the author, 2020.
8. Ibid.
9. Donnacha Ó Beacháin, *From Partition to Brexit: The Irish Government and Brexit* (Manchester: Manchester University Press, 2018), p. 218.
10. *The Irish News*, 3 August 2020.
11. Duignan, *One Spin on the Merry-go-round* (1996), p. 106.

CHAPTER TWENTY-ONE
1. Finlay, *Snakes & Ladders* (1998), p. 201.
2. Ibid.
3. Ibid., p. 203.
4. Noel Gallagher, interview with the author, 2020.
5. Ibid.
6. Mallie and McKittrick, *Endgame in Ireland* (2002), p. 162.
7. Duignan, *One Spin on the Merry-go-round* (1996), p. 127.

CHAPTER TWENTY-TWO
1. Mallie and McKittrick, *Endgame in Ireland* (2002), p. 169.
2. John Major quoted in Reynolds, *My Autobiography* (2009), p. 319.
3. Joe O'Meara, Clifden, interview with the author, 2020. O'Meara acted as part of an intermediary group and link to people like Charlie Murphy, a former Adjutant General of the IRA and Dublin publican Tommy Smith. O'Meara has retained some of the notes and documents from these meetings in his personal archive.
4. Mallie and McKittrick, *Endgame in Ireland* (2002), p. 179.
5. *The Larry King Show*, February 1994.
6. Bill Clinton quoted in Reynolds, *My Autobiography* (2009).

CHAPTER TWENTY-THREE
1. Shane Harrison, BBC Dublin correspondent, interview with the author, 2020.
2. Mallie and McKittrick, *Endgame in Ireland* (2002), p. 200.
3. Ibid., p. 201.
4. Billy Hutchinson, *My Life in Loyalism* (Dublin: Merrion Press, 2020), p. 189.
5. Quoted in Duignan, *One Spin on the Merry-go-round* (1996), p. 152.
6. Phillip Hannon and Jackie Gallagher (eds), *Taking the Long View: 70 years of Fianna Fáil* (Dublin: Blackwater Press, 1996), p. 131.
7. *The Irish Times*, 26 September 1994.
8. Collins, *The Power Game* (2000), p. 273.

CHAPTER TWENTY-FOUR

1. Dáil Debates, 16 November 1994.
2. Collins, *The Power Game* (2000), pp. 273–4.
3. Seán Duignan, interview with the author, 2020.
4. Finlay, *Snakes and Ladders* (1998), p. 256.
5. Vincent Brown quoted in Reynolds, *My Autobiography* (2009), p. 414.
6. Dan Wallace quoted in Reynolds, *My Autobiography* (2009), pp. 423–4.
7. Leo Enright, former BBC correspondent, interview with the author, 2020.
8. Ibid.
9. Duignan, *One Spin on the Merry-go-round* (1996), p. 160.
10. Ibid., p. 162.

CHAPTER TWENTY-FIVE

1. Seán Duignan, interview with the author, 2020.
2. Ibid.
3. Willie O'Dea, former minister, interview with the author, 2020.
4. Bertie Ahern, former Taoiseach, interview with the author, 2020.
5. Hannon and Gallagher (eds), *Taking the Long View* (1996), pp. 132–3.
6. Finlay, *Snakes & Ladders* (1998), p. 264.
7. Donal Cronin, interview with author, 2020.
8. Johnny Fallon, writer and analyst, interview with the author, 2020.
9. Willie O'Dea, interview with the author, 2020.
10. Finlay, *Snakes & Ladders* (1998), p. 265.
11. Dunlop, *Yes Taoiseach* (2004), p. 320.
12. Noel Whelan, *Fianna Fáil: A Biography of the Party* (Dublin: Gill & Macmillan, 2011), pp. 285–6.

CHAPTER TWENTY-SIX

1. Diplomat Roderic Lyne quoted in the state papers and referred to in *The Irish Times*, Friday 28 December 2018.
2. Ibid.
3. Roger Stott in a discussion with the author, while a TD, attending a dinner at Castle Lesley, County Monaghan, on the occasion of a meeting of the British–Irish Parliamentary Body.
4. Rafter, *Martin Mansergh* (2002), p. 284.
5. David Harvey, interview with the author, 2020.
6. Ahern, *The Autobiography* (2009), pp. 204–5.
7. Johnny Fallon, writer and analyst, interview with the author, 2020.
8. Ahern, *The Autobiography* (2009), p. 205.
9. David Harvey, interview with the author, 2020.

CHAPTER TWENTY-SEVEN

1. *The Irish Times*, 20 November 1996.

2.   Quoted from the libel trial in *The Irish Times*, 15 October 1996.
3.   Ibid.
4.   Finlay, *Snakes & Ladders* (1998), p. 312.
5.   Ibid., p. 264.
6.   Ibid., p. 265.
7.   Dessie Hynes, interview with the author, 2020.
8.   Duignan, *One Spin on the Merry-go-round* (1996), p. 40.
9.   Dessie Hynes, interview with the author, 2020.
10.   Businessman Eamon Monahan of the Capital Showband, interview with the author, 2020.
11.   *Irish Independent*, 23 September 2000.
12.   Ibid.

CHAPTER TWENTY-EIGHT

1.   *Irish Independent*, 14 September 2002.
2.   *Sunday Tribune*, 11 February 1996.
3.   *Irish Independent*, 14 September 2002.
4.   Gerry Purcell of Purcell Meats, interview with the author, 2020.
5.   *Irish Examiner*, 24 March 2012.
6.   *The Irish Times,* 30 July 2008.
7.   Interview with Phillip Reynolds on Shannonside FM as quoted in the *Irish Examiner*, 17 December 2013.
8.   Ibid.

CHAPTER TWENTY-NINE

1.   Ó Beacháin, *From Partition to Brexit* (2019), p. 218.
2.   Collins, *The Power Game* (2000), pp. 237–8.

CHAPTER THIRTY

1.   The Ronson was a flashy but popular cigarette lighter at the time.
2.   Johnny Fallon, writer and analyst, interview with the author, 2020.
3.   Sheridan, *The Irish Times*, 22 August 2014.

CHAPTER THIRTY-ONE

1.   *The Irish Times*, 26 August 2014.
2.   Fr Brian D'Arcy, interview with the author, 2020.
3.   Louis Turley, interview with the author, 2020.

Index